Frontispiece Sebastian jumping

Connections

In all places and at all times people are making connections. This ground-breaking work investigates what gets connected (antecedent and subsequent social events knotted together into what the author dubs 'string being') and what does the connecting (linked neural circuits in the brain that run on culture like an engine runs on fuel).

Connections boldly unites two warring intellectual traditions – hermeneutics and cognitive neuroscience – proposing that brain structures form a cultural neurohermeneutic system which functions like a bow firing arrows linking past and future realities. This system is a connector in human affairs and can explain everyday life. Its precise anatomy remains speculative, but enough is known to hypothesize that it functions as an interpretive hierarchy that permits individuals to make increasingly complex interpretations of social events on the basis of cultural memory.

The book also marries another odd couple. Because 'string being' involves people's actions, and because these are understood to be social phenomena, the anthropology outlined here is very much a social one. However, Reyna argues that it is also Boasian, because it recognizes and embraces the relationship between the biological and cultural. He proposes that a Boasian social anthropology might be a way to make anthropology the central social, cultural, and biological discipline for studying the human condition.

This challenging work rethinks a number of topics crucial to understanding the human condition – brain, mind, culture, the social, and causality. Written in an accessible and entertaining style, it will be essential reading for anyone studying and practicing anthropology, as well as philosophers of the mind, psychologists, and cognitive scientists.

Stephen P. Reyna is Professor of Anthropology at the University of New Hampshire, USA and Visiting Senior Research Professor at the Max Planck Institute for Social Anthropology, Germany.

Connections

Brain, mind, and culture in a
social anthropology

Stephen P. Reyna

London and New York

First published 2002
by Routledge
11 New Fetter Lane, London EC4P 4EE

Simultaneously published in the USA and Canada
by Routledge
29 West 25th Street, New York, NY 10001

Routledge is an imprint of the Taylor & Francis Group

Typeset in Goudy and Gill by BC Typesetting, Bristol
Printed and bound in Great Britain by
The Cromwell Press, Trowbridge, Wiltshire

British Library Cataloguing in Publication Data
A catalogue record for this book is available from the British Library

Library of Congress Cataloging in Publication Data
Reyna, Stephen P.
   Connections: brain, mind, and culture in a social anthropology/
  Stephen P. Reyna.
     p.   cm.
  Includes bibliographical references and index.
   1. Culture. 2. Cognition and culture. 3. Ethnopsychology.
  4. Neurobiology. 5. Hermeneutics. I. Title.

GN357.R49 2002
306–dc21   2001048454

ISBN 0–415–27154–1 (hbk)
ISBN 0–415–27155–X (pbk)

Contents

Illustrations

Preface

This is an epoch when anthropology is seen by many to be largely ethnography. I formally 'took' anthropological theory as a student in Marvin Harris's 'History of Anthropology' course when he was finishing the *Rise of Anthropological Theory* (1968) and gained from him a conviction that theory counts. Ethnographers – lacking theory and lacking understanding of how to ground theory in observation – resemble infants without language, cute but babbling. However, Harris liked to caution against different abominations of theory construction, and one of his direst admonitions concerned the sin of eclecticism.

Perhaps, he would read the present text and note that it bunks, in a common argumentative bed, the pre-Socratic materialist Empedocles with the idealist Kant; the historical particularist Boas with the conjectural hermeneutist Geertz; the Marxist Louis Althusser with the non-Marxist Wesley Salmon; not to mention a whole gaggle of cognitive neuroscientists who get thrown in. So Harris – on realization that all these different thinkers cavorted in a common bed – might thunder: eclectic orgy!

However, the position is not eclectic. I come from New Hampshire, where you take your Robert Frost seriously, and the old poet once said something to the effect that, 'A poem is something you have seen a thousand times and never seen before.' What you are about to read is no poem. However, its bits and pieces – facts and generalizations – have been around, just as the bits and pieces – words and images – of a poem have been around; but, as in a poem, the bits and pieces have never before been assembled, so you could not have seen them. The present text does some assembling and helps you see something you might not have seen before, how social realities get connected.

Specifically, the text theorizes about how antecedent social events get strung to subsequent ones. Social events that are connected are called 'string being'. What is explained, then, is how the connections that make string being are forged – hence the book's title, *Connections*. It is theorized that certain structures in the brain, which run on culture, make the connections. These structures are called a 'cultural neurohermeneutic system'. The study of them is 'cultural neurohermeneutics'. Thus, to vastly oversimplify, the book's argument is that cultural hermeneutics helps to explain string being. Because string being involves people's actions, and because these are understood to be social phenomena, *Connections* ultimately contributes to a social anthropology. However, it is a far cry from pre-World War II social anthropology and, because it seeks to integrate social, cultural, and biological matters in a common analytic framework, as did Franz Boas, I choose to call it a Boasian social anthropology.

A word is in order about the text's style. Theory is hard. Readers are required to consider philosophical literatures that begin in pre-Socratic Greece, tarry with Descartes and Kant, and press on to nineteenth- and twentieth-century hermeneutists and philosophers of science. They inspect recent proposals of neuroscience and consult events ranging from Chad to the New York Police Department, while learning something of the history of social and cultural anthropology. So I have resolved to write as clearly as possible and to illustrate my points ethnographically.

Daumier, the nineteenth-century etcher, who brilliantly skewered French society, has been a stylistic source. When you are invited to 'come up and see my etchings', it will be to experience sharp ethnographic engravings that illustrate the argument. Certain sentences and judgments are provocative; intentionally so, in order to grab readers' attention, stimulate reflection, incite protest. However, the goal of such language is not to replace one orthodoxy with another. Rather, it is provocation of restless inquiry, hopefully in the direction of truer, more elegant generalization. Kindly note, the names of individuals mentioned in the text and their residences are pseudonyms, unless they have previously been made part of some public record.

A Senior Faculty Fellowship from the Center for Humanities at the University of New Hampshire provided greatly appreciated time to devote to this project in 1997–8. Fragments of the book's arguments were offered in symposia. These included the 14th International Congress of Anthropological and Ethnological Science in Williamsburg, Virginia (1998); the Faculty Fellowship Lectures Series of the Center for Humanities, Durham, New Hampshire (1999); Boston University's Anthropology Department's Departmental Seminar (2000); and the Inaugural Conference of the International Social Theory Consortium in Lexington, Kentucky (2000). These were fine sessions. I greatly learned from the questioners. Roy D'Andrade, Terrence Deacon, Victor de Munck, Richard Fox, Jonathan Friedman, Hanna Lessinger, Charles Lindholm, David Sutton, and Joan Vincent have made comments that, though they may not have realized it, influenced the direction of *Connections*. Stephanie Smith was instrumental in putting the references together. I spent a wonderful time at the Max Planck Institute for Social Anthropology in Halle/ Saale, Germany, between October 2000 and January 2002. The Directors of this Institute, Günter Schlee and Chris Hann, provided intelligent support for this project.

Three final, deep debts: the first is to fathers and sons. L.J. Reyna, my father, came from a Harlem orphanage to become an experimental psychologist. He has long held an interest in scientific epistemology. Equally, he used to take his kids to the movies in Ayer, Massachusetts when Little John was our dog. Later I took my kids – Braden, Damon, and Alexander – to the movies in Somersworth, New Hampshire when Sebastian was our dog. Movies, epistemology, Sebastian, and our restless spirits, all find their way into the text. The second debt is to R.E. Downs who has read and challenged my work over the years. He has taught me patience and clarity; qualities that he firmly believes need strengthening in my case. Finally, my wife Nina Glick Schiller is an anthropologist of extraordinary skill. From her I learn what will just *not* do. This book is dedicated to our family.

Durham, New Hampshire, USA
and Halle (Saale), Germany

Abbreviations

AAD	antecedent attachment device
ACC	anterior cingulate cortex
ANS	autonomic nervous system
ATF	*After the Fact* (Geertz 1995)
CAT	computerized axial tomography
CC	*The Apotheosis of Captain Cook* (Obeyesekere 1992)
CNS	central nervous system
CPR	*Culture and Practical Reason* (Sahlins 1976a)
EEG	electroencephalography
ERP	event-related potential
fMRI	functional magnetic resonance imaging
HMO	health maintenance organization
HNT	*How 'Natives' Think* (Sahlins 1995)
IC	*The Interpretation of Cultures* (Geertz 1973)
LGN	lateral geniculate nucleus
LK	*Local Knowledge* (Geertz 1983)
LP	*The Logic of Social Practice* (Bourdieu 1990)
MGN	medial geniculate nucleus
PET	positron emission tomography
PFC	prefrontal cortex
R&R	*Of Revelation and Revolution* (Comaroff and Comaroff 1991)
rCBF	regional cerebral blood flow
SAD	subsequent attachment device
SE	*Les Structures élémentaires de la parenté* (Lévi-Strauss 1949)
TD	transforming device
V1	primary visual cortex
WL	*Works and Lives* (Geertz 1988)

Chapter 1

Introduction

Only connect.

(E.M. Forster, *Howard's End*, Chapter 22)

This book introduces cultural neurohermeneutics as a way of accounting for how people go about making connections, and it is the chore of this chapter to indicate how the case for such a hermeneutics will be made. The chapter oscillates back and forth between sentimental memories that are part of everyday life, and the terms of a project for investigating connections in such life. Let us begin with the sentimentality. I live in an old New England country house. The other day it was hot. I was throwing a stick for Sebastian to fetch. Sebastian was an old dog who acted as if it were his duty to humor people, up to a point; and owing to his age he believed that point was very quickly reached when they had him fetching their sticks. So Sebastian took his stick and went to cool himself under a honeysuckle between the house and the barn. It was midday and the dark green honeysuckle looked inviting. The dog had the right idea. I crawled in and sat beside him. He looked at me, puzzled, but when he realized that my presence did not signify the resumption of the stick game he put his head down and was soon asleep. I adjusted to the world under the bush. A dove cooed, as another had thirty years before.

It was 1969. Dazed from the intense hurly-burly of fieldwork, I walked out of the tiny Chadian village of Bémbassa – some mud huts arranged in thirty or so households on the banks of the Shari River – on a path that went east; passed the fields where there had been sorghum at the last harvest; and on a mile or so to a vale that flooded during the rains and afterwards stayed green when everything else was bleached and arid. The day was hot, 100-degree Fahrenheit heat. A huge *mas*, a tamarind, was in the center of the meadow. As with the honeysuckle, I went and sat under it. When I looked up, there had been a rush of the sensation of the leaves' deep greenery, more enveloping than that under the honeysuckle. Far above, dappled sunlight streamed through the topmost branches of the tree. I knew I was under a tamarind and that the Barma of Bémbassa believed that their story, the history of the Kingdom of Bagirmi, had begun under a tamarind. Thinking about these Barma roots had triggered family memories.

One summer in the 1950s we traveled to my grandparents for a vacation in Iowa. Des Moines in August was hot like Chad, only more boring. My mother showed me photographs that were her mother's. My grandmother had been born before the turn of the century, but the pictures were from an even earlier time, of relatives who had flourished after the US Civil War. The pictures were mostly of men, some women, a few of a whole family – staring out at you from the faded space of the photograph. My mother was a storyteller, so she connected, as best she could, the people in the pictures with their lives.

Among the women there had been a line of Priscillas. The first lived about the time of the Civil War, another a generation or so later, and finally my mother, who was born in 1918. The family had lived in West Virginia during the Civil War. There were six sons. Three fought for the Union. Three fought for the Confederacy. The six sons' mother tended the sick and wounded during the war, riding out at night – not sidesaddle, 'like a woman', my mother was careful to note, 'but astride, like a man'. At the very end of the war, amidst the chaos of disintegrating armies, she was riding home from her nursing when a man jumped out of the darkness, grabbing her horse's bridle. She slashed at him with her riding crop – a 'good cavalry saber cut', my mother editorialized. He collapsed. It was a son badly wounded.

I remember coming across the faded picture of a dour woman just after my mother had told me this, and asking, 'Was that her?' To which the response came, 'I don't know.' In the end, after looking at all the pictures, most of the time she did not 'know' anything about them and she commented – part joke, part irony – 'They're not really moving pictures.' The pictures were a disappointment, stories untold. The boredom of Des Moines returned. That was almost forty-five years ago. Now there is a picture of my mother, an old Priscilla, staring out with a silent smile, seeming about to say something – she who has been dead for nearly two decades. The family album consists of disconnected photographs: a dour woman of the 1860s, a smiling one of the 1960s.

The preceding has depicted everyday lives summoned in sentimental memories. It is time to proceed to develop some terms for the investigation of such life. A region where there are families, clans, governments, or other sorts of institutions, is a space of human structures. Now there are antecedent regions of human structure, and there are subsequent ones, and antecedent regions become subsequent ones. The photographs framed spaces of family. There was the earlier picture of the dour woman and the later one of my mother. Somehow the two spaces, separated in geography and time, were connected. This book takes the injunction 'Only connect' terribly seriously, offering a view of a connector that strings structural antecedents to their consequents, making string being possible for human structures. Let us elaborate by specifying what is meant by this term, an elaboration that will return us both to the honey-suckle and the tamarind.

STRING BEING

I became an anthropologist because of a need shared with my mother: to tell true stories about people. Actually, I became something of a hybrid: a Boasian social anthropologist. In the winter of 1883 Franz Boas had been frozen into Baffin Island in the Canadian Arctic.[1] This obliged him to live for a year with the Eskimos. He discovered, as he told his fiancée in a letter to her in 1884, that 'I am now truly just like an Eskimo' (in Müller-Wille 1998: 17), and he believed that this 'filled up the lacunae of my knowledge' about them (in Collins 1964: viii). The greater knowledge Boas acquired of a people, whom earlier anthropologists had called 'savages', and whom he now knew to not be 'uncivilized' (Müller-Wille 1998: 17), led to his questioning of these anthropologists.

Consequently, *Doctoraluk* – Big Doctor, as the Eskimos called him – at Columbia University at the turn of the twentieth century, devised an anthropology that, like the New York buildings being constructed around him, was colossal: the grandest human science explaining social, cultural, and biological phenomena, and their inter-relations, in all places and over all times. So vast an enterprise had to have four fields – cultural anthropology, archeology, linguistics, and biological anthropology – in order to realize these explanatory goals. The first three fields were to help anthropologists understand social and cultural phenomena. The fourth was to facilitate an understanding of human biology; and it was believed that by nesting all these fields together in a common discipline, understanding would be forthcoming of the intimacies between biological and sociocultural realities.

Most of my 1960s Columbia University professors – including Marvin Harris, then occupying Boas's office – raged at Boas, but in the end it was an anger of sons. They might not like Daddy, but they were like him. They were formulating a cultural materialism, but it was a materialism adjusted to the confines of the four-field approach and to understanding relations between the biological and the cultural. There were endless examinations that demanded: 'Defend the four-field approach'; and defend it I did, becoming in the process a Boasian.

Social anthropology, on the other hand, was a British enterprise. It had begun in earnest in 1922 with the publication of A.R. Radcliffe-Brown's *The Andaman Islanders* and Bronislaw Malinowski's *Argonauts of the Western Pacific*, and had focused more narrowly upon explaining the structure and function of particular 'primitives' at specific points in time.[2] By the 1960s my Columbia professors all agreed with the apostate social anthropologist Edmund Leach that it was a time for *Rethinking Anthropology* (1961), which, in their revisionism, meant that social anthropology was the past, cultural ecology the now. But I intended to work in Africa, and African anthropology at the time was largely British social anthropology. This meant reading Radcliffe-Brown, Evans-Pritchard, Fortes. So, if not a bona fide product, in the sense of being trained by one of these masters, I certainly knew what they were about, and fully intended to base my Barma ethnography upon sound social anthropological principles, by making a contribution to descent group theory. Serendipitously, then, I became something of a Boasian social anthropologist. This work seeks to end the serendipity by offering a rationale for such anthropology. Study of the Barma had begun in 1968.

Now it was three decades later. I was a *gada* – what the Barma called a 'whitebeard' – sitting under an old bush with an ancient dog, reminiscing. Remembering that New York City police were abusing people of color. An officer with a broomstick had sodomized a Haitian in a Brooklyn police station. Another guy, who had committed the crime of trying to get into his apartment building, was shot forty-three times by an elite police squad. Remembrance of one butchery evoked another. I had been reading about European struggles for mastery of the world at the beginning of the nineteenth century. These had been decided at the Battle of Waterloo, where the Emperor Napoleon and the Duke of Wellington fought, slaughtering thousands upon thousands upon thousands in the process. One moment the Emperor was up, his cavalry charging; the next he was down, his cavalry mangled corpses. Great Britain was the hegemon.

These memories under the honeysuckle elicited recollections of being under the tamarind and of first fieldwork. I remembered upon arrival in Bémbassa, politely but firmly demanding to be taken to their unilineal descent groups. The villagers, upon hearing this demand, looked at me with uncomprehending incredulity, the sort that postmodernists reserve for metanarratives. The next six months revealed that, while the Barma might once have had lineages, I had probably missed them by a century or so, which put a crimp in any desire to contribute to descent group theory.

So I had gone back to basics, trying to make sense of the everyday lives of people who lived in Bagirmi. Ahmet's marital tribulations came to mind. Ahmet was a young man in the village married to a still younger Amina. Her body had a lithe elegance that stimulated *miyawa* ('adolescent male') imaginations up and down the Shari River. She was *pusa noko ojo*, a 'real knockout', and she was smart enough to know that this was the case. Ahmet, on the other hand, was too young to have amassed himself the considerable bridewealth it took to marry her. In fact, he was an unambitious guy, who sat around all day with an overturned cardboard box in front of him, on top of which were a few kola nuts, some tea, and sugar for sale. Ahmet sold little. He was diffident. Some of the villagers thought of him as a 'loser'. He had only been able to marry Amina because his family was wealthy by Bémbassa standards and had paid his bridewealth. Amina may have realized that she was stuck with a loser. She left.

This was during the dry season when last year's fields were being burnt and elephants were in the vicinity, noisily bending trees back and forth – like dentists extracting teeth – to get at their soft innards. Ahmet, on recognizing Amina's departure, stood up behind his box, stripped naked and ran for it – east, in the direction of the tamarind, into a bush full of hazy smoke and elephants working their trees. Now it is not the height of rationality to run bare-assed through the drifting haze of elephant-studded burning fields. Ahmet had cracked. Village mates ran off after him, caught him, and returned him to his mud house.

Remembering Ahmet's story brought back Musa's. Part of my investigations of Bagirmi had been on the margins of the kingdom to try to understand how tributary groups were organized into the polity. In order to make this study, I had lived with the Abu Krider, an Arab 'tribe', who sometimes were and sometimes were not loyal tributaries. Musa, sadly now dead, worked with me on this phase of the research. Musa and I were something of a roadshow wandering from village to village doing fieldwork. We must have seemed an odd couple. He, with flowing robe and dark aviator glasses, was tall and slender. I, attired in short pants and a sweaty T-shirt, was rotund with a beard; to one observer 'Père Noël bizarre'. Musa was debonair, and a bachelor, normally at dusk it was goodbye Steve, hello young ladies – and, perhaps, with nasip (luck) there would be some niknik (intercourse). Then, it all changed. It became a time of masass (sorcery). Goodbye niknik, hello celibacy and the solace of anti-sorcery medicines.

As I sat under the honeysuckle, these memories were like old photos. Frozen moments: people of color in New York going about their ordinary lives, then blasted; Napoleon going about his extraordinary life before Waterloo, then blasted; Ahmet with Amina, then nuts; Musa, before sorcery, then a frightened celibate – snapshots of realities once vivid, now fading, hinting at stories just as had my family pictures.

There was a problem. The problem was ontological. Ontology is the branch of philosophy that philosophers up to the eighteenth century used to call meta-physics, and that positivists since Comte in the nineteenth century condemn as balderdash. This later judgment seems excessive. Ontology 'aims at dis-covering a framework for understanding the kinds of things that constitute the world's structure' (Fetzer and Almeder 1993: 101). Now some frameworks for understanding the world are better than others, and it is the search for these that gives ontological investigations merit.

The ontological problem arises because the world is just not constituted as isolated photographs. The snapshots succeeded each other, one after another. First photograph: there were some people of color in New York living their lives. Second photograph: they were sodomized or dead. First photograph, Napoleon was Emperor; then, photograph two, he was not. Once Ahmet and Amina, photograph one, were together; then, photograph two, they were not and Ahmet was catatonic. Once Musa, photograph one, sought nocturnal *niknik*; then, photograph two, he fought sorcery. The everyday hustle and bustle of people going about their business – social ontology, if you will – is strung out over time, like a movie. This stringing of antecedent to subsequent social being might be playfully imagined as 'string being'. What in a preliminary fashion is such being? String being is a characteristic of human events. Henri Lefebvre developed a 'science of space' (1991 [1974]: 7) for the social sciences. Such a notion is important for understanding string being. However, in order to understand space, a further concept, that of abstraction, requires explication because, as I use the concept of space, it can involve abstraction. The dictionary defines 'abstract' as something 'derived' or 'extracted'. An abstraction is some form of symbol, or groups of symbols, derived either from reality or from other symbols. A 'symbol' is something that stands for something else. The 'something else' that a symbol stands for is what it is derived from. Ideas and concepts are abstractions. The concept of a 'dog' is a symbol that is derived from – that is, stands for – the reality of Sebastian.

There are levels of abstraction distinguished in terms of how near a concept is to reality. The notion of 'closeness' to reality refers to how much thought has to be performed after one senses reality before one arrives at the abstraction. Concepts that 'directly report' reality are those that give a name to sensations of realities, with no further thought required. 'Observation' is the term for the sensing – that is, seeing, smelling, hearing – of reality. Less abstract concepts are reports of observation. You sense something. You say what it is. See a dog, say it is a 'dog', no further thought required.

Concepts that do not directly report reality, but which are derived from those that more or less do, are more abstract. So, for example, you can directly see somebody 'running', but you cannot see their 'speed'. The term 'informational sentences', as used here, refers to directions that tell people how to derive more abstract concepts from observations, or vice versa.[3] To calculate runners' speed, you have first to see where they started, then see where they ended, to get the distance they ran. Next you have to see how long it took them to do the running, to get the amount of time it took them to run. Finally, to derive their speed from these observations, you have to divide the time the running occurred into the distance run. 'Running' you observe. 'Speed' is a greater abstraction you can get by performing various calculations about what you observe of the running.

'Space' is place. It is place in a double sense. 'Abstract space' is the places where different abstractions about reality occur. It might be thought of as being like a photograph. 'Real space' is the reality from which abstract space is derived. It is whatever has been captured in the photograph. 'Social space' is abstract or real places of human interactions. The mother after the Civil

War striking her son, Napoleon battling Wellington, occur in real social space. There is a key informational sentence that instructs how to derive abstract from real social space: *events in real social space must be demonstrated to exhibit structure, before they can be welcomed into some abstract social space.* Events exhibit structure if it is demonstrated in some way that they are enduringly organized as either parts, or relationships that connect the parts. The mother striking her son was an event with two parts, 'mother' and 'son', and one relationship, the 'striking'. So it was an event within a domestic structure. Napoleon fighting Wellington was an event where there were also two parts – the opposing armies of the two commanders – and one relationship, that of fighting. Thus it was an event in a political structure. Different spaces can be named after what the structure in them does. Mother and son, Napoleon and Wellington respectively occupy domestic and political spaces. (Hereafter, if the term 'social space' is used without the qualifiers 'real' or 'abstract', reference is being made to both these types of spaces.)

Social spaces occur in time. 'Time' is the order of occurrence of events in reality. Two sorts of temporal orders can be distinguished: those in which realities are unrelated, and those in which they are related. Temporal sequences of social space in which there is a connection between the earlier and later occurrences in the sequence are said to be 'strings'. The existence of such strings means that these sorts of realities might be thought of as a 'string being'. The fact of string being means that the 'photographs' of social space are connected. Photographs that are strung together make movies, which is why social reality is better imagined as like movies than like photographs. *Connections* seeks to explain how string being is possible.

THE APPROACH

This explanation integrates four intellectual traditions – two of which appear to be at each other's throats, a third declared by some to be *déjà passé*, and a fourth explicitly interested in making connections. Additionally, the explanation, at least initially, slights one tradition that certain readers might believe should take pride of place, so this apparent snub needs to be accounted for. The two traditions perceived as adversaries are hermeneutics and neuroscience.

Hermeneutics, since the end of the 1960s, has been extremely important, considerably inspiring postmodern canon, dominating much of literary criticism, the arts, as well as certain areas of philosophy, the social sciences, and history. Nowhere has hermeneutics been more important than in cultural anthropology, which has been said to take the 'interpretive turn' (Rabinow and Sullivan 1987). Neuroscience, for its part since the 1990s, largely due to the inventions of new technologies for observing the living, normal brain, has produced 'Exciting findings . . . concerning the neural underpinnings of cognitive functions', especially pertaining to 'the influence of emotion and motivation upon cognition' (Nichols and Newsome 1999: c35). This new knowledge of the brain has deeply influenced psychology, psychiatry, artificial intelligence, and linguistics. Investigators of mental realms are obliged to keep the brain in mind.

These two traditions have been treated as adversaries because hermeneutics is imagined as something of an art, and neuroscience – well, the name says it – is a science. Further, hermeneutics is an idealism, dealing in the realm of incorporeal ideas. Neuroscience is a materialism because the object of its study, the brain, is a physical object about the size of a grapefruit and the most complex material structure for its size in the universe. So hermeneutics and neuroscience are considered mutually exclusive. If you do one, you do not do the other. However, I shall put them together, though in a materialist fashion that might have some old hermeneutists, like Heidegger, spinning in their graves. So much the better.

The over-the-hill intellectual tradition to be resuscitated is that of causality. A number of philosophers and scientists, starting at the beginning of the twentieth century, decided that causality, which had been critical to explanations of nature since Aristotle, was obsolete. Bertrand Russell at one point, for example, maintained that 'the word "cause" is so inextricably bound up with misleading associations as to make its complete extrusion from the philosophical vocabulary desirable' (1953: 387). Russell volunteered perceptive insights on many topics. Causality was not one of them. I argue, as has Harriet Whitehead (2000), that recent developments in the understanding of causality return it to its ancient position as *a* central notion for explaining the world. Hence, Russellian 'extrusion' is explanatory lobotomy.

Versions of all of these three traditions are helpful when explaining string being, for the following reasons. Causality seems most obviously needed because, if one understands it, one comprehends generally how causes come to have their effects, which helps to explain how antecedent spaces can connect with consequent ones. Hermeneutics is relevant because, after all, interpretation is rarely exegesis of the meaning of literary texts, and more often figuring out what just happened to know what to do next. Now 'what happened' occurred in an antecedent space, while 'what to do' will happen in a subsequent one. Interpretation, then, figures out what happened to further figure out what to do and thereby is a sort of causality that connects past spaces with future ones; and if you cannot make the connection you cannot understand string being.

But why neuroscience? Before proceeding to answer this question, it should be observed that neuroscience is undergoing rapid growth because of the acquisition of new tools for studying the brain. Gerald Edelman, a distinguished developmental neuroscientist, speculates about some of the prospects for this growth when he says, 'We are at the beginning of the neuroscientific revolution. At its end we shall know how the mind works, what governs our nature, and how we know the world. Indeed, what is going on in neuroscience may be looked at as a prelude to the largest possible scientific revolution' (1992: xiii).

With this explosion of neuroscientific knowledge in mind, it is possible to respond to the query, why neuroscience? But the answer to this question hinges upon recognizing the virtue of the insight, 'Something has got to happen someplace.' Interpretation, as will be shown, is something; and it occurs all the time, everywhere in individuals' lives. So it has got to happen somewhere. Furthermore, an elementary grasp of biology makes it clear that interpretation does not happen in the big toe and that it does occur in the brain. Hence, neuroscience provides knowledge of the someplace where a causal hermeneutics connects the past with its future.

Finally, the fourth intellectual tradition to which the present approach is indebted is connectionism. As Strauss and Quinn observe, there are 'many types of connectionists' (1997: 66), so it is important to precisely locate the present project within the hubbub of alternative connectionisms. The entire approach goes back to the work of the pioneering nineteenth-century research of the neuroscientists Santiago Ramón y Cajal and Karl Wernicke, who developed a position that came to be called 'cellular connectionism'. According to their views, individual nerve cells, organized in functional groups that connect with one another in a precise manner, are the units of brain function. Cellular connectionism has been validated and its very success has given rise since the 1980s to formal connectionisms in the disciplines influenced by neuroscience.

Formal connectionisms emphasize mathematical modeling. Such positions are strongly developed in artificial intelligence (Rummelhart and McClelland 1986), and exist in psychology (MacDonald and MacDonald 1995), linguistics (Pinker and Prince 1988) and philosophy (Fodor and Pylyshyn 1988). These positions tend to begin with 'neural metaphors' (Strauss and Quinn 1997: 51); ideas about the nature of neural networks within the brain, most importantly that they involve parallel distributed processing. Then formal models of cognition are elaborated on the basis of these 'metaphors'. My views are in one sense connectionist in the manner of both the cellular and the formal connectionists, but in another sense quite different.

First the similarity: this can be stated quickly and simply. I shall be interested in neural networks. Now the differences: this takes more explanation. There are two. First, readers will find no mathematical representation of connections proposed in this text. Such representations have their place, but when a reality is still metaphorical, it seems imprudent to put a mathematical cart before an empirical horse. It is true that there have been enormous advances in the study of the brain. It is equally correct that very little is still known, especially concerning the 'microcircuitry' of neural networks because observation of such networks remains 'most vexing' (Nichols and Newsome 1999: c37). This means, even though 'Connectionist systems claim to be "neurally plausible"', the fact remains that 'direct neurophysiological evidence for the existence of any specific kind of net or connectionist architecture in the brain is difficult to obtain' (Eiser 1994: 197). Hence, emphasis upon formalization risks sending a cart of speculative equations careening ahead of the neural horses that should draw that cart.

The second difference between past connectionisms and the present concerns the extent of the connections discussed. Previous connectionists have been interested only in connections within the brain. I am interested in these, but I am further interested in how the internal space of the brain connects with other, external spaces in string being. This means that the scope of this analysis goes beyond the brain. Hence, the variety of connectionist theory proposed is one of string being. Such theory must answer two questions: *what gets connected* and *what is the connector*? Responses to the former question are generalizations about the social forms in external spaces. Responses to the latter question are generalizations about what it is that makes the connections between such forms.

It is time to discuss the intellectual tradition that appears jilted in the explanation of string being. This is cognitive anthropology, an approach that seeks to strengthen an understanding of culture through the utilization of the findings of cognitive science. Cognitive anthropology, since the publication of Steven Tyler's (1969) work of the same title, has progressed in two different non-Darwinian and neo-Darwinian directions. The non-Darwinians include US and British branches. The American non-Darwinians are a diverse group – ranging from Lave's emphasis upon cultural cognition in everyday settings (1988), to Hutchins's model of Trobriand land tenure (1980) and Holland and Skinner's schemas of romance (1987). These approaches, though different, share an emphasis upon cultural schema or model theory (D'Andrade 1995). Recently, there has been a wedding of schema theory to a form of connectionism (Strauss and Quinn 1997: 48–84). Maurice Bloch, himself something of a connectionist (1998), and Christina Toren, influenced by Piaget (1999), have been important in British cognitive anthropology.

The neo-Darwinians, influenced in varying degrees by Dan Sperber (1996), include Pascal Boyer (1994), Scott Atran (1990, 1998), Lawrence Hirschfeld (1996, 1999), and Harriet Whitehead (2000). Their position, reminiscent of some of the last work of Victor Turner (1985: 249–89), joins with that of evolutionary psychology in suggesting that 'much more human knowledge is innate than . . . previously supposed' (Strauss and Quinn 1997: 79). They are neo-Darwinians because they take natural selection into a realm that Darwin did not consider: that of the human brain. Specifically, they argue that the brain is composed of different modules, resultant from the operation of genes existent because of natural selection, which function in different cognitive domains to produce different sorts of cultural representations.

The work of cognitive anthropologists is important. However, it will be largely set aside, at least until the final two chapters. The reason for this is that the explanandum of *Connections* is different from that of the cognitive anthropologists. The 'explanandum' of an explanation is, what is to be explained? The 'explanans' is, what does the explaining? In a detective story, the corpse is the explanandum, a mystery to be resolved. The fact that the butler did it is the explanans. Now, in cognitive anthropology the explanandum tends to be some form of a cultural mind that is accounted for by an explanans indebted to Piaget, as in the case of Torens, or heavy on modularity, as in the case of the neo-Darwinians. However, what is to be explained in *Connections* is something else. The explanandum is connections that are made between social events. The explanans of this explanandum is the connector, which will turn out to be a number of connected brain structures, themselves ultimately strung together with antecedent and subsequent social being. This being the case, the emphasis is upon research dealing with the brain and not mind.

So the present volume is in search of a connector. Specifically, it is proposed that a cultural neurohermeneutic system is a connector making connections between external spaces in string being. Thus the approach argues the importance of a particular neurohermeneutics – a cultural one – for explaining everyday life. Let us below outline the arguments from causality, hermeneutics and neuroscience that recommend such a conclusion. In so doing, I rehearse the book's argument.

THE ARGUMENT

The argument in the text is simple. First, it is shown that anthropology should be *the* central human science, but that this has been impossible due to a problem with its major theoretical projects; and then it is demonstrated how a cultural neurohermeneutic system eliminates the problem. How is the argument made? There is a type of film called a 'road movie', such as *Bonnie and Clyde*. Directors of such films put the protagonists in a car and let them drive to lots of scenic places. So viewers get two benefits for the price of one. They enjoy great scenery, plus they get the movie's story. Actually, the road movie as a way of developing a narrative is old stuff. Both the *Odyssey* and *Candide* were road shows. Odysseus took a Mediterranean tour; while Candide and his tutor, Pangloss, benefited from a rather more extended global jaunt. This is pretty good company, so *Connections*' position is developed on the road, with different chapters of the argument formulated in different picturesque (intellectual) vistas. Readers enter a 'twilight' zone, encounter a 'ghost', get stuck in and freed from the 'cement of the universe', take time out for some archery, and finally come to cultivate a garden.

Chapter 2 opens the argument and travels to what Marshall Sahlins has termed a 'twilight' zone. The chapter develops a method for locating problems in theory, applies the method to certain aspects of anthropology, and discovers problems. The method proposed for analyzing theoretical problems is called 'agnoiology'. Two current theoretical projects are explored agnoiologically: those of conjectural hermeneutics, derived from Geertz, and Cartesian dualism, whose genealogy ascends to René Descartes, but whose recent practitioners include Pierre Bourdieu, Jean and John Comaroff, Claude Lévi-Strauss, and Marshall Sahlins. It is shown that anthropology is in a twilight zone because these approaches bungle making the connections necessary to account for string being. There is a consequence of this twilight of bungled connections. Because of it, anthropological theory offers no credible candidate for the connector between antecedent and subsequent spaces. The remainder of the text is an excursion in search of the candidate.

Chapter 3 travels to a place that Gilbert Ryle has said is haunted by a 'ghost'. The apparition bedevils Cartesian dualism – which dualism Sartre had said was 'insurmountable'. The chapter duels the dualism, largely with data from neuroscience, and shows what is mistaken about it, thereby exorcising the ghost. This frees readers to discover that what was previously judged to be two different realities – a dualism – is a single reality – a monism. It is then shown that this monism is a social one composed of I-space, structures internal to the body, and E-space, those external to it. Neurohermeneutics investigates how a connector holds together the string being in this social monism. The remainder of the book's chapters argue that a cultural neurohermeneutic system in I-space is a connector that generates desire to act upon antecedent E-spaces in ways that produce subsequent E-spaces.

Chapter 4 voyages to the 'cement of the universe'. This was Hume's term for causality, and one of the labors of this chapter is to get rid of the cement. The chapter first addresses the conjectural hermeneutists' disdain for connection by formally posing the question 'What is a connection?' It answers this question by suggesting that ultimately connection is causation. A knotty approach to causation is then developed based upon the philosopher of science Wesley Salmon's notion of physical causality and the Marxist Louis Althusser's conception of structural causality. Knotty causation gets readers out of Humean cement. Investigators using this approach to causation look for material structures that tie together antecedent and subsequent realities. Such structures are called 'connectors'. The remainder of the chapter travels the streets of different sorts of hermeneutics, because it is here that a connector may be found. It is argued that there is a neurohermeneutic system in I-space, composed of linked neural circuits in the brain that interpret antecedent events in E-space to make actions that become the basis of subsequent events in E-space. This is the connector, but it is not yet fully constructed.

Chapter 5 goes on the road again to finish the labor of building the connector by bringing culture into the analysis. It travels to a land where, as the poet William Blake put it, there are 'arrows of desire'. The chapter begins with a discussion of Immanuel Kant's approach to interpretation. This discussion leads to the realization that hermeneutics does not produce 'all or nothing' interpretations so that a hermeneutist knows 'This means that, and that's that!' Rather, interpretation normally results in multiple shades of meaning. Such an appreciation leads to the suggestion that hermeneutics should be understood as some sort of a hierarchical causal process, with different levels in the hierarchy producing different shades of meanings.

This recognition leads both back to culture and to neuroscience. First, it is argued that culture comes in two 'neuronal' and 'discursive' forms. Next, it is proposed that the neurohermeneutic system is actually a *cultural* neuro-hermeneutic system. This proposal is based upon the integration of ideas about neuronal culture, with elements of the Kantian hermeneutic, and with a particular neuroscientific, 'associationist' approach to learned memory. The cultural neurohermeneutic system works through a neural circuitry that takes information about antecedent events from E-space into an interpretive hier-archy in I-space. The interpretive hierarchy utilizes learned cultural memories of past realities to represent the antecedent events in ways that form the basis of desires about future realities. Then the circuitry of the cultural neuro-hermeneutic system translates these desires into actions that lead out of I-space to become events in E-space. These are the old poet's 'arrows' that connect antecedent with subsequent E-space. So the chapter concludes by proposing that the cultural neurohermeneutic system functions as a bow firing arrows linking past to future realities.

After the hurly-burly of being on the road to the connector the final two chapters go home, to speculate upon what it might mean to cultivate neuro-hermeneutics in a 'garden' of string being. Chapter 6 locates cultural neuro-hermeneutics in a broader theoretical context. It discusses what it is not and what it is. It is argued that such hermeneutics is not an *über*-determinism. The case of the neo-Darwinian cognitive anthropologists is discussed when seeking to define this variety of determinism. It is concluded that cultural neuro-hermeneutics is neither a biological nor a cultural *über*-determinism. It is really a rather knotty causal determinism.

Chapter 7 explores the type of anthropology implied by this approach. It is proposed that this is a Boasian social anthropology. One aspect of this pro-posal involves integrating certain aspects of the work of the cognitive anthro-pologists into the inquiry, showing how their interest in mind can be used in an analysis of the brain to make a stronger cultural neurohermeneutics and, concomitantly, a stronger Boasian anthropology. A final note of reassurance is required here. The old Boasians and social anthropologists often imagined themselves to be ferociously opposed. So it may seem a cruel kindness, an oxymoron, to marry the two anthropologies. However, it will be shown that the approach argued in *Connections* combines elements of the two traditions, so that what at first sight appears a very odd couple, on reflection might just be a way to make anthropology *the* central social, cultural, and biological discipline studying the human condition.

So no more fading photographs, waning memories, *Connections* motors through a twilight zone of bungled connections on to the connector and, then, home to the garden. Along the way you will hear more stories of people set upon by the New York police, of Ahmet, of Musa, even of the Emperor and the Duke. It is time to be out and about, making connections.

Part I

Bungled connections

Chapter 2

Conjectural hermeneutics and 'insurmountable dualism'

> Bungle: 1. To do or make in a clumsy or unskilled manner . . .
> (*Oxford English Dictionary*)

Mario Bunge, a philosopher of social science and not an anthropologist, hence with the level-headed gaze of a non-partisan specialist, terms anthropology – and he really means Boasian anthropology with its four fields – the 'broadest', most 'basic and comprehensive' of the human sciences. It is the central discipline in the study of humanity. Other disciplines are merely 'branch' offices (Bunge 1998: 47). Given this centrality, one might expect things to have gone well for anthropology.

They have not, at least according to some of its distinguished practitioners, who debate whether the discipline is 'self destructing' (Knauft 1996: 1). Marshall Sahlins warns that '"Culture" . . . is in the twilight of its career, and anthropology with it' (1995: 14). Eric Wolf deplores its 'general retreatism' (in Friedman 1987: 116). Clifford Geertz prophesies that the discipline will disappear in about fifty years (in Handler 1991: 612). Knauft states that such opinions appear 'widely shared' (1996: 296). A discipline that goes about its intellectual business in an unskilled fashion may be said to bungle. The fact that anthropology, the most 'basic' of the human sciences, is judged to be 'self destructing' suggests bungling. This indicates that a useful activity for securing any future for anthropology is to investigate, why the bungling?

Sherry Ortner, very much a partisan insider for anthropology, wrote an influential article, 'Theory in Anthropology since the Sixties', which claimed the discipline to be theoretically 'a thing of shreds and patches' (1984: 126). Bunge, the informed outsider, concurs with Ortner's judgment, reporting anthropology to be 'theoretically underdeveloped' (1998: 57). This chapter reviews four theoretical projects in anthropology. The first project is Clifford Geertz's conjectural hermeneutics, especially as presented in *Works and Lives* (1988) and *After the Fact* (1995). The second project is Pierre Bourdieu's practice theory, as argued in perhaps its most complete form in the *Logic of Social Practice* (1990). The third project is one of a Gramscian idealism that has been proposed by Jean and John Comaroff in their *Of Revelation and Revolution* (1991). The final project is Lévi-Straussian, including the original version offered in *Les Structures élémentaires de la parenté* (1949) and a variant developed by Sahlins in the rebarbative *How 'Natives' Think* (1995). Though these projects have their origins in the 1940s, and though they do not exhaust the theoretical possibilities in current anthropology, they are arguably among the most important theoretical alternatives caterwauling for space in the anthropological imagination at the turn of the millennium.[1]

The chapter is organized into three parts. Section one offers elements of an 'agnoiological method', for the discovery of weaknesses in theory. This methodology operates by discovering information concerning what is *unknown but which needs to be known* to strengthen theory. Then, this methodology is applied in the second and third sections. Section two explores aspects of Geertz's thought. It argues that Geertz and his followers operate a conjectural hermeneutics that is weak, because it rejects the utility of bothering to know how events in reality might be connected. Section three reveals that elements of Bourdieu's, the Comaroffs', Lévi-Strauss's, and Sahlins's work all exhibit a Cartesian ontology that divides reality into objective and subjective spaces. However, agnoiological analysis suggests that the generalizations they develop to explain events in this ontology fall into an agnoiological hole of 'insurmountable dualism', to use Sartre's term for it. This means that, even though they dearly want to connect the objective and subjective, they bungle it. The chapter concludes with proposals for addressing this bungling. The work of the chapter begins in the next section by explaining the virtues of agnoiology.

AGNOIOLOGY

> Knowledge and human power are synonymous, since the ignorance of cause frustrates the effect.
>
> (Francis Bacon, *The Great Instauration*, 1690)

As modern times dawned, where Bacon was defining the nature of a new science, he made one point very clearly. The preceding quotation expresses that point: knowledge is power. However, implicit in this doctrine is a further one about ignorance: in order to know something, you must know you are ignorant of it. Agnoiological doctrine consists of instructions that guide scientific practice during validation of theory to provide knowledge about what knowledge is *absent* in the theory. In order to understand agnoiology we need to acquire a sense of science and of the role of validation in it. What follows is not a technical treatise defending a particular Comtean positivist, logical positivist, or post-positivist philosophy of science. Rather, the view of science present is vulcanized. Vulcan was the Roman god of crafts. The understanding of science might be called 'vulcanized' because it is that of a craftsperson struggling to describe what they actually do when practicing their art. The idea that science might be an art is not original. Back when Bacon was offering his ideas for a new science, he spoke of it as 'The art which I introduce' (1980 [1620]: 21).

Art creates splendors of the imagination. Different arts, different imaginations.[2] Artists use their imaginations to conjure creations, paintings, and the beauty they create pertains to these. Scientists, too, use their imaginations to conjure creations, generalizations, to which the beauty they produce belongs. Rubens imagined magnificent bottoms; Einstein a theory of relativity. Relativity has its beauty, just as does a Rubens bottom. Let us set aside the baroque bottom to pose the austere question, what is scientific beauty?

This question is answered by posing another question, what is a generalization? Generalizations, at their simplest, result from the practice of linking concepts together into statements that take particulars and maintain them more generally. 'Sebastian liked Braden, Damon and Alexander' is a particularity. Sebastian, it will be recalled, was the dog in the introduction. He was given as a puppy to my sons, who loved him dearly. 'Dogs and people exhibit generalized reciprocity based upon affection' is a generalization that expresses more broadly the relationship between the boys and dogs.

Further, generalizations are statements that express relationships in verbal or quantitative form which explain why there are connections in some space of reality. Such statements have two parts, *concepts of reality* and *concepts of connections* in reality. 'The more peoples' interests are opposed, the greater their likelihood of conflict' is a generalization that expresses how the concepts of 'opposing interests' and 'levels of conflict' are related in a positive fashion, so that as one goes up, the other also goes up. Additionally, it explains why there are often different forms of disputes ranging from verbal harassment to naked violence in spaces in which pro-abortion and anti-abortion activists find themselves.

So understood, the scientific imagination is about conceiving connections, with the creations of this imagination expressed in generalizations. The connections in generalizations are relationships between concepts, concepts that represent that certain events will happen in specific ways in the world. Those generalizations which are relatively low in abstraction and scope and that are derived from observations are termed 'empirical generalizations'. Those that are inductively derived from empirical generalizations and which, thus, are higher in abstraction and scope are 'theories'. Generalizations that are deductively derived from theories and that are of lower scope and abstraction are 'hypotheses'. The concept of a theory is enormously contested. From a vulcanized perspective, theory is any of these three sorts of generalizations. 'Theorizing' is making generalizations. 'Theory' is generalizations made.

Now it is possible to distinguish the beauty of theoretical creations from those in other arts. A generalization's beauty is about how accurately it provides knowledge of reality. A Picasso can bend reality a good bit and still have its beauty, but generalizations must be 'realistic' to qualify as beautiful. So the aesthetics of science – expressed more generally, by philosophies of science; less generally, by scientific methods; and least generally, by particular techniques employed in specific sciences – offer information about how to formulate generalizations that accurately correspond to the realities with which they are imagined to correspond. A generalization in which there is no such correspondence is said to be purely conjectural, a guess. This brings us to the concept of truth.

Truth is central to the scientific aesthetic because it is the tool humans possess for distinguishing what *is* from what is conjectured. The following incident helps to illustrate this point. During the 1988 US presidential campaign between George Bush, Sr, and Michael Dukakis, Bush's supporters hired an advertising agency to make what has come to be known as the 'Willie Horton' commercial. This was shown on television during the campaign and represented a reality that made voters not want to vote for Dukakis. The commercial used a *cinéma-vérité* style to reveal a frightening man being freed from prison at the instigation of the then Governor of Massachusetts, Dukakis. The man released was Willie Horton, a black murderer, who, the film informed its viewers, proceeded to rape a nice, white, suburban, middle-class woman. The commercial conjured a reality where 'Niggers rape white chicks, even in the burbs, and the Democrat helped them do it!' Dukakis lost.

A statement is 'true' when 'what it asserts to be the case is the case' (Fetzer and Almeder 1993: 135).[3] The commercial's message – 'the Democrat helped them do it' – is something of an empirical generalization. However, the observations that Horton was not released by Dukakis and that African-American men upon prison release do not uniformly sprint for the suburbs to rape bourgeois women suggests that observed events do not occur as the commercial has them. The advertisement may have its beauty from the perspective of a film aesthetic. However, from that of a scientific aesthetic it is an ugly racist conjuring of the sorts of untruths that provoke lynching. Perhaps, because it is so important to distinguish what *is* from what is *conjectured*, even as determined a skeptic as Derrida insists, 'we must have truth' (1981).

Truth in scientific aesthetics results from validation. Validation, sometimes called 'confirmation' or 'verification', involves procedures that guide the making of observations so that observers can know how well what a generalization asserts to be the case is the case. One way in which this is done is through the creation of procedures that foster objectivity, a concept with 'a large number of interrelated senses' (Mautner 1996: 298). Two ontological and epistemological senses, however, are fundamental and need to be distinguished. The *Oxford English Dictionary* offers a definition of objectivity as 'the object of perception or thought' (in Sahlins 1995: 162). Here is a first, ontological sense of the term where it is used in opposition to subjectivity. The subjective is a realm within a person of consciousness, of perceptions and thought. The objective is an external realm of the objects of perceptions and thoughts. I shall be interested in this meaning of objectivity later in the chapter. However, there is a second meaning of the term that is of present interest.

The epistemological meaning of objectivity is the making of observations that exhibit 'independence of awareness' and/or 'impartiality of judgment' (Mautner 1996: 298–9).[4] Objectivity is desired because otherwise there is bias that can produce untruths. A study of people that observes only men exhibits gender bias and would be likely to produce unreliable judgments concerning women. Objectivity does not mean that either science or scientists are value neutral. Scientists have their biases. However, scientists who seek objectivity pursue an epistemic tolerance by suspending, as much as is possible, ego-centrisms, phallocentrisms, and ethnocentrisms. They do this by creating validation procedures that eliminate, where possible, such centrisms.

What are such procedures? They are numerous and, among others, include random sampling and different techniques of controlling for bias. Do they work? This is a bit like inquiring: do contraceptive techniques work? At present, there is no such thing as a foolproof contraceptive. Nor are there procedures to eliminate bias perfectly. But simple precautions do reduce the risks of unwanted pregnancies or biased conclusions. Gender bias is reduced if one observes as many women as men. Racial bias would have been reduced in the Willie Horton commercial if observations had been made of how often black men as compared to white men raped white women in the suburbs.

Validation procedures must not only strive for objectivity; they must also do so in situations that are contested and approximate – contested, in that there are different generalizations that compete to explain the same events and in this contestation the prize goes to those statements which are 'approximately true' (Miller 1987). These are generalizations for which observations better fit the case than they do for competing generalizations. Generalizations that better fit the case have *more* events that occur the way they are supposed to than their rivals and so might be said to be 'approximately truer'. Einstein's relativity is, in this sense, approximately truer than Newton's mechanics. This brings us to the Scottish philosopher James Frederick Ferrier.

Ferrier introduced the expression 'epistemology' into English in his *Institutes of Metaphysic* (1854: 397–440). Less well known is that, in the same work, he also proposed the term 'agnoiology'. Epistemology has long been a staple of philosophic discourse. Perhaps, agnoiology languished because it is fiendishly difficult to pronounce and philosophers, reluctant to face ridicule, refrained from spitting it out in the heat of *parole*. But spat out it should be. Agnoiology deals with an aspect of knowing that seems neglected. Epistemology concerns knowledge; agnoiology the 'nature and character' of ignorance (ibid.: 400). Ferrier believed that 'the most important proposition in agnoiology' is that 'there can be ignorance only of that of which there can be knowledge' (ibid.: 405). Agnoiological doctrine, then, specifies methods that proceed by revealing ignorance: what one does not know, but needs to know, in order to possess fuller knowledge. Ignorance consists of unrealistic concepts and what investigators need to know are gaps, voids, gaffes and holes, because it is these that reveal different flaws in the conception of reality.

The trope of a necklace is helpful in explicating gaps, voids, and so on. A generalization – be it an empirical generalization, a theory, or a hypothesis – is like a necklace. Its concepts of what is are its jewels, and its concepts of the connections between what is are its strands. A beautiful 'generalization necklace' is a flawless representation of a real-world necklace. 'Flawless' here means approximately true. A theoretical 'gap' occurs when observation reveals that there is some space of existence where events happen, for which there are *no* concepts of what happens or of how they are connected. For example, the existence of men and women has not been a secret, though concepts that depict this reality typically failed to play a part in social theory until the 1970s. Similarly, it has been obvious that people possess different amounts of economic resources and that these are related to a number of other different realities ranging from life span to taste. However, concepts of economic difference, as of class, tend to be missing in neo-classical economic theory. A gap, then, is a situation where a generalization necklace has not been completed, because the jewels and/or the strands are missing.

The notion of a void is related to that of a gap. In a 'void' a space of existence has been given a concept, but there is knowledge either that observations indicate that there are realities which have not been fully observed pertaining to this concept; or that the concept is so vague that it is unclear how it might correspond to realities. Before microscopes were invented one could not see the tiny bugs that ran riot in human bodies. However, after their invention investigators detected a few such bugs and gave them a name, 'microbes'. It was observed that these might be related to illnesses. This, then, led to the knowledge that there was a void, and that further observation of microbial realities would lead to more complete understanding of illness. This knowledge, when acquired, reduced the void and made possible a germ theory of illness.

Consider a further example of the value of knowing of the existence of a void. Many have long held the impression that smoking was harmful. However, in the late 1950s it became known that there was a non-chance, statistical relationship between smoking and lung cancer. Further, because it was evident that the onset of cancer did not suddenly induce people to smoke, it was suspected that the association between smoking and cancer was because the former caused the latter. This suggested the generalization 'smoking causes lung cancer'. The two concepts, the jewels, in this generalization necklace are 'smoking' and 'lung cancer'. However, there is a missing strand. It is known that it is unknown how smoking causes cancer; that is, the relationship between smoking and cancer remains a mystery. This knowledge is the void.

A second way in which voids occur is when concepts are supposed to represent something happening in reality but it is terribly obscure what that something might be. Such voids are those of ambiguity. For example, political science textbooks hold the US up as a model of a democracy even though persons of great wealth and high political position considerably influence what happens in government. Can it be that democracies are also oligarchies? These textbooks do not address this issue, which means that in them the concept of 'democracy' remains ambiguous and, hence, something of a void. Concepts like 'culture', 'power', 'deconstruction', which have multiple meanings, which are not necessarily voids, become so when the investigators who utilize them fail to specify exactly what they mean when they use the terms.

Attention now turns to generalizations in which there are gaffes. These occur when observation reveals that there are concepts and/or relationships in a generalization that do not accurately represent observed realities. A 'gaffe' is a situation where they have got it wrong. A generalization necklace has been completed, but is composed of the wrong jewels and strands. Consider, for example, that up to the eighteenth century the dominant theory of the origin of rocks held that 'rocks' resulted as 'precipitates from a universal chaotic fluid' (Bynum et al. 1981: 441). Nobody ever found the fluid. It was a real gaffe. Consider, further, that the Comte de Gobineau believed 'every race capable of developing a civilization develops one peculiar to itself' (1856: 438). Such opinions as this formed the basis of a nineteenth-century racism which insisted that 'racial difference produced cultural difference'. In this generalization necklace there are two concepts, 'race' and 'culture', and one relationship, that of 'production'. However, Boasian anthropology provided evidence that failed to observe any connection between race and cultural change (Boas 1911; Stocking 1968). The gaffe, then, is that the concept of 'race' does not accurately represent whatever it is that produces cultural difference.

Gaps, voids, and gaffes concern the generalizations of a single thinker. 'Holes' are located when it is observed that a number of thinkers have similar gaps, voids, and gaffes in their theorizing. For example, it has been appreciated from the very beginning of capitalism that not everybody is able to find work in such economies. However, as Myrdal has remarked, the concept of 'unemployment' did not enter economic theory until the late nineteenth century (1969: 45). This means, because no economic theorist employed a notion of unemployment, that this gap kept reappearing in economic generalizations, suggesting that there was a theoretical hole concerning employment. Consider, further, that Gobineau was not alone in his racism. Many others – including Comte, Spencer, and Tylor – subscribed in varying degrees to his view that race was a source of cultural difference. Gobineau's gaffe, then, was reiterated in nineteenth-century cultural theory suggesting that it was sunk in a deep, racist hole.

Let us clarify what you can know you do not know if you apply agnoio-logical procedures during validation. If you know your ignorance is that of a gap, you know you need a concept, or concepts, to fill the gap. If you know your ignorance involves a void, you know you need more observations before you will be able to formulate concepts to fill the void. If you know that you are so ignorant as to have made a gaffe, then you know you will need new concepts and probably further observations to remove the gaffe. The identifi-cation of holes is the discovery of a particular type of unobjectivity. Much intellectual bias is the proclivity to think *about* particular subjects. For example, starting with Sigmund Freud, many twentieth-century theorists were preoccupied with sex. The discovery of holes provides knowledge of a reverse bias, of the obsession of an intellectual community to ignore certain matters. Nineteenth-century Victorians ignored sex. Holes, then, as deep spaces of ignorance are promising places for the scientific Vulcans to set up shop, observing and theorizing, to craft more objective jewels and strands of generalization necklaces. It is time to turn an agnoiological gaze on con-jectural hermeneutics.

A CONJECTURALIST WORLD OF IMPRESSION MANAGEMENT

> It grew out of the cultural anthropology of the 1960s. . . . It has a major spokesman in Clifford Geertz, whose work has made it the most influential style of anthropology among the wider intellectual public.
> (G. Marcus and M. Fischer, *Anthropology as Cultural Critique*, 1986: 16)

Something is conjectured, as was noted in the previous section, if it is just guessed at without concern for the truth of the guess. The first 'It' of the above quotation is a conjectural hermeneutics. In the decade between the publication of *The Interpretation of Cultures* (1973, hereafter IC) and *Local Knowledge* (1983, hereafter LK), Geertz rejected science, saying he 'never really bought' it (Handler 1991: 608), thereby initiating anthropology into this hermeneutics. Let us explore a bit where, and how, it is that Geertz parts company with science, for it is here that his hermeneutics becomes conjectural.[5]

Geertz actually called for the validation of interpretations according to 'systematic modes of assessment' (1973: 24). Now Spencer has said that Geertz expends 'considerable energy on the problem of the validation of differing interpretations' on page 30 of IC (1989: 159). A single page hardly seems to allow enough space to develop any mode of validation, let alone one that is 'systematic'. Further, my reading of the page in question is that it offers no procedures for arriving at valid attributions of meaning. There appears to be no other student of Geertz who proposes that they have formulated validation procedures. Further, I take Geertz at his word when he tells readers in LK that they would not find 'much' in the way of 'theory and methodology' in his hermeneutics (1983: 5). So D'Andrade's judgment that Geertz's approach exhibits 'no method of validation' (1995: 248) seems sensible, which means that even though Geertz called for 'systematic modes of assessment' he never crafted them.

Similarly, Geertz reveals a lack of concern with objectivity. This is evident in certain aspects of his Indonesian ethnography. Indonesian society, at the time Geertz studied it, was riven by great differences of wealth and position. However, Geertz made no systematic attempt to inform readers when information was from the viewpoint of the gentry, peasants, or for that matter from himself. Readers, then, do not know whether they are being presented with the biases of landowners, workers, or of a Cold War liberal (Reyna 1998).

As for truth, Geertz's position is not that true statements do not exist. He implicitly assures readers that they do when, following consideration of certain assertions made by Evans-Pritchard, he says, 'The question is not the truth of such statements (though I have my doubts about those Bedouins and those women)' (1988: 63). Rather, his attitude is one of indifference to truth in the sense that he acts as if distinguishing truth from untruth is unimportant. So why bother with questions of validation, which, of course, explains why he failed to deliver upon the promised modes of assessment. Such indifference means that, when it comes to establishing the truth of interpretations, 'You either grasp an interpretation or you do not, see the point or you do not' (1973: 24).

This suggests, as Crapanzano has observed, that Geertz's interpretations were made in the absence of 'specifiable evidence' (1992: 67), which means that they are pretty much 'conjectural, unverifiable' (Cohen 1974: 5). This judgment is shared by Bunge, who states, 'we are never told how to interpret "interpretation", from the examples used one gathers that it is just conjecturing' (1998: 57). It might be objected that Geertz provided intellectual underpinnings of interpretation with his discussion of 'thick description' with its ethic of sticking 'experience near'. However, these concepts were derived from the philosopher Gilbert Ryle in a manner which has been shown to be muddled (Descombes 1998). Further, regardless of whether Geertz got his philosophic rationale right, Crapanzano's, Cohen's and Bunge's judgment remains: no account of how to 'interpret "interpretations"' disturbs thick description. If Geertz's hermeneutics is something of a guessing game, then it is appropriate to label it conjectural. So hereafter, I shall refer to it as conjectural hermeneutics and its practitioners as conjecturalists. This leads us to the question, what is the conjecturalist aesthetic; that is to say, how and what should they use their imaginations to conjecture?

Geertz might be construed in *Works and Lives* (hereafter WL) to be arguing that conjectural hermeneutics should conjure up knowledge judged, in considerable measure, by its rhetorical effectiveness. WL examines great anthropologists seeking to comprehend what made them exceptional. At one point in the text Geertz states 'that the separation of what someone says from how they say it . . . substance from rhetoric . . . is as mischievous in anthropology as it is in poetry, painting, or political oratory' (1988: 27). In fact, Geertz does separate substance and rhetoric in WL because he ignores the substance of his subjects' work and is completely indifferent to what might be true in it. Rather, his only concern is with 'how they say it', which implies that he holds an aesthetic where the beauty of what is created in an anthropological text depends on its rhetoric. Hence, writing of Lévi-Strauss, Geertz says, 'It was not the odd facts or even odder explanations Lévi-Strauss brought forth that made of him . . . an intellectual hero. It was the mode of discourse he invented to display those facts and frame those explanations' (ibid.: 26). Here, what Geertz asserts is that what made Lévi-Strauss a 'hero' was not his substance ('facts . . . and explanations') but his rhetoric ('mode of discourse').

This poses the question, how does one appraise the beauty of rhetoric? Geertz answers this question by noting that 'we listen to some voices and ignore others' (ibid.: 6), and that the factor governing what gets 'listened to' is that:

> some ethnographers are more effective than others in conveying in their prose the impression that they have had close-in contact with far out lives. . . . In discovering how . . . such an impression is created, we shall discover, at the same time, the criteria by which to judge them.
>
> (ibid.: 6)

Geertz proposes in this quotation that 'the criteria by which to judge' anthropological rhetoric is that of how 'effective' it is in the manufacture of impressions; and impressions, like advertising copy, are to be assessed in terms of whether they are 'listened to'.

Geertz, then – nonchalant about validation, objectivity, and truth – is a bit like those advertising executives who made the Willie Horton commercial. They too were in the business of manufacturing 'effective' impressions. Essentially, Geertz is suggesting an aesthetic whose central canon is: textual conjuring will be judged in terms of how 'effective' it is in creating impressions. The Horton commercial by this aesthetic was a real thing of beauty. It made a great impression. What, then, was there left to say when you had decided that your contribution to anthropology was to exhort its practitioners to get into the field of impression management?

What was left to say was said in *After the Fact* (hereafter ATF), and is an expression of an ontology that goes a long way towards helping us to understand the rejection of science. Perhaps its core is contained in his 'It is

Heraclitus cubed and worse' (1995: 2). 'Time' is 'larger and smaller streams, twisting and turning and now and then crossing, running together for a while, separating again' (ibid.: 2). There are no histories or biographies, 'but a confusion of histories, a swarm of biographies' (ibid.: 2). Consequently, the anthropologist must be satisfied with a world of 'accidental dramas' (ibid.: 2), 'particular events', and 'unique occasions' (ibid.: 3). This is a sociocultural ontology of evanescent 'confusion' in which reality is 'twisting', 'turning', 'accidental', 'particular', and 'unique'. An appropriate question to pose at this juncture is, what reasons does Geertz advance to justify this position? The answer to the question is that in ATF being is as Geertz says it is, take it or leave it. Further, given that reality is 'confusion', is it surprising that Geertz confides to his readers, 'I have always thought that understanding social life entails not an advance toward an omega point, "Truth", "Reality", "Being", or "the World", but the restless making and unmaking of facts and ideas' (ibid.: 117)? Everywhere, at all times and in all places social 'understanding . . . entails not an advance'.

Conjectural hermeneutics has been enormously influential. There emerged in US anthropology throughout the 1980s and early 1990s, according to Marcus, 'a distinctive interpretive approach . . . unique in the social sciences or humanities' (1994: 43).[6] What is distinctive, if not unique, about this approach, is that its practitioners, like Geertz, reject science and validation. James Boon's discussion of falsifiability in *Other Tribes, Other Scribes* illustrates how such conjecturalists treat validation. Here, after explaining to readers that anthropology was to a significant degree a literary discipline, he popped the question, 'what becomes of the issues of falsifiability and accuracy?' His response to this question was simple: 'They are . . . complexly conventionalized' (1982: 20). Absent is further discussion of how different conventions lead to greater or lesser falsifiability and, hence, accuracy. What Boon does here is to stop the discussion of falsifiability just when it is getting interesting. Certainly, there are 'complexly conventionalized' conventions of falsifiability. Now tell us which are the better ones? But Boon, and other conjecturalists, responds to this question with silence. So, theirs, like Geertz's, is a conjectural hermeneutics that can only evaluate claims of what happens in social being literarily in terms of 'the emotional impact of rhetoric' (Kuznar 1997: ix).

It should come as no surprise that these conjecturalists do not 'need' what Marcus termed 'conventional social theory' (1994: 47). Rather, what conjecturalists do, as Marcus and Fischer candidly confide, 'is *at best* conversation across cultural codes, at a minimum a written form of public lecture adjusting style and content to the intelligence of the audience' (1986: 29; emphasis added). When they do these there is 'motivation to develop more effective ways of describing and analyzing cross-cultural experience' that 'makes use of more explicit fictional narrative devices tempting' (ibid.: 76). Marcus and Fischer are honest: conjectural hermeneutists are 'at best' conversationalists.

What may be distinctive of conjectural compared to other forms of hermeneutics is the inattention to truth. Gadamer has written, 'no one would dream
of putting in doubt the immanent criteria of what we call scientific knowledge'
(1987: 111–12). Even Derrida had insisted there 'must' be truth. However,
there is no place in any of Geertz's texts where he confronts the literature
concerning validation, objectivity, and truth and demonstrates why truth is
impossible. He just 'never really bought' it. Rosaldo has asserted that 'conceptions of truth and objectivity have eroded' (1989: 21). The erosion of such
'conceptions' would seem to be grounds for their clarification – a task Rosaldo
ignores, perhaps because he does not show evidence of any familiarity with
the relevant literature. James Clifford, following Nietzsche, apparently unaware
that Nietzsche had repudiated himself (Westphal 1984), decided that there
was no truth (1988: 93).

In sum, conjecturalists do not know the reasoning for, or against, different
understandings of truth. Hence, they are in no position to formulate
arguments against truth; but they do know it to be true that truth has 'eroded'.
Consequently, though they do not seek truthful theory, they truly know that
they represent the Other better than do scientific anthropologies. So, missionaries, they proselytize anthropologists to repudiate scientific approaches as
'archaic' and 'surviving' in 'degraded form' (Tyler 1986: 123), the better to slip
into a conjectural program with 'fictional . . . devices' that are so 'tempting'.

It is time to specify the nature of the conjecturalists' bungling. Hermeneutics
for them is a guessing game because they are indifferent to validation. Some
of their guesses evoke vivid impressions of connections in reality but, being
nonchalant about the truth of these impressions, who knows whether the connections exist or are just another case of effective impression management,
like the Willie Horton commercial, based upon use of 'fictional . . . devices'?

Further, remember that in the preceding chapter it was suggested that
reality is strung out over time – with antecedents linked to consequents – in a
sort of string being. Agnoiologically, if those antecedents and their sequelae
are likened to jewels, the trouble with conjectural hermeneutics is that the
jewels can never be connected because conjecturalists refuse to validate
whether anything is connected to anything else. Conjecturalist doctrine
exhorts impression management at the expense of validation. Their bungling
results from refusal even to try to string the jewels together, to bother to
observe whether antecedents have consequents. So being can never get to be
string being.

Now it is time to investigate another species of bungling. Bourdieu, the
Comaroffs, Lévi-Strauss, and Sahlins held diverse views on the nature of
science, but none was anti-scientific like the conjecturalists. Validation is fine.
If there are jewels out there to connect, connect them. But, as the following
section argues, all four theorists share a theoretical descent, with modification,

from Descartes into a hole of Cartesian dualism; with a ghost bungling around at the bottom of it.

CARTESIAN DUALISM

> Few views are as central to Western philosophy as Descartes's dualism.
>
> (M. Rozemond, *Descartes's Dualism*, 1998: xi)

Rozemond makes it clear. René Descartes (1596–1650) authored one of the 'central' positions in modern Western philosophy. But in order to grasp Descartes, mention must first be made of Baron Verulam, Francis Bacon (1561–1626). Modernity got a rousing send-off in his works. These championed three premises that were most succinctly expressed in *The Great Instauration* (1620). First, nature is the author of what happens in nature. Second, science is the tool to 'conquer' nature. Third, 'human Power' increases with nature 'commanded', making possible progress, or increases in 'the fortune of the human race' (1980 [1620]: 21, 31, 32). There is an imperious humanism in this modernism, for as one commentator on Bacon has noted, it is 'a world freed from God's providence' (Weinberger 1980: ix), where humans command nature, not gods.[7]

Descartes, a generation Bacon's junior, shared with the good Lord the beliefs that natural realities account for each other and that science provides truer knowledge of these realities. Indeed, the subtitle of his *A Discourse on Method* (1649) states that the text is concerned with 'the discovery of the Truth in the Sciences'. However, there is an element of Descartes's thought that seems a survival from a medieval scholasticism that was itself an amalgam of Aristotelian philosophy and Christian theology.[8] This aspect of his thought is best approached through Descartes's understanding of what it meant to be human.

'Man', he believed, is 'a combination of mind and body' (Descartes 1985 [1649]: 61). The key insistence here is that there are two different realities, one of mind and the other of body. Further note, Descartes used the terms 'mind' and 'soul' interchangeably and that, speaking of himself, but having himself stand for every person, he insisted:

> [I] knew I was a substance whose whole essence or nature is simply to think, and which does not require any place, or depend on any material thing, in order to exist. Accordingly this 'I' – that is, the soul by which I am what I am – is entirely distinct from the body.
>
> (ibid.: 127)

The Cartesian 'I' – an incorporeal mind–soul, which consciously thinks, is the 'essence' of a person and is 'entirely distinct' from material body – is the starting point of modern views of ontological subjectivity (Judovitz 1988). However, this view of mind as soul seems directly derived from Christian theology. Thomas Aquinas in *Summa theologica* insisted, 'the human soul, which is called intellect or mind, is something incorporeal and subsisting' (in Rozemond 1998: 45). Descartes added to Bacon's conception of modernity, and the value added by Descartes's position was the mind–soul. Thus, lurking in a 'central' space of modernity is something unmodern, a medieval throwback. Remember, the humanism in modernism made humans the chief actors in nature. Now, if minds are souls, and the soul partakes of divinity, then, human actors swagger about the playing fields of nature clothed in a simply divine fashion. It is time to consider certain ontological implications of the throwback.

The conception of 'man' as both body and soul means that Descartes's is a two-realities ontology. At this point the second, ontological definition of the subjective–objective dyad becomes relevant. The inner, incorporeal space of soul–mind will be termed the 'subjective'. The space external to soul–mind of material body, and of the physical things with which the body interacts, will be understood as the 'objective'. So Descartes's ontology of body and soul really dichotomizes reality into objective and subjective spaces. Now, a dualism is the view that in a domain there are two mutually irreducible substances; and Descartes's insistence that there are two realms of being – body and soul, objective and subjective – that are 'entirely distinct', but in 'combination', makes this a Cartesian dualism.

A problem with this dualism was how the 'combination' of soul and body actually worked. Descartes was not certain, but he had a hunch. Let us then conceive that the soul has its principal seat in the little gland which exists in the middle of the brain, from whence it radiates forth through all the remainder of the body by means of the animal spirits, nerves, and even the blood, which, participating in the impressions of the spirits, can carry them by the arteries into all the members (in Restak 1979: 234). Descartes's 'little gland' was the pineal gland. Biology has not been kind to Descartes's hunch. Nobody ever found 'spirits' working out of the pineal gland to do the soul's bidding. Rather, the pineal gland appears to function in helping the body to maintain circadian rhythms. Hence a trouble with Cartesian dualism, from the very beginning, was that his explanation of the mind–matter connection was a big gaffe.

G.W.F. Hegel, writing in the early nineteenth century subsequent to the devastation of Germany by France, and Jean-Paul Sartre, writing in the mid-twentieth century subsequent to the return devastation of France by Germany, continued and amplified Cartesian dualism. Hegel had said in his *Phenomenology of Mind* (1967[1807]) that there was a reality of a thing 'itself' (*an sich*) as well as one 'for consciousness' (*für es*); that is, that there is existence as it is, and as people are aware of it. Sartre argued that there were two varieties of reality. 'On the one side', as his able commentators, Gilson et al. say:

> there stands being *en soi*, 'in itself', a monolithic mass of sheer reality, blind to itself, pitiless, inexorable in its absolute being there; on the other stands the reality which we ourselves are, being *pour soi*, 'for itself', able to gather itself up for a fleeting moment into an act of self-awareness, and because aware, because of this capacity to separate itself off from the necessary course of things, able to direct its own future.
>
> (1966: 382)

This was Hegel's ontology that, of course, was Descartes's ontology because it involves a *double* reality. There was first a reality of events outside people – monolithic, pitiless, inexorable. For Sartre it was the reality of Nazi occupation. Then there was a second inner reality, one of conscious mind. This was that of Sartre contemplating Fascist soldiers, before scribbling another few lines about being that was *en soi* and *pour soi*.

So Cartesian dualism might be likened to an old dog that has hunted far and wide. Other ontological visions – ether in the natural and *élan vitale* in the biological sciences – have come and gone. But Cartesian dualism, present at the beginning of modernity, doggedly hunts on. Even recent neuroscientists and philosophers of science flirt with it. For example, John Eccles and Karl Popper, both knighted for acts of 'hard' science beyond the call of duty, argued that the 'self' – the conscious being that is 'me' – is essentially non-material (1977). In the philosopher Gilbert Ryle's terms it became 'Official Doctrine' of modern intellectual hunters (1949: 11).

In agnoiological terms Cartesian dualism consists of theories with generalization necklaces whose jewels are hard diamonds of the objective linked by golden strands to pearls of the subjective. There are, thus, in these necklaces two concepts and two relationships. The concepts are those of the objective and subjective. The relationships are the strand stringing the objective to the subjective and vice versa; respectively referred to as the 'object–subject' and the 'subject–object' connections. Problems with this dualism have concerned conceptualization of the pearl of subjectivity and of the nature of the connections between the two jewels. Ryle, who authored one of the devastating critiques of Cartesian dualism, argued that Descartes's view of 'how a person's mind and body influence one another is notoriously charged with theoretical difficulties', so that the connection between the two remains 'mysterious' (ibid.: 12). A key problem was with the way Descartes had conceptualized mind. It was something that both was, and was not, there. This was because, according to Ryle, mind was in 'its own place' but this place was 'not witnessable' as it was 'private' (ibid.: 11, 12). So mind, wandering invisibly in the subjective, was 'the Ghost in the Machine' (ibid.: 15–16).

Sartre, like Ryle, brooded about Cartesian dualism. At the end of *Being and Nothingness* he worried, 'it appeared to us difficult to establish a bond between them (the objective and subjective), and we feared that we might fall into an insurmountable dualism' (1966 [1943]: 755). This dualism was 'insurmountable' because a ghost marching invisible rounds cannot be attached to anything. Sartre's recognition of an 'insurmountable dualism' suggests trouble with the 'Official Doctrine'. Below, working agnoiologically, I determine whether three theoretical projects in anthropology have imagined variants of Cartesian dualism. The analysis proceeds first by ascertaining if Bourdieu's, the Comaroffs', Lévi-Strauss's, and Sahlins's views are variants of the Cartesian generalization necklace, and then by noting if these views contain gaps, voids, and gaffes. The discussion begins with practice theory.

Practice theory

The Logic of Practice (hereafter LP), originally published in French in 1980, and only available to English readers in the 1990s, was a clarification and expansion of the text that had introduced practice theory to anthropology, *Outline of a Theory of Practice* (1977).[9] Bourdieu is explicit in LP that there is an interrelationship between the social and the subjective. This interrelationship is described as a 'dialectic of objective structures and incorporated [subjective] structures which operates in every practical action' (1990: 41). This 'dialectic' is represented by six concepts: field, practice, capital, *habitus*, practical sense, and practical logic.

Field is the major concept Bourdieu employs when considering social realities. Such realities occur in a 'social topology' (1989b: 163) composed of different fields. There are economic, political, religious, educational, and other fields. These are sets of objective, historical relations between positions varying according 'to the overall volume of capital they possess and . . . according to the structure of their capital' (ibid.: 17). Capital, as Bourdieu says elsewhere, is his term for power (1986: 243). The 'social physics' of fields involves the playing of a 'game' (1987: 248). This is the 'struggle' between organizations of positions with different amounts of capital to achieve different outcomes. A field, then, is a topology of powers in contention with each other.

Let us turn now to the subjective, or what Bourdieu calls 'social phenomenology'. It is with this realm that the bulk of the text in LP is concerned. Ultimately what 'produced individual and collective practices' is the '*habitus*' (1990: 54). This latter is 'embodied history, internalized as second nature' (ibid.: 56); a 'system of structured, structuring dispositions' (ibid.: 52) that are 'deposited in each organism in the form of schemes of perception, thought and action' (ibid.: 54).

Bourdieu links *habitus* to field when he asserts that 'The conditionings associated with a particular class of conditions of existence produce *habitus*' (ibid.: 93); because the dispositions composing *habitus* are 'durably inculcated by the possibilities and impossibilities, freedoms and necessities, opportunities and probabilities inscribed in the objective conditions' (ibid.: 54) of the fields in which people participate. Bourdieu shares Marx's insistence upon the centrality of considering such social positions as class. Thus the poor display a different *habitus* from the wealthy because of different 'objective conditions' of their positions in economic fields.

Bourdieu connects *habitus* to practice when he states, 'The genesis of a system of works or practices . . . arises from the necessary yet predictable confrontation between the *habitus* and the event' (ibid.: 55). However, it is not so much *habitus* that produces practice, because when the confrontation actually occurs, it is between the 'second nature' of *habitus*, practical sense and events; and it is this practical sense that actually 'causes practices' (ibid.: 69). Practical sense, perhaps Bourdieu's most engaging notion, is unconscious 'adjustment to the demands of a field' involving a 'feel for the game' (ibid.: 66). It is a goalie in soccer 'sensing' what to do the instant a ball is launched at the net. Practical sense, as an aspect of *habitus*, varies with social position. A rich person's practical sense of how to deal with a cop who has pulled her over for speeding will vary from that of a poor person.

Because practices occur in the manner just suggested, Bourdieu thinks that they exhibit logics. These, however, are not those of the logician; namely, the conscious formulation of conclusions based upon the application of the rules of a particular formal logic. Rather, because practices are the result of the dis-positions of *habitus*, social scientists may 'construct generative models which reproduce in their own terms the logic' (ibid.: 92) of the dispositions that structure practice. Such generative models, inspired by Chomskian linguistics, because they use the dispositions of a *habitus* as the formulae of a generative calculus of practice, are what Bourdieu terms a 'practical logic'. Why does the preceding partake of 'Official Doctrine'? Practice theory is a variant of the Cartesian dualism because it seeks to explain how the objective (fields) influences the subjective (the *habitus*) that in turn influence the objective (this time in the form of the practices that are the games played in fields).

Below I consider how effectively Bourdieu connects the objective with the subjective. Bourdieu's generalization necklace consists of three concepts; field, *habitus*, and practice. He stipulates that these concepts are connected when he announces that the practical sense of *habitus* 'causes' practice and that 'the conditionings associated with a particular class of conditions' of fields 'produce *habitus*' (ibid.: 53). Thus, if fields produce *habitus* and *habitus* causes practice, then both the objective and subjective are strung to each other. However, let us inspect more closely a single strand in this theory, that of the field–*habitus* relationship.

If it is asserted that 'conditionings associated with a particular class of conditions produce *habitus*', then the following questions require answers: what 'conditionings' are being discussed under what 'conditions'? Bourdieu's use of the term 'conditioning' is ambiguous. The term is the central concept in behaviorist thought and refers to contingencies of reinforcement that do create different behavioral dispositions, under different environmental conditions (Skinner 1961). However, Bourdieu does not indicate whether he is using it in a behaviorist manner. My sense is that he is not. For example, in one place in LP he says that *habitus* 'is a relation of *conditioning*: the field structures the *habitus*, which is the product of the embodiment of the immanent necessity of a field (or of a hierarchically interacting set of fields)' (1990: 44). Now, behaviorists never talk of subjective phenomena and the faintest suggestion that anything might be the 'embodiment' of an 'immanent necessity' would strike them as twaddle.

If it is unclear how Bourdieu uses conditioning, he is equally vague as to the conditions to which conditioning is subject. Readers are told that the *habitus* is 'a product of history' (ibid.: 54); and that it is 'inculcated by the possibilities and impossibilities, freedoms and necessities, opportunities and prohibitions' (ibid.: 54) of the objective conditions of fields. But 'history' is a pretty vast term, and readers are never told of what histories the *habitus* is a product, or by what 'possibilities and impossibilities', and so on, it is inculcated; or how this inculation occurs. Given the preceding, I conclude that the field–*habitus* relationship is ambiguous.

It might be objected that LP appeared at a time in Bourdieu's career when he had not fully developed his views on the field. Certainly he has thought more about fields in *Distinction* (1984) and in *La Misère du monde* (1993); and he speaks (evoking Heidegger and Merleau-Ponty) of an 'ontological complicity: between the field and *habitus*' (in Wacquant 1989: 43). Nevertheless, though Bourdieu is clear that a field 'structures' or 'produces' a *habitus*, how this might occur remains conceptually unclear. So there appears to be a void between Bourdieu's field and *habitus*. Just what are the concepts that represent the realities that make field and *habitus* ontologically complicit?

For that matter, the concept of *habitus* itself seems a mystery. It 'is the product of the embodiment of the immanent necessity of a field', a 'product of history'. It 'causes' practices. This is in effect saying what something is caused by and what, in turn, it causes, but nothing about the *it* that is both caused and causes. In my reading of Bourdieu I am unable to discover what it is that is *habitus*. Now there is nothing apparently wrong with Bourdieu's concept of *habitus*. So it is not a gaffe. But we really know very little about it. So we need further observations to know more fully to what it corresponds in reality. In agnoiological terms, *habitus* is a void. In Ryle's terms, Bourdieu's pearl of subjectivity is ghostly. This means that, regardless of his intentions, Bourdieu has not discovered much about the subjective and how the objective connects to it. It is time to consider the work of the Comaroffs.

A Gramscian idealism

Jean and John Comaroff in *Of Revelation and Revolution* (hereafter R&R
describe their project as the writing of 'history in the anthropological mode', a
mode which accounts 'for the making of a social and a cultural world'. They
believe that such a project commits them to exploring 'the relationship of
matter and meaning' (1991: 38–9). The realm of 'matter' and the 'social'
correspond to the objective; that of culture and meaning – because meaning
is normally understood to be incorporeal – corresponds to the subjective. Note
that these two realms enjoy a 'relationship'. Thus, the Comaroffs, too, adhere
to a Cartesian dualism; for their generalization necklace, like Bourdieu's,
ultimately consists of objective and subjective jewels connected in a
'relationship'.

Their project derives from attempts that flourished in England in the 1970s
and 1980s to utilize the work of the Italian Marxist Antonio Gramsci and his
concept of hegemony (see Hall 1986; Williams 1977). The Comaroffs claim
to follow in 'the *Geist* of Gramsci' (1991: 21). They do so by situating the
notion of hegemony within the context of a cultural field. I shall argue that
their account of a cultural field approaches a theory of the subjective realm;
that this theory produces an account of history as a 'long conversation' – a
view that is a Gramscian idealism, with only a passing concern for objective
social realities.

Seven concepts are important to understanding cultural fields: culture,
ideology, hegemony, agentive power, non-agentive power, contradictory
consciousness, and resistance. Culture is 'the space of signifying practice, the
semantic ground on which human beings seek to construct and represent
themselves and others – and, hence, society and history' (ibid.: 21). They
think of this space as a field, specifically a 'historically situated field of signifiers' (ibid.: 21). (The following distinction can be made between Bourdieu's
and the Comaroffs' fields. The former's fields are organizations of capital or
power. The latter's are organizations of signifiers.) Cultural fields have 'two
modalities' (ibid.: 27); one of hegemony and the other of ideology. The
differences between ideology and hegemony depend upon an understanding of
the way the Comaroffs view power.

They assert that there are two varieties of power, and that ideology and
hegemony are each associated with one of these. Agentive power is 'the
relative capacity of human beings to shape the actions and perceptions of
others by exercising control over the production, circulation and consumption
of signs and objects of the making of subjectivities and realities' (ibid.: 22).
Non-agentive power 'proliferates outside the realm of institutional politics . . .
and its effects are rarely wrought by overt compulsion' (ibid.). Its effects
'are internalized, in their negative guise as constraints; in their neutral guise,
as conventions; and in their positive guise, as values' (ibid.). There are no
human agents in command of other humans in this second type of power,

because the control is 'internalized', and so the Comaroffs believe it is appropriate to term this variety of power non-agentive. Hegemony is associated with non-agentive and ideology with agentive power, for reasons detailed below.

The Comaroffs define ideology, following Raymond Williams, as a '"worldview" of any social grouping' (ibid.: 24). What makes such a worldview an ideology is that it is 'of' a group (ibid.), whose members are its agents. Different groups, drawing upon the same culture, construct different ideologies, as is illustrated by pro- and anti-abortionist groups in the United States. Ideologies are explicitly communicated by their agents so that people are conscious of their existence. Following Marx and Engels, the Comaroffs assert that 'the regnant ideology of any period or place will be that of the dominant group' (ibid.).

If ideology is conscious, hegemony is unconscious. It is 'that order of signs and practices, relations and distinctions, images and epistemologies – drawn from an historically situated cultural field – that comes to be taken-for-granted as the natural and received shape of the world and everything that inhabits it' (ibid.: 23). Hegemony is 'shared . . . throughout a political community' (ibid.: 24) and, like Bourdieu's notion of *habitus*, as the Comaroffs acknowledge, 'consists . . . of things that go without saying because, being axiomatic, they come without saying' (ibid.: 23). It is in this sense that hegemonies are 'ineffable' (ibid.: 24): the unvoiced, unconscious forms of perception and conception of social and natural being.

The Comaroffs believe that ideology and hegemony exist 'in reciprocal interdependence' within a cultural field (ibid.: 25). This interdependence appears to be that of a 'long conversation'. Sometimes in these conversations, 'Between the conscious and the unconscious', the 'silent signifiers and unmarked practices' of hegemony 'rise to the level of explicit consciousness, of ideological assertion' (ibid.: 29). Then, the more successful groups are in asserting 'control over various modes of symbolic production' (ibid.: 25), 'the more their ideology will disappear into the domain of the hegemonic' (ibid.: 26). Hegemonies, however, once made can also be transformed back into ideology. To understand how this might occur, a notion of contradictory consciousness is needed.

Gramsci appropriated this concept from Marx and Engels, as do the Comaroffs from Gramsci. In their version, contradictory consciousness is 'the discontinuity between (1) the world as hegemonically constituted and (2) the world as practically apprehended, and ideologically represented, by subordinate people' (ibid.: 26). For the Comaroffs, the greater the contradictory consciousness (that is, the greater the gap between the way a hegemony posits things should be and the way they are actually apprehended), 'the more that unremarked truth and unspoken conventions will become remarked, reopened for debate' (ibid.: 26). This thrusts previously hegemonic ideas into a hurly-burly of ideological struggle because as contradictory consciousness 'gives way to ever more acute, articulate consciousness of contradictions, it may also be a source of more acute, articulate resistance' (ibid.: 26).

What, then, is history? History is largely in R&R what happens in cultural fields, and what happens in such fields as the Comaroffs reiterate in a number of places is the 'long conversation' just described (ibid.: 171, 198, 213, 243). If idealism is a view that reality 'depends upon (finite or infinite) minds or (particular or transcendent) ideas' (Bynum et al. 1981: 199), then the Comaroffs' theory of historical realities as a 'long conversation' oscillating between ideological and hegemonic ideas certainly seems an idealism. Such an idealism may not be especially Gramscian.

Gramsci never offered, as the Comaroffs are aware, a precise definition of hegemony (Lears 1985: 568). He was, however, a Leninist rotting in a Fascist jail, with a keen sense that history ultimately resulted from changes in different 'relations of force'. These changes involved continual fluctuation 'between the first and the third moment, with the mediation of the second' (Gramsci 1988: 207). Without launching into an exegesis of the Gramscian moment, readers should grasp that the third moment is that of 'military forces' (ibid.: 207). The Comaroffs' understanding of hegemony has people acquiring hegemony after a 'long conversation' and, then, because hegemonies are 'unconscious', ineffably consenting to their domination. Gramsci's hegemony involved 'a combination of force and consent' that allowed a 'dominant, fundamental group' to impose a 'general direction . . . on social life' (1971: 80, 12). This force, as just noted, was often violent. The Comaroffs think they follow the *Geist* of Gramsci. I suggest, because they ignore force, that they are chasing a *poltergeist*. The analysis now turns to the handling of objective social realities in R&R.

I have two concerns: (1) the Comaroffs de-emphasize observations that need conceptualization; and (2) they emphasize concepts whose empirical significance has not been established. Consider, for example, the case of violent force. They acknowledge the significance of violence when they say they do not 'deny the coercive, violent bases of class antagonism and racial inequality here (in southern Africa)' (1991: 4). However, though they do not deny the actuality of violent force, they do downplay it. For example, they insist that the European missionaries 'were to prove themselves every bit as effective, in making subjects, as were the storm-troops of colonialism' (ibid.: 200). This allows them to conclude that 'The European colonization of Africa was often less directly coercive a conquest than a persuasive attempt to colonize consciousness' (ibid.: 313). Such an assertion, of course, underplays colonization's violence because it insists that colonization was 'less' coercive than persuasive.

Why diminish the importance of violence? After all, Jean Comaroff had herself acknowledged that there had been a *'realpolitik* of oppression' (1985: 261). This involved the slaughter, wounding, rape, and imprisonment of African children, women, and men by Europeans. It was a product of the systematic application by Boer and British of physical violence for 400 years. Colonial southern Africa may have had its 'long conversation' but it equally had its long butchery. The Comaroffs provide *no* evidence demonstrating that the former was more important than the latter in producing hegemony. Rather, they merely assert that this was the case.

The Comaroffs offer an account of how the objective influences hegemony with two generalizations: the first suggesting what happened, and the second identifying the agents of what happened. What happened was that 'colonialism . . . gave rise to a new hegemony amidst – and despite – cultural contestation' (1991: 18). More specifically, missionaries were 'the most active cultural agents of empire' (ibid.: 6), parts of whose 'evangelical message insinuated themselves into the warp and weft of an emerging hegemony' (ibid.: 12). Readers might detect a similarity between a major nineteenth-century ideological justification for colonialism and these two generalizations. Imperial propagandists justified colonialism because they believed it brought civilization to benighted folk. Of course, what these ideologies meant by 'civilization' was European conceptions. Such a view of civilization resembles the Comaroffs' definition of hegemony as a 'dominant conception' (ibid.: 23). This means that their doctrine that colonialism produced European hegemony (namely, civilization) rather resembles that of the nineteenth-century jingoists who asserted that colonialism produced civilization (that is, European hegemony).

However, skepticism seems justified with regard to the Comaroffs' belief that missionaries were the key agents of the insinuation of hegemony. This is because their own observations suggest it is by no means certain that missionaries really were all that important. The Comaroffs say that European missionaries did not actually convert 'many' (ibid.: 311). They quote a nineteenth-century observer who describes services in which 'Some would be snoring; others laughing; some working' (ibid.: 247). In addition, there were teachers, merchants, journalists, and military personnel who also dispensed European notions. The relative significance of these latter agents of hegemony compared to that of European missionaries is nowhere established in R&R. Clearly, it is premature to offer conclusions concerning the importance of European missionaries as hegemonic agents until observations have been made that clearly establish the relative causal importance of other suspected agents.

The preceding suggests a gaffe in the Comaroffs' position. Observation of southern African history reveals a reality of a long butchery. This is an objective reality and might be thought to be relevant to producing hegemony. However, violent force goes unrepresented in the Comaroffs' account. Rather, hegemony 'took root' as a result of the 'long conversation' conducted by missionaries, but the Comaroffs themselves furnish evidence that suggests this may be something of a misrepresentation. Hence, R&R downplays objective realities known to be important, those pertaining to violent force, while emphasizing others, missionaries, of unestablished importance. Here, then, is a gaffe.

There also appears to be a problem with the specification of how hegemony influences objective social realities. R&R states that new hegemonies 'seem to have the capacity to generate new substantive practices' (ibid.: 30). The word 'generate' is a synonym for cause. This means that the Comaroffs are tentatively offering the generalization that changed hegemonies cause changed practices. This may well be the case, but there is no elaboration of how this might occur; that is to say, there are no concepts to represent how changes in hegemonies are connected to changes in practices. There is a strand missing in the generalization necklace that connects the subjective concept of hege-mony to the objective one of practice. This is a gap.

It is clear that what the Comaroffs do want to theorize about – missionaries holding long conversations – does not represent an important objective reality, violent force. This is a gaffe. Furthermore, they seem reluctant to address how the subjective is linked to the objective. This is a gap. In con-clusion, the Comaroffs' version of Cartesian dualism comes with a gap and a gaffe. Earlier it was suggested that R&R had an idealist tilt. Perhaps because of this they are unable to think either about the objective or about how it connects with the subjective – hegemonies in cultural fields. Attention turns to Lévi-Straussian structuralism.

Lévi-Straussian structuralism

Initially imagined among Amazon peoples in the 1930s, researched in New York city libraries during World War II, and published as *Les Structures élémentaires de la parenté* (1949, hereafter SE), Lévi-Strauss offered a structuralism that, in the end, was another descendant of Cartesian dualism. No theoretical approach since the end of World War II has been as important as that of Claude Lévi-Strauss. Below I explore the 1949 version of this structuralism and then Sahlins's 1980s emendation of it.

Lévi-Strauss's approach was to begin by making observations of things that were out there in objective realms of less complex peoples – people then called 'primitive', without states and stratification. Where others saw chaos of cultural particularity, Lévi-Strauss discerned structure. Kin groups, marriage rules, gift giving, myth, ritual, and art all seemed to have structures. Then, on the basis of analysis of some particular social being in objective space, such as dual organization in the Amazon or marriage among the Kariera of Australia, he would infer an abstract structure that corresponded to what had been observed.

Only one abstract structure emerged out of the welter of different transfor-mations of kin groups, myths, marriage rules that existed among different, less complex peoples. Lévi-Strauss was using the term 'transformations' in its logical or mathematical sense where it means formulas used to express the different relations between elements that form iterations of a given, common structure. There were a number of transformations that were the 'elementary structures' of less complex societies. But these transformations were all iterations of a common abstract structure which was 'binary', in the sense that whatever it was that was the structure it had only two parts. For example, dual organization as found in the Amazon was based upon two descent groups linked in a moiety organization. Further, the binary structures exhibited 'reciprocity' in the sense that whatever the two parts might be, their relationship was always one of mutual exchange of roughly equal valuables. The descent groups in moieties, for example, were at the same time wife-givers and wife-receivers and, thus, linked in reciprocal exchange of precious women.

SE was compelling because it took everyone else's views of kinship in less complex societies – be it those of Maine, Morgan, Westermarck, McLennan, Spencer, Lubbock, Durkheim, Radcliffe-Brown, Lowie, or Kroeber – and showed them to be either incorrect or in some way consistent with Lévi-Strauss's structuralism. Further, it argued this on the basis of observations from an enormous global sample of less complex populations that had required reference to 'more than 7000 books and articles' (Lévi-Strauss 1967: xxviii).

If Lévi-Strauss's binary structures of reciprocity were an abstract model of a portion of objective reality, how did this objective realm come about? SE spent very little time responding to this question. However, Lévi-Strauss did say that, 'To understand' the elementary structures that were transformations of his abstract model, 'inquiry must be directed to certain fundamental structures of the human mind, rather than to some privileged region of the world or to a certain period in the history of civilization' (1969 [1949]: 75). Here was a Cartesian dualism.

There was an objective realm, 'the world' or a historically particular time of a 'civilization'. This was external to a subjective realm of the 'fundamental structures of the human mind'. Lévi-Strauss's dualism, then, was a mind–world one which was strongly idealist, because it was to the mind that 'inquiry must be directed' to understand the abstract binary structures that had been inferred to be out there in the 'world'. The key here is that somehow what goes on in the world is a product of the fundamental structures of the mind.

There are two problems with this dualism. The first of these resembles that with Bourdieu's *habitus*. Lévi-Strauss's mind has 'fundamental structures', but just as Bourdieu refrains from telling readers what *habitus* might be, so Lévi-Strauss says little about his 'fundamental structures'. Vincent Descombes put the matter as follows, 'The notion of "human mind" [in Lévi-Strauss] is so vague that perhaps it would be wiser not to look for its meaning' (1980: 122).[10] Thus, in agnoiological terms the 'fundamental structures' are a void. They are one of Ryle's phantoms, something that is, but we are not told what it is.

The second problem with this dualism is that Lévi-Strauss intimates that the mind's 'fundamental structures' are somehow connected with the 'elementary structures' out in the world. Perhaps, the 'fundamental structures' might be likened to a movie projector that projects ideas about how matter should be organized out into the objective world, thereby creating the interactions that logical inference can show to be the 'elementary structures' of the abstract model. But, then again, perhaps not. Lévi-Strauss actually tells his readers nothing about the nature of the connection, merely suggesting that further 'inquiry' is needed. But he never provides the concepts that explain this connection. Agnoiologically, this is a gap. Thus, in the generalization necklace of Lévi-Strauss's Cartesian dualism there is a strand that attaches the jewel of the mind to that of the world. But the jewel of the mind is a void, and the strand linking mind to the world is a gap. Lévi-Strauss is fencing damaged goods, a flawed generalization necklace. Let us turn now to Sahlins.

Sahlins went on the road to Paris in the 1960s, a cultural materialist, and returned transformed, a Lévi-Straussian structuralist. *Culture and Practical Reason* (1976a, hereafter CPR), which justified this metamorphosis, argued that there had been, and were, two firmly established theoretical orders, those of practical and cultural reason. Practical reason amounted to explanations which insisted that culture was 'formulated out of practical activity' (ibid.: vii), be it of economic or ecological varieties. Cultural reason involved explanations which insisted that practical activity was formulated out of autonomous culture, with culture understood to be symbolic schemes. Sahlins in CPR found every theory of practical reason wanting. He further claimed to have discovered that *Doctoraluk* Boas had believed in a cultural reason. Over the years following publication of CPR, Sahlins used Oceanic peoples to show how cultural reason facilitated the understanding of Pacific realities (1981, 1985).

Then came a problem. Gananath Obeyesekere developed an 'ire' (1992: 8) regarding one aspect of Sahlins's work. It appears that he heard Sahlins speak about his (Sahlins's) interpretations of Hawaiian interpretations of why they cannibalized Captain Cook. Sahlins's understanding is that this happened because Hawaiians believed that Cook was their god Lono. Obeyesekere thought this was wrong, and wrote *The Apotheosis of Captain Cook* (1992, hereafter CC) to reveal why. Additionally, he suggested that Sahlins was, in Sahlins's recounting of the affair, an agent of 'Western violence and imperialism' (Sahlins 1995: 18). This was too much, Sahlins responded furiously. *How 'Natives' Think, About Captain Cook for Example* (1995, hereafter HNT) expressed that fury. Commentary upon the polemics in HNT and CC has been of a 'boxing commentator' variety, with the chief goal to fathom which of the combatants got in the most telling blows. I shall not discuss HNT in this manner because I am convinced that its value lies in the theory Sahlins cobbled together to support his interpretation of Cook's murder. This theory might be termed neo-Lévi-Straussian because it adds something new to the old structuralism, though retaining its Cartesian dualism. Indeed, what is striking about Sahlins is that he is aware in CPR that his project is in the tradition of such 'antique dualisms' (1976a: ix). However, he is confident that he has left them 'behind' (ibid.: ix).

Later in Lévi-Strauss's career, by the time of his *La Pensée sauvage* (1962), the notion of 'fundamental structures' was replaced by that of a 'conceptual scheme' which 'governs and defines practice' (1966 [1962]: 130). There is no indication that Lévi-Strauss meant anything different by the concept of a conceptual scheme than he had by fundamental structures. Both were what went on in the human mind. The term 'governs' is strong. A conceptual scheme did not merely influence practices; it governed them. Something that governs something else brings about what the something else does. However, Lévi-Strauss was unconcerned with *how* this governance occurred, so that the mind–world gap continued.

Now, when Sahlins had returned home from Paris and published CPR he had decided that there were cultural reasons for practices. He further believed that cultural reason involves the existence in people of 'a definite symbolic scheme' (1976a: viii), and that the way people lived was 'according' to this scheme because it 'organizes' their lives (ibid.: 176). Since concepts involve symbols, Sahlins's 'symbolic scheme' was Lévi-Strauss's 'conceptual scheme'. Further, just as Lévi-Strauss's scheme 'governed', Sahlins's scheme 'organized'. So Australian foragers *à la* Lévi-Strauss had their binary schemes which governed their marriage classes; while Americans *à la* Sahlins had their schemes of lipiderotic cultural reason that organized their colossal consumption of fat-saturated death patties (namely, hamburgers). Sahlins, then, had become Lévi-Straussian by accepting the proposition 'Schema brings about practices'.

However, like Lévi-Strauss, Sahlins in CPR expressed no opinion as to how schemas governed practice. If the term 'agency' refers to how humans do things, then both Lévi-Strauss and the Sahlins of CPR were indifferent to questions of agency. Starting in the 1970s, a number of scholars, from Bourdieu (1988, 1989a) to E.P. Thompson (1979), began to complain that an inability to deal with questions of agency was an intolerable defect of structuralism. In agnoiological terms this faulting of structuralism for its lack of conceptualization of agency was a recognition that there was a gap between the subjective mind, in which there were schemas, and the objective world, in which there were practices. HNT tried to put some agency into the pencil of Lévi-Straussian structuralism by trying to fill this gap.

This occurred when Sahlins sought to convince readers that there was a 'cultural organization of empirical objectivity' (1995: 160); that is, that objectivity was 'culturally constituted' (ibid.: 169). His argument was as follows. Humans make 'sense perceptions'. They see, smell, and so forth. From these they make 'empirical judgments'. They see a goose, smell a goose cooking, and so on. Now, and this is crucial, 'a sensory perception is not yet an empirical judgment' because what a perception comes to be judged as depends on 'criteria of objectivity' (ibid.: 162). These latter 'criteria' are understandings of the objects of perceptions that are 'culturally constituted'. This is because the particular schemas of particular cultural reasons confer properties upon perceptions, be these perceptions of the external world or those of one's own thoughts. Thus, when Hawaiians experienced sensory perceptions of the object, Cook, because of their Hawaiian schema of things, Cook was awarded the empirical judgment, Lono – a judgment that pretty much cooked his goose!

What people actually do when they formulate empirical judgments out of sense perceptions is dealt with in an *en passant* fashion by Sahlins. When comparing Hawaiian with Melanesian schemas, as they operated during early contacts with Europeans, he notes, 'In ways reminiscent of the story of Cook . . . direct reports of Melanesians show them scanning their traditional knowledge . . . to find whatever parallels they could . . . and thus achieve a satisfactory interpretation' or empirical judgment (ibid.: 180). Sahlins appears to be on to something with the notion of 'scanning'. Sahlins does not divulge how scanning operates.

However, it would appear to be a process whereby people take their sensory perceptions and scroll them across the corpus of their schema to arrive at an empirical judgment. It is a process of taking sensation of objects and looking through the cultural definitions of sensations – namely, their understandings – in one's schema to match the perception with its cultural understanding. For example, an English person on scanning Cook – through an eighteenth-century British schema that understood different sorts of gold braid to be associated with different naval ranks – might interpret him as a 'captain'. Hawaiians, according to Sahlins, interpreted him through their very different schema as 'Lono'.

Now we are in a position to offer a few statements which can begin to put some agency into the proposition that 'schema bring about practices'. These statements are that: (1) people make sensory perceptions; (2) perceptions are scanned across the understandings in schema to form empirical judgments; (3) empirical judgments form the basis of practices. The second statement might be called the scanning generalization, and it is this that makes Sahlins a neo-Lévi-Straussian because it adds something new, the realization that it is scanning that translates schema into practice. This project, of course, is Cartesian because it has a generalization necklace composed of two jewels; a subjective schema and an objective practice, with the jewel of subjectivity strung to that of the objective by the process of scanning.

How comfortable can investigators be with the scanning generalization? This question is answered by posing another, what is scanning? This question goes completely unanswered in HNT. The term is never mentioned in the index. When used it is undefined. There is no attempt to specify the precise relationships between events that correspond to scanning. The readers are left to their own devices to speculate, as I did, that scanning involves scrolling of perception across the elements of a schema. But what does it really mean to 'scroll across a schema'? There is, thus, a void in Sahlins's understanding of how subjective schemas connect with objective practices.

There is, I believe, another void. This time it is with the conceptual pearl which Sahlins uses to represent the subjective. This concept, of course, is 'symbolic scheme'. The problem is that readers are not told what the term refers to in reality in HNT. Sahlins uses other terms in CPR to mean symbolic scheme. These are 'cultural scheme', 'symbolic order', and 'cultural order'. I have examined each page in CPR in which these four terms appear and have reached the following conclusions. Readers are told in CPR that schemas have a 'fundamental autonomy' (1976a: 57). Further, readers are informed about what they do. They 'organize' practices, as we have just discussed. However, readers of CPR are never told what it is that does the organizing. We are told that organizing occurs. We think it might be the result of scanning. But we are never told what it is that does the organizing.

Sahlins wrote two further books – *Historical Metaphors and Mythical Realities* (1981) and *Islands of History* (1985) – in which the concept of schema is important. However, neither work specifies what is a schema. Now it might be objected that this notion is an abstraction and that abstractions do not exist in the world. Fair enough, but Sahlins insists that schema 'organize'. There must be something that does the organizing. It is here that Sahlins is silent.[11] The problem with such muteness is that it is like characterizing the heart as autonomous and as the organ that pumps blood without bothering to conceptualize the organ itself. Such a treatment of schema means that there is a void at the heart of Sahlins's position. Who knows what a schema is? Agnoiological analysis, then, reveals two voids in Sahlins's structuralism. So Sahlins does not appear to have left those 'antique dualisms' as far behind as he thought. It is time to inquire into whether there is a hole in the Cartesian dualism of this anthropological theory.

A ghost in the hole?

The preceding agnoiological analysis, though incomplete, nevertheless revealed gaps, voids, and gaffes in the positions of Bourdieu, the Comaroffs, Lévi-Strauss, and Sahlins. Remember that Cartesian dualism is distinguished by having (1) two concepts, the objective (represented by social phenomena in the work under consideration) and the subjective, and (2) two connections representing how the objective relates to the subjective and the reverse. The subjective concepts were those of *habitus* for Bourdieu, cultural field for the Comaroffs, fundamental structures of the mind and schema for Lévi-Strauss and Sahlins. The objective concepts were field and practice for Bourdieu, missionaries or practice for the Comaroffs, the world for Lévi-Strauss, and practice for Sahlins.

Two voids were identified in Bourdieu's practice theory. The first void was in the notion of *habitus*. This subjective space was given a name and, hence, was not a gap; but it was a name about which nothing was said and, so, was a void. The second void was in the connection between *habitus* and field. Such a connection was posited to exist but it was conceptually ambiguous, which meant that it was not clear how *habitus* actually connected with a field.

A gap and a gaffe were identified in the Comaroffs' Gramscian idealism. The gap pertained to how changes in hegemony related to changes in practices. Such a connection was postulated to exist, but no concepts were presented to explain how the connection occurred. The gaffe occurred in the theorizing about the connection between the objective and subjective realms. Long conversations by missionaries out in the objective world were supposed to connect with the rise of hegemony in that of subjectivity. However, the existence of a long butchery seemed just as likely to explain why southern Africans might have wanted to adopt new hegemony, suggesting that the Comaroffs' talk of long conversations was a bit of a gaffe.

A gap and a void were noted in Lévi-Strauss's structuralism. The gap concerned how fundamental structures connected with the world. Such a connection was implicit but concepts detailed how this occurred; that is, there was a gap in the fundamental structures–world connection. The void pertained to Lévi-Strauss's chief subjective notion, fundamental structures of the mind. The concept was named so it was not a gap but, as with Bourdieu's *habitus*, nothing was said about it, so it was a looming void. Finally, consider Sahlins's term 'scanning'. This was a concept that appeared to fill the gap in Lévi-Strauss's void by explaining how fundamental structures connected with the world. They did it by scanning. However, Sahlins went no further in explaining what scanning might be. So it too was a mystery concept, a real void.

Let us summarize the findings of agnoiological analysis. Two gaffes were found pertaining to how the objective connects with the subjective, one each in Bourdieu's practice theory and the Comaroffs' Gramscian idealism. Two gaps were located in the converse connection of how the subjective connects with the objective, one again in the Comaroffs' Gramscism and the other in Lévi-Strauss's structuralism. This leads to a judgment. Sartre was correct. The old ontology of Descartes, when it had hunted as far and as wide as late twentieth-century anthropological theory, disappeared in a hole of an 'insurmountable dualism', unable to connect the objective and subjective.

Finally, anthropological Cartesian dualists know there is a subjective. They can name it – *habitus*, fundamental structures of the mind, symbolic schema – but when it comes to theorizing about the nature of it, nothing more gets said. Why is this so? Perhaps, because Cartesian dualists imagine the subjective as incorporeal, they are obliged to imagine that there is nothing to it because the incorporeal is immaterial – that is, nothing. So, lurking at the bottom of the hole is a subjective void. Something that is nothing that does a lot. It is as if there is a ghost at the bottom of the hole. What conclusions might be drawn from the analysis of this chapter?

CONCLUSION

We have visited in Marshall Sahlins's terms a 'twilight' zone, and one conclusion from this visit seems clear. Many anthropologists currently bungle
making connections about what goes on in reality for two reasons. Conjectural
hermeneutists bungle because they just do not 'get it'. They see no necessity
for making connections; warranting the conclusion that one of anthropology's
troubles is the popularity of a project which, indifferent to truth, intolerant of
those seeking it, explicitly rejects any project that imagines there might be
connections in reality and then uses validation techniques to establish the
truth of these. The second reason for the bungling is quite different. The
Cartesian dualists dearly want to make connections between the objective and
subjective. But they botch the job because they have descended into a hole of
'insurmountable dualism', complete with a ghost at the bottom.

A cruel reality had best be faced now. If a discipline that advertises it will
tell you something about a particular reality cannot do so, then 'Frankly my
dear', who gives a damn about it? This goes a long way to explaining why
anthropology, positioned to be the central social science, but unable to connect anything to anything else, is, like Scarlett O'Hara's plantation in *Gone
with the Wind*, 'destructing'. Otherwise put, anthropology's survival depends
upon its practitioners becoming connectionists.

Two proposals seem promising for helping anthropologists to learn this art.
The first of these pertains to Cartesian dualism. Let us discover exactly what
it is in this dualism that inhibits connecting the objective and subjective
and, then, use this knowledge to move on to a more connection-friendly
ontology. This is the next chapter's topic. The second proposal pertains to
conjectural hermeneutics. One way of redressing their cavalier attitude towards
connections is to re-analyze the very concept of 'connection' to formulate an
opinion as to what it means for antecedents to be connected to their
subsequents. This analysis is performed in the chapter following the next,
which introduces a knotty approach to connection.

Chapter 3

Confronting the 'insurmountable'

... and we feared we might fall into an insurmountable dualism.
(J.-P. Sartre, *Being and Nothingness*, 1966 [1943]: 755)

The argument against Cartesian dualism is straightforward. You overcome the insurmountable by going somewhere else (ontologically). You do this because what it is that is supposed to be surmounted does not exist, and why bother to surmount a chimera? Thus, the chief burden of such an argument is to demonstrate that there is something chimerical in Cartesian dualism, posing the question: how does one identify a chimera?

This is really a question of how to identify an ontological ghost. Identification follows from a sort of revelation. If it is discovered that a reality differs from what some intellectual opinion claims it to be, then the ideas constituting the opinion are revealed to be an ontological ghost because they stand for nothing. Exorcism follows because everybody knows, ghosts are not real. Remember, Cartesian dualism makes the following claims – that either are, or are not, ghosts – about reality:

1   that being is a dual reality composed of different, connected realms of the subjective and objective;
2   that subjective being consists of immaterial mind;
3   that objective being consists of material objects, like the human body.

The remainder of the chapter consists of three sections – one very short, another very long, and a final short one. The first short section examines the plausibility of the first of these claims. It explains how the subjective and objective are the same reality. Next, the terribly long section investigates the second claim. This takes a long time because it is argued that the immaterial mind is material, and demonstration of the plausibility of this view requires a considerable corpus of material evidence. However, once this evidence is presented, then the Cartesian dualism is revealed to be a ghost, corresponding with no reality. Further, it is revealed that what does exist is not a double but a single reality, so that if one wants to understand the being in which humans act, forget Cartesian dualism, embrace monism. In effect, then, the first two sections move forward by a process of ghost busting. A third, brief section introduces a particular *social* monism that replaces the old dog no longer able to hunt.

GHOST BUSTERS I

'One and the same can be both'

The first claim of Cartesian dualists, that being is dual, is scrutinized and dismissed in this section, 'Ghost Busters I'. Let us begin this argument. The soul of the Cartesian position is that the subjective and objective are obdurate antinomies – different and opposed beings. However, Paul Churchland, who with his wife Patricia Churchland (1986), has pioneered the field of neurophilosophy, has argued that this is incorrect, insisting, 'there is simply no conflict between objective and subjective. One and the same state can be both' (1995: 225). In order to make this point, it is important that we be clear about ontological usage of the terms 'objective' and 'subjective'.

The concepts 'objective' and 'subjective' are employed in their ontological sense, according to Searle, when they are 'predicates of entities and types of entities, and they ascribe modes of existence' (1995: 8). A mode of existence, or entity, is ontologically subjective if it exists somewhere internal to the subject, in her or his mind. Thoughts are subjective entities, because their mode of existence depends upon their being within subjects. A mode of existence is ontologically objective if it exists external to the subject, and can be the object of what the subjective mind contemplates. Elephants, in contrast to thoughts, are ontologically objective because their mode of existence lumbers on external to any particular subject or mental state of that subject's mind.

Now reality is ontologically *both* objective *and* subjective at the same time. This seems to strain readers' credulity because it posits that they accept that a situation can be both itself and its opposite at the same time; an apparent logical abomination, like saying life is death. However, what might be termed a 'locational relativist' argument clarifies that the objective is not to the subjective as life is to death. The argument begins by asking the reader to grasp that the ontological apprehensions of objective and subjective are the result of different observational locations of the nature of being and not the nature of being itself. This is because being that is ontologically subjective has an existence defined by its location *within* a subject. Hence, your subjectivity is the reality that is within you, and whatever it is that is within you – a thought or flatulence rushing to come out – is just as real as that which is outside of you. But, as I stand looking at you, your subjectivity, the actuality within you, is a reality that is to me out there, as objective as an elephant. Thus, understood observationally, the ontological terms of objective and subjective refer to who is observing whose being.

For example, I am occasionally classified as Hispanic because of my name. You may be a salesperson targeting sales to Spanish-speakers who, upon hearing my name, believes that I am 'one of them'. Your belief that Reyna is a 'Hispanic' is located within you. It is ontologically subjective. However, the belief is in you, and you are external to me. Thus, at the same time that the belief is ontologically subjective it is equally ontologically objective. Further, I can ask you, 'Do you really think I am a person of Hispanic descent?' and get some epistemically objective idea as to whether you truly believe this. For example, you might reply, 'Yeah, because of your name.' If your reply was heard by others beside myself, it is a safe bet (another term for approximate truth) that you really do construct me as a 'Hispanic'. Hence your belief is epistemically objective. This means that it can be observed that it is epistemically objectively true that reality can be ontologically objective and subjective.

The preceding has consequences for Cartesian dualism. What maintained the dualism was the possibility that the subjective and objective were ontological opposites. However, they are actually the same thing. Any location is either objective or subjective relative to the location of who is observing whom occupying it. What is subjective to you is objective to me. Thus, these terms are the same spaces differently observed in a common reality. Otherwise put, the terms 'objective' and 'subjective' do not denote realities. They merely report the relative place of who is reporting those realities, the observer or the observed, which explains why the argument is a locational relativist one. However, what is the reality of this subjective that is objective? The answer to this question leads us to 'Ghost Busters II' and to the contemplation of certain basics of the human brain.

GHOST BUSTERS II

Brain and mind

> To know the brain is the same thing as knowing the material course of thought and will, the same thing as discovering the intimate history of life in its perpetual duel with eternal forces.
>
> (Ramón y Cajal, in Levitan and Kaczmarek,
> *The Neuron, Cell and Molecular Biology*, 1997: 478)

Some might say, still hunting with the dog of Cartesian dualism, that the conclusion of the preceding section ignores the fact that the subjective involves the mind; that the mind involves willful consciousness; and that the conscious mind is different. It is a realm of thought bearing no material reality; and so the dualism of the objective, as a place of material realities, and the subjective, as a place of immaterial minds, is preserved. 'Of course', as George

Herbert Mead had famously remarked, 'the mind is a very ambiguous term' (1977: 181) and as Stephen Kosslyn and Richard Andersen, echoing Mead, recently added, 'The term thinking is notoriously vague' (1995: 959). So the concept of mind is 'ambiguous' because that of thought is 'vague'. A materialist approach to thought is advanced in what follows which supports the claim of the pioneering nineteenth-century neuroscientist, Ramón y Cajal, that the brain minds 'the material course of thought and will'.

Let us begin by noting that the elaboration of such an approach is enhanced by recent developments in the tools for observing the normal brain. This is because for much of the twentieth century normal brains could not be investigated without gravely harming them. So brain researchers tended to observe deceased or damaged brains. However, recent advances in observational techniques allow brain scientists to observe what is happening in the brain as it actually performs normal functions. The key innovations were the development of electroencephalography (EEG) in the 1950s, followed by computerized axial tomography (CAT), regional cerebral blood flow (rCBF), functional magnetic resonance imaging (fMRI), and positron emission tomography (PET) by the late 1980s. These provide 'real-time' recordings and, in the case of fMRI and PET, an actual image of the brain as it thinks. As a result, a cognitive neuroscience began to flourish in the 1990s as part of a 'brain science revolution' (Lister and Weingartner 1991: 5). This revolution engages both neurology and cognitive science, the latter being an amalgam of cognitive psychology, linguistics (especially semantics), information theory, and computer modeling. Introductions to the discipline can be found in Gazzaniga (1995, 1999), Kosslyn and Koenig (1992), and Kandel et al. (1995).[1]

Certain limitations of the new observational techniques need to be specified. They do not allow neuroscientists actually to observe what happens *within* the organs of the nervous system as they actually happen. This means that brain states at molecular levels go unrecorded. Nevertheless, cognitive neuroscience has made progress in observing people minding their own business, as they consciously perceive, remember, emote, reason, and will. Such observations allow scholars to discuss credibly the ambiguities of the mind, of which one of the most perplexing is whether the immaterial mind is 'material', as Ramón y Cajal said it was. Such an inquiry is undertaken below.

Gross anatomy: information and representation

[T]he general and lasting features of the external world are represented in the brain by relatively lasting configurations of synaptic connections.
(Paul Churchland, *The Engine of Reason, the Seat of the Soul*, 1995: 6)

Let us begin by asking, what is the most decisive function performed by the brain? The philosopher Daniel Dennett responded to this question calling brains 'anticipation machines' whose 'fundamental purpose is to produce the future' (1991: 177). Dennett is perceptive here, though I would put the matter somewhat differently. Humans, like other animals, as opposed to granite, act. Actions involve doing this and that, here and there, over a past, a now, and a future. 'Now' is the time to organize things about the future. The 'past' is the *only* predictor of that future, and the brain is the organ which evolved, especially among humans, literally to embody the lived past to have it around to be analyzed to organize future actions.[2] The 'future' is what happens after events in the now that include contemplating the past. This means that Dennett got it half right. Indeed, brains are anticipation machines, but they are just as much retrospection machines; and they anticipate because they retrospect. I shall argue below that brains are able to be such machines because, as Paul Churchland suggests, they represent 'the world' in 'configurations of synaptic connections'. This is the *re*-presentation of events in E-space in structures of synaptic connections in the brain's I-space. In order to support this suggestion it is necessary to show how the various structures of the brain in the (k)now use the past to make future action over space and time.

The human nervous system has two major subsystems, the autonomic (ANS) and the central nervous system (CNS). The ANS is the web of nerves in the body that controls its internal business. There are two parts to the ANS, the sympathetic and parasympathetic nervous systems, which tend to operate in opposite manners. The sympathetic nervous system is activated by a group of neurotransmitters called catecholamines, most importantly norepinephrine, largely coming from the adrenal medulla in the brain. These are important in emotions, especially in 'flight or fight' emergencies – where the heart rate picks up, adrenalin flows, and blood is shifted from the skin and viscera to the brain and muscles. The parasympathetic nervous system, in effect, tells the body to 'chill out' after the rigors of the operation of the sympathetic nervous system.

The CNS 'minds' the ANS's internal business and the body's external business. The brain is one of two CNS organs, the other being the spinal cord. The spinal cord serves three major roles. Simple reflexes (such as knee jerks) are mediated within the spinal cord. Rhythmic movements (such as walking) are also mediated within the spinal cord; and information transfer from the external environment to the brain and vice versa occurs along the spinal cord. The spinal cord, in fulfilling this final function, might be likened to an extension cord plugging the brain into external reality.

The brain is the place where 'all higher nervous system functions' occur (Dowling 1998: 84). The first of these is to perceive reality now; that is, to apprehend information about events roughly as they occur. The second function is to learn about that now so that it can become memory, information about the past. Present nows, as opposed to past nows, are a real headache. You have to do something about them. The third function of the brain is to deal with the headache, and figure out what to do about now. This is

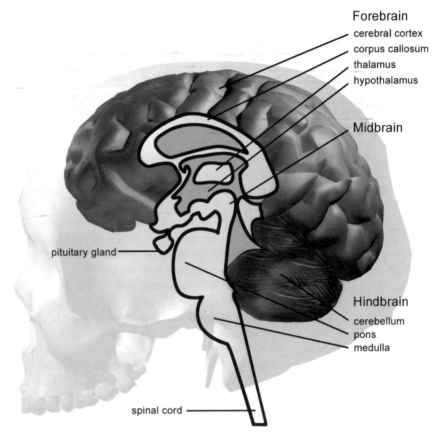

Figure 3.1 Longitudinal section of brain
Source: Dowling (1998: 90); *Artist:* A.N. Reyna

reasoning about perceptions of present realities in terms of embodied past realities. The fourth function is to do it, to act, which is what creates futures. These four functions are performed in three major structures: the forebrain, midbrain, and hindbrain.

The hindbrain emerges from the spinal cord and has three main parts: the medulla, pons, and cerebellum. The medulla is involved with regulating vital body functions, often through the ANS, including heart rate and respiration. The cerebellum is important for coordinating and integrating motor activity, that is, the timing and smoothing of muscle movements to act. The pons relays information from structures in the forebrain, especially the cortex, to the cerebellum. The midbrain is relatively small in humans and, as its name suggests, is situated between the hindbrain and the forebrain. It includes the thalamus and hypothalamus. The thalamus is the central sensory clearing-

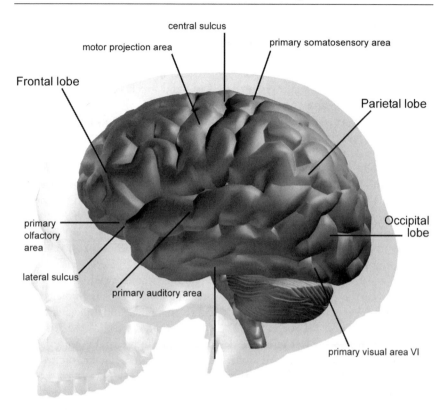

Figure 3.2 A left-side view of the outside surface of the cortex
Source: Dowling (1998: 97); *Artist:* A.N. Reyna

house. Certain parts of it relay information from the senses to the cortex. Other parts relay back information concerning the senses from the cortex to the muscles. The hypothalamus is the brain's principal regulatory center for basic drives and emotions, such as those involved in eating, drinking, body temperature, and sexual activity.

The forebrain accounts for roughly 75 percent of a person's brain. It contains two major regions. The first of these is the cerebral cortex that is itself divided into four major subregions (sometimes called lobes): frontal, parietal, temporal, and occipital. The four cortical subregions are themselves divided into smaller regions. Further, all these regions tend to be demarcated by grooves – sulci (pl.), sulcus (sing.) – within which there are rounded elevations – gyri (pl.), gyrus (sing.).

Perception, reason, and the initiation of motor activities – that is, actions – largely occur in the cortex. A deep infolding, the central sulcus, divides the front of the cortex from the back. The posterior part of the cortex, the sensory lobe, is largely concerned with receiving and analyzing sensory information involving seeing, hearing, smelling, tasting, and touching. Seeing occurs in the primary visual area in the occipital lobe (also called the visual cortex); hearing, in the primary auditory area of the temporal lobe along the lateral sulcus (also called the auditory cortex). Taste and touch occur in the primary somatosensory area along the central sulcus.

The anterior part of the cortex, the frontal lobe, is involved in analyzing information, and then translating it into motor activities. There are two major parts of this cortex. The prefrontal cortex (PFC) is in the front, the anterior portion. Behind – that is, posterior to – the PFC are various motor regions. Further, smell occurs in the primary olfactory area in the frontal lobe. Just what the PFC does has been one of the 'more debated' questions in neurobiology (Deacon 1997: 259). Strikingly, the PFC by comparison to that in other animals is disproportionately enlarged.[3] Further, it is heavily interconnected to all other portions of the brain (Fuster 1989: 12–26). The PFC does not appear to be directly involved in intelligence.[4] There can be severe damage to it and intelligence remains relatively unchanged. Nor does it appear to be the place where meanings are established, because damage to it does not appear to destroy a person's ability to understand the meaning of words or sentences (Deacon 1997: 265). Rather, goal-directed behavior involving will appears lost after the destruction of the prefrontal cortex.[5] So I shall argue later in this chapter that the PFC, like a conductor, orchestrates information in ways that create action.

Motor activities involve the utilization of muscles and, as such, might be said to 'motor' bodies through reality, thereby creating action. Information about will – what to do about some present now based upon remembrance of past nows – is transmitted back from the PFC to the motor projection areas, which are on the frontal side of the central sulcus opposite the primary somatosensory area. Here this information goes to the pre-motor and then to the motor areas, where it is translated into increasingly precise directions about how to achieve goals. The information of these directions is then conveyed to other portions of the nervous system, especially the spinal cord, whence it is forwarded to muscles to become movements that 'motor' the body along to goal attainment.

The areas between the motor projection and various sensory areas are called the association cortices. These regions, especially that part in the PFC, are restricted in other animals. It is here that the brain mostly performs a third of its functions, analyzing present perceptions in terms of past realities. This is done because 'Here . . . sensory perceptions are married with appropriate cognitive associations – the perception of a knife, for example, is joined with concepts of stabbing, eating, slicing, and so on' (R. Carter 1998: 108). The perception 'knife' is the now. The cognitive associations – for example, 'slicing' – are remembrances of knives past. Because the association areas in humans are roughly 200 times greater than in other animals, people are better able to analyze the present in terms of the past and thereby to plan for the future.

The second part of the forebrain is beneath the cortex, and hence is often called subcortical, and includes the amygdala, the hippocampus, the basal ganglia, and the septum. The amygdala remembers and regulates emotion and reinforcement. The hippocampus remembers events. What is striking about it is that it receives inputs from practically every region of the cortex through the entorhinal cortex. Further, it has outputs that loop back through the entorhinal cortex to the cortical areas that the inputs originated from. What are all these interconnections about? It appears that they are necessary for the learning, and recall, of long-term memories. If a person's hippocampus is surgically removed, that person will remember events up to the operation, but will be unable to recall ones that occurred just a short time prior to it.

The basal ganglia receives inputs from the cortex and feeds information back to it by way of the thalamus. It is, thus, involved in the initiation and execution of movements that are smoothed out by the cerebellum. Parkinson's disease, which involves difficulties initiating movement and tremors, results in part from the destruction of a part of the basal ganglia called the substantia nigra. The septum appears to be related to awareness and emotional expression.

These four subcortical areas are interconnected and additionally are connected with the thalamus and hypothalamus in the midbrain in what has been called the 'limbic system'. P.D. MacLean, who introduced this term (1952), suggested that this was the 'visceral' or emotional brain. Although the idea that there is a single limbic system which is in charge of all emotion is 'not acceptable' (LeDoux 1996: 99), it is true that the different parts of the limbic system, complexly interacting with each other, are involved in the integration of emotion and thought. The preceding discussion has in a very rudimentary manner described only the major parts of the central nervous system.[6] However, a question remains: how do the parts get connected?

The response to this question leads us to neurons. These are the physical wiring of which the different brain parts are composed, and it is they that get connected to make the ANS and CNS. Consideration of neurons and their connections will in turn help further understanding of the nature of representation and information in the brain. There are estimated to be 100 billion to 1,000 billion neurons (nerve cells) in the nervous system (Dowling 1998: 6).[7] Neurons consist of three parts: the nucleus (the cell body); dendrites (short fibers with branching networks at the end); and axons (relatively long fibers that end near other nerve cells in the brain, near other nerve cells in the spinal cord, or in an organ such as muscles somewhere in the body). Synapses are the regions of contact between neurons and other cells. Here axons from one neuron are in close proximity to dendrites from another neuron in a synapse. Axons are the senders, dendrites the receivers in these synaptic connections. Dendritic and axonal branching allows a neuron to synaptically connect with many other neurons, with each neuron having in the order of 100 to 10,000 connections.

The organization of connections between neurons variously involves modules, circuits, networks, pathways, or systems. These terms need to be sorted out. This is especially true of the notion of 'module', because the view that the brain was somehow modular and that, therefore, cognitive processes exhibit modularity has been said by Massimo Pintelli to be 'arguably . . . the single most important discovery of cognitive science' (in Fodor 1998: 11). More neurological and more cognitive versions of brain modularity can be distinguished. Cognitive scientists tend to begin by examining different examples of cognition. For example, they might examine a particular language to discover its grammar, and from its grammar infer what is indicated about human cognitive abilities. Then, on the basis of their judgments concerning these, they draw certain conclusions about the entity that produces such abilities. The neuroscientists directly inquire into this entity, the brain.

These more neurological versions of modularity derive from Vernon Mountcastle's research concerning the organization of neurons in the cerebral cortex. Mountcastle in the 1950s found that different vertically oriented clusters of connected neurons a few millimeters square performed remarkably specific brain functions. He originally called these neuron clusters 'columns'. Restak (1994: 32–5) provides an accessible account of this work. These columns came to be called modules (Mountcastle 1979), and it came to be believed that the brain was organized 'into' modules that were 'relatively independent functioning units that work in parallel' (Gazzaniga 1985: 4). Modules perform narrow functions that are components of larger, superordinate ones. For example, the V2 module (the 'V' is for vision) in the visual cortex creates stereo vision. The V4 module produces color. Together these two modules are components with perhaps twenty or so other modules that perform the superordinate function of seeing.

Just what sorts of neurological modules exist in the cerebral cortex is very much open to question. It is claimed – for example, by Persinger (1987: 9–23) – that there is a module for religious experience, apparently located in the temporal lobe which when triggered is able 'to produce intense feelings of spiritual transcendence, combined with a sense of some mystical presence' (R. Carter 1998: 13). Harriet Whitehead asserts that there is a 'sexuality' module (2000: 6). In the more neurological variant of modularity, the exact neuroanatomy of the functional unit that is believed to be a module should be known, and it should be in the cerebral cortex.

The more cognitively oriented view of modularity derives most importantly from Jerry Fodor's *Modularity of the Mind* (1983), via Noam Chomsky's (1980) belief that there was a module for language in the brain, and, perhaps, ultimately from Immanuel Kant's different 'faculties' of cognition (1781). A 'module' is a 'special-purpose, computational system' (Fodor 1998). A 'mind' in this view, as Karmiloff-Smith puts it, is a gaggle of 'genetically specified, independently functioning modules' (1999: 558). These are 'deemed to be hardwired . . . of fixed neural architecture (specified genetically), domain specific . . . and insensitive to central cognitive goals' (ibid.: 558). The view that modules exhibit domain-specific cognitive abilities is important.

Domain-general cognitive capacities are reasoning abilities that apply to any cognitive task. If humans have such cognitive capacities, then they are endowed with a *single* set of reasoning abilities that they apply to *all* cognitive tasks. For example, Piaget's (1983) theory of cognitive development is domain general, because a single type of reasoning characterizes each level of a child's cognitive development. Most theories of the mind in the past tended to be domain general. Domain-specific cognitive abilities are those that address different cognitive tasks with different modes of reasoning, structures of knowledge, and mechanisms for acquiring that knowledge (Gelman 1999: 238). Modularity approaches insist that each module have its specific domain of cognition. Hirschfeld and Gelman (1994) present an overview of such approaches. Elman et al. (1996) critique them.

When it is necessary to distinguish the two views of modularity, the more neurological variant will be called just that, 'neurological modularity', while the Fodorian variant will be called 'domain-specific modularity'. Finally, it should be noted that both approaches concern the same reality, that of the module, and that this reality might be imagined as functionally like a morpheme. Morphemes are the smallest concatenations of sound that function to distinguish meaning. Modules are the smallest connections of neurons that function to distinguish cognitive ability. Now, no module is an island.

'Circuits', 'networks', 'pathways', and 'systems' are terms that refer to synaptic linkages between different modules. Thus, they refer to the tying together of regions of different function so that smaller, more specific functions can work together to perform larger, more general ones. Following the lead of Damasio (1994: 30), a distinction will be made between collections of connected neurons that are microscopic versus those that are macroscopic. Circuits and networks are microscopic. Pathways and systems are macroscopic. Generally, networks, pathways, or systems are named after the parts of the brain that get connected or after the functions they perform. Thus, for example, connections between neurons in different parts of the cortex are said to be part of 'corticocortical' networks, while those involved in memory are termed 'memory networks', and those producing emotion are a 'limbic' system.

The concept of 'wiring' will be used to denote any and all synaptic connections within the CNS. This means that the CNS's wiring consists of billions upon billions of neurons synaptically connected in perhaps a trillion or so ways, in modules within circuits within pathways that run from the organs of the body which sense reality to the brain and back again to those organs that motor us along in that reality. What goes on within this wiring?

Flows of electrical and chemical energy move within it. This is because each neuron is capable of developing energy that is propagated as an electric current, along its fibers. The currents start at dendrites and flow to axons. At the ends of axons, at the synapses, electrical energy is changed into chemical energy and transmitted to the body of another nerve cell to fire off energy in it. The chemicals that do the job of synaptic transmission are called neurotransmitters. Acetylcholine, serotonin, dopamine, and norepinephrine are important among these. The brain, then, is a place of transmission, termed 'triggering' or 'firing', of electrochemical energy, called 'signals', from cell to cell. Neurons bringing signals into and out of the brain areas are respectively called 'afferent' and 'efferent'. One is not speaking metaphorically, then, when one describes individuals as alive with nervous energy.

Electrochemical energy moves along a wiring organized in feedforward, feedback, parallel, lateral, convergent, divergent, and hierarchical manners. 'Feedforward' connections are those where there is a synapse such that an axon of neuron A is joined with a dendrite of neuron B so that electrochemical activity in A can trigger such activity in B. 'Feedback' is the reverse situation, where not only can A excite B, but B can do the same to A. Feedforward and feedback can occur not only between two neurons, but between hundreds of thousands of them. Especially important in this regard are signals that feedforward from subcortical regions of the brain to the cortex, such as the thalamus or the amygdala, to the cortex and, then, feedback to the subcortex. Regions of neurons connected in feedforward/feedback fashion are said to exhibit 'feedback loops'. The thalamus and the cortex are connected in a 'cortical-thalamic' feedback circuitry.

'Parallel' neuronal arrangements occur where there are a number of neuronal circuits that function at roughly the same time. The cortical-thalamic feedback loop, for example, consists of neurons organized to do parallel processing of different sensory stimuli. This means that certain neurons are arranged in circuits going from the thalamus to the occipital lobe in the sensory cortex to process visual stimuli. Other neurons are arranged in other parallel circuits from the thalamus to the temporal lobe for hearing and the parietal lobe for touch. Further, parallel processing may occur within the modules of a circuit that is itself arrayed parallel to another circuit. For example, within visual circuitry different modules analyze form, color, movement, and so on at the same time while a similar parallel processing is occurring with sound in auditory circuitry. This arrangement of neurons in parallel circuits distinguishes brains from computers, which work in a more linear fashion. Computers, thus, have to do one thing at a time. Brains with extensive parallel wiring can do many things at the same time, like seeing and hearing.

Parallel neuronal patterns exhibit hierarchies where there is convergence and divergence. 'Hierarchical' neuronal patterns are those in which information is transmitted through convergent or divergent levels of neurons. The circuitry in the sensory and motor pathways is arguably the two central hierarchical systems in the CNS. Stimuli are brought in the sensory pathway into the CNS by receptor cells (one level in the hierarchy), passed on to the thalamus (a second level), and thence on to the cortex (a third level), and finally on to certain areas in the prefrontal cortex (a fourth level), to contemplate the sensory stimuli. In the motor pathway, on the other hand, stimuli leave from the prefrontal cortex (one level), for the motor cortex (another level), thence on to the spinal cord via the thalamus and cerebellum (still another level), and finally on to the muscles, for some action vis-à-vis the original visual stimuli.

The sensory hierarchy that runs from receptor cells throughout the body and feeds into the PFC is 'convergent', because neurons from all over the body converge upon on a single spot. Conversely, the motor hierarchy that runs from the PFC out to all the nerves that trigger muscles throughout the body is 'divergent', because neurons from one region diverge to all the nooks and crannies of the body. Different association areas of the cortex are named after the neurons that converge and diverge there. Areas where neurons meet from different senses are said to be 'polysensory'. Areas that are junctions of different modes of brain function are said to be 'multimodal'. Finally, converging and diverging pathways are sometimes called 'ascending' and 'descending', and it is important to recognize that sensory and motor pathways ascend to and descend from the same room in the attic, the PFC.

It is time to explain what is going on as energy surges through this wiring. The electrochemical events in neural networks involve the transmission of information. This term now requires a formal definition. 'Information' might be thought of as material *re*-presentations of what is and what to do about it in the experienced past, the present, and the future. Past information is memory. Present information is perception. Future information concerns desires, plans of places to go, people to meet, things to do. A key to understanding such information is to know what kind of reality it is that has the capacity to be a material *re*-presentation of other realities.

This reality is 'the *depolarization pattern*, the set of firing rates of the neurons in a specific collection of neurons' (Baron 1987: 28; emphasis in the original). Depolarization is the flow of electricity in a single neuron. However, information in neural circuits is never the depolarization of a single cell. Rather, it is a 'pattern' specified by 'the rate of firing of each neuron in the collection' of neurons in a module (ibid.: 29). Depolarization patterns are dependent on the particular connections that exist between neurons. Paul Churchland, whose quotation began this section, calls these 'configurations of synaptic connections' (1995: 6). What might such patterns or configurations look like?

The illustration provided is oversimplified but nevertheless explains these configurations. Imagine a module of three rows of synaptically connected neurons. The first row consists of neurons whose dendrites received neuronal transmissions either from events outside the body, or from other modules within the body. This row of neurons is said to be the 'input units'. The axons from this unit connect with the dendrites of the second row and the axons of

the second row connect with the dendrites of the third row, whose axons connect with neurons in another module. The third row of neurons, because its
electrical transmissions travel to other modules, is said to consist of 'output
units'. The second row of neurons secreted between the input and output rows
is said to consist of 'hidden units'.

Now the connections between neurons in a module may be of two kinds.
Either the flow of electricity from one neuron turns off or on the flow of electricity in the neurons to which it is attached. The former sort of connections
are said to be 'inhibitory', the latter 'excitatory'. In addition, each connection
has a 'weight' (strength); the greater the weight (excitatory or inhibitory) on a
connection, the more vigorously will a neuron turn off or on when signaled by
the neurons to which its dendrites attach. Now 'information' is the different
patterns of firings that can be activated in the neurons connected in modules.
To illustrate: consider seeing our friend from the first chapter, the dog
Sebastian. The actual image of him results from patterns of activations of his
shaggy black being in modules in the retina transmitted along the optic nerve
to modules in the lateral geniculate nucleus (LGN) in the thalamus, and on
from there to modules in the visual cortex, whose activated patterns are the
information that is the image of Sebastian.

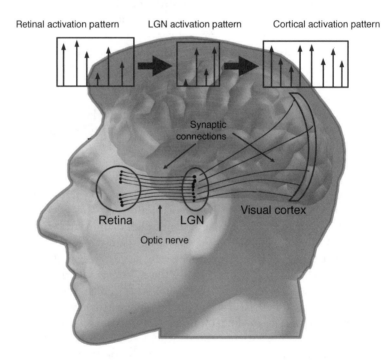

Figure 3.3 Synaptic connections between retina and visual cortex
Source: Paul Churchland (1995: 10); *Artist:* A.N. Reyna

The previous discussion of information has been hypothetical. Let us talk about an event that actually occurred.

Consider, for example, the case of a young black man from Guinea in Africa in a rough neighborhood in New York City on a cold night the winter before the new millennium.[8] Amadou was not a bad guy. He was going into the entryway of the building in which he lived. Four cops came along. He was an external reality to these guys. They saw him and heard him and through these sensations *re*-presented him in the modules that led down the pathways of their CNSs. In this new state of Amadou, he was information, a particular pattern of firings in circuits and pathways of the cops' CNSs.

The preceding, it might be appreciated, involves a revision of the term 'representation'. Now the concept does not refer to faithful mirroring of, or a correspondence with, reality; an understanding of the term that Rorty had complained about (1979). Rather, it denotes the taking of a reality that is in one material form and giving it another material form – that is, literally taking one thing and *re*-presenting it as something else. Neuronal representation takes external and internal bodily realities and *re*-presents them as patterns of firing in modules of connected circuits and pathways in the CNS. Perhaps, four cops lumbering up to the Guinean fired off his limbic system. He felt fear. This put him into a 'flight or fight' mode. He reached for his wallet. This act of the young black man was *re*-presented as particular patterns of firings in the sensory pathways of the four cops; and those patterns appear to have represented him as drawing for a gun, because they triggered a further pattern of firing in the cops' motor pathways, which triggered *their* guns, which blew him away. Thus, these cops were literally, not metaphorically, quick on the trigger. This ends, due to its brevity, a rather 'gross anatomy' of the brain; but one adducing sufficient evidence to suggest that the brain is an information-processing machine that works by *re*-presenting events in E-space – like Amadou reaching for his wallet – as events in I-space – like the depolarization patterns in the neural circuits and systems of the cops' brains.

The remaining parts of this section investigate the type of information the brain *re*-presents. They successively argue that perceiving consists of material representations of perceptual and emotional nows; that memory involves material representations of the perceptual and emotional pasts; that emotion is a type of perception consisting of material representations of the reinforcing properties of reality; and, finally, that reason and will ultimately function as material anticipations of the future. So it is suggested that there are two sorts of perceptions and that these provide information concerning 'what is' right now. Next, it is advised that there are two sorts of memories and that these provide retrospection concerning 'what was' back then, as well as what was done about it. Finally, it is proposed that reason is neuronal anticipations of what to do in the future based on perceptions of the now and memories of the then.

Three particularities distinguish this approach. First, it treats emotion as a type of perception. Second, it insists that now is a learned then; that is, that the present in the brain is built upon memories of a learned past. Third, this means that what the brain does as a retrospection machine in the business of anticipation is to produce the future which, if now is then, has to be then again. Let us begin with perception, and go back to Empedocles at the dawn of Western philosophy.

Perception

SOCRATES: Do you agree with Empedocles that existing things give off a
sort of effluence?
MENO: Certainly.
SOCRATES: And that they have pores into which and through which the
effluences travel?
MENO: Yes.
SOCRATES: And of the effluences, some fit some of the pores, while
others are too small or too big?
MENO: That's right.
SOCRATES: And there is something you call sight?
MENO: There is.
SOCRATES: From this . . . color is an effluence from things which is fitted
to sight and perceptible.

(Plato, Meno)

Plato in this fragment from the Meno has Socrates use Meno as a straight man to present Empedocles' pre-Socratic explanation of perception. Things in reality, like the page you are reading, emit 'effluences', minute particles. As these strike your body some of them fit through your 'pores' to make the pages 'perceptible'. Note that this conception of perception is thoroughly material-istic. Perception results from 'effluences' that are things that go through other things, 'pores'. The approach to perception proposed below is Empedoclean in that it identifies the effluences and pores involved in the embodiment of information about things happening as they happen.

Information processing originates at 'receptors'. These are specialized cells that act as transducers – devices that transform one form of energy into some other form – with the recognition that the energies serve as the medium con-taining information. Receptors transduce energy bearing information about external reality beyond the nervous system into its neuronal form. Let us pay a brief visit to external reality. There things emit or reflect energies. Some of these might be radiant energies, involving light waves, which you can see. Others might be acoustical energies, involving sound waves, which you can hear. The properties of these energies, such as their amplitude and frequency, contain information about the things that radiate them. Energies that contact receptors act as 'stimuli', because the contact triggers – in the sense of 'starts the operation of' – the receptors.

Stimuli contact two types of receptor cells. 'Interoceptors' receive energy in the form of stimuli that are internal to the body; 'exteroceptors' receive energy in the form of stimuli that are external to the body. There are extero-ceptors for the different senses: in the retina for seeing, in the cochlea for hearing, in the olfactory epithelium for smelling, in the tastebuds for tasting, and in a number of different touch receptors for touching. There are also receptors for temperature and pain. The dendrites of sensory neurons connect with receptor cells, and it is across the synapses of these two types of cells that whatever form of energy that stimulated the receptor cell is transduced into neuronal electrochemical energy within the CNS. Thus the information contained in the incoming stimuli now is embodied and *re*-presented as signals.

In order for perception to occur, sensory neurons transmit signals along neural pathways to the sensory cortex. To illustrate, take the cases of vision and hearing. Visual stimuli coming in the form of light waves contact rods and cones – the receptors – in the retina. There they are transduced from radiant energy in the external world to neuronal electrochemical energy that is transmitted along the optic nerve which takes the signal to the LGN in the thalamus whose axons pass it on to the primary visual cortex (V1), located at the very back of the brain at the end of the occipital lobe. Neurons from V1 fan forward to other parts of the visual cortex that perform different tasks in processing visual signals into visual images. There are believed to be up to twenty-five of these visual cortex areas, each called V2, V3, and so on, and each processes different aspects of the electrochemical signal to make a more complete image of the external reality that stimulated the rods and cones. For example, V2 and V4 participate in color-processing fabricating 'what we know as the experience of color' (Damasio and Damasio 1992: 90). Further, these 'areas participate', according to Dowling,

> in two major pathways of visual information flow. One pathway pro-gresses from the occipital lobe dorsally into the parietal lobe. Known as the *where* pathway, it analyzes such things as where an object is. The other pathway flows from the occipital lobe ventrally into the temporal lobe. It is know as the *what* pathway; it identifies objects.
>
> (1998: 117)

There are feedback loops between the visual cortex and other cortical regions in association areas, making possible the simultaneous production of infor-mation created by these regions. I see, smell, and hear the wind under the honeysuckle all at the same time.

Hearing has been less completely researched than seeing, but enough is known to establish that auditory pathways are roughly parallel to those of vision. Sound waves, be they from a songbird or from speech, strike the eardrum setting it to vibrating. These vibrations are ultimately transmitted to auditory receptors in the cochlea where they are transduced into neuronal signals. These move along the auditory nerve where most arrive at the medial geniculate nucleus (MGN) in the thalamus, whence they are relayed on to the auditory cortex in the temporal lobe. As in the visual cortex, there are different areas for processing different aspects of auditory signals. This includes a 'core auditory cortex (A1) and at least four other zones surrounding it' (Kolb and Whishaw 1990: 217). The other senses work in roughly the same manner as do sight and vision. Receptor cells transduce information from the external world into electrochemical neuronal information which is shipped along pathways that bring them into the sensory cortices where they are processed.

The preceding allows us to distinguish detection from perception. The former is the first part of the processing of sensed information about external reality. It is the taking of information from reality and moving it to a place where it can be processed to a point where a person can be aware of it. So understood, 'detection' is 'the result of activity of receptors and their associated afferent pathways to the corresponding . . . [cortical] sensory areas' (ibid.: 223). Perception is a second part of the processing of information about external reality. It is the *re*-presentation of polarization patterns brought to the sensory cortex as a result of detection as images, smells, tastes, feels, or sounds of which persons can be aware. It should be clear that one of the sorts of realities perceived is that of language. What people have perceived – images, smells, tastes, sounds, and so on – will be said to be 'sensations'. Sensations of E-space, other than those pertaining to language, will be said to be 'worldly'. Sensations of language – hearing or reading texts – will be said to be 'semantic'.

So Empedocles has been vindicated. His 'effluences' are the material photons in light waves or air molecules in sound waves. His 'pores', of course, are the receptors. And he would have been delighted to know of the nerves that connect to the sensory areas where perceptions are displayed. All these, of course, are a material reality.

Before proceeding, a point needs to be made explicit. The nows *re*-presented are those containing information about the world that comes from the five senses. They are thus a particular type of sensory perception. Of course, I have suggested that perception of the now is constructed from perceptions of the past. In order to understand how this might be the case it is necessary to consider memory; after which we shall be in a position to consider another, emotional sort of perception.

Memory

> For to remember is to perceive anything with memory.
> (John Locke, *An Essay Concerning Human Understanding*, 1690)

[A]ll memory is essentially *associative*.
(Joaquín Fuster, *Memory in the Cerebral Cortex*, 1995)

The view of memory outlined below is broadly Lockean with a Fusterian twist.
John Locke, the Enlightenment philosopher, linked memory with perception,
Joaquín Fuster, the contemporary neuroscientist, links it with associations.
First, I shall discuss the Lockean and then the Fusterian aspects of memory.
The approach is Lockean, in the sense that memory is understood in terms of
what happens to certain perceptions. What happens to them is that they get
stored. Memory is the storage of past perceptions to conserve them for
retrieval, more or less, as needed.[9] William James (1890) recognized that there
appear to be two basic types of memory. A 'short-term' – sometimes called
'primary', or 'working' – memory is 'what you are conscious of now' (LeDoux
1996: 185), while a 'long-term' memory is 'one lasting from minutes to a lifetime' (ibid.: 184–5). Long-term memories may be part of short-term working
memories. For example, I am thinking right now about my mother. The short-
term memory holds a long-term memory; an image of 'Peter', my mother, a
woman who was so fierce that they gave her a man's nickname.

Long-term memory can be either 'explicit' or 'implicit'. The former
memories are 'conscious recollections'; those of the latter sort cannot 'be
brought to mind and described verbally' (ibid.: 181). Peter teaching me to ride
a bike is an explicit memory; knowing how to do it is an implicit memory.
Explicit, long-term memory is said to be perceptual (or as it is also called,
declarative). 'Perceptual' memory is perception of past 'events and facts'
(Fuster 1995: 17). It may be further subdivided into episodic or semantic
(Tulving 1972). 'Episodic' memory concerns 'past events in an individual's
life'. It is remembrance of my mother in Iowa showing the pictures in the
1950s, of sitting under the tamarind in 1969, of sitting under the honeysuckle in 1999. Chapter 5 connects semantic memory with culture. However,
for the moment it need only be known that semantic memory stores
'knowledge of the world' and 'represents organized information such as facts,
concepts, and vocabulary' (Squire 1987: 169). It is memory of what is a
'mother', a 'tamarind', and a 'honeysuckle'.

The distinction between these two forms of perceptual memories needs to
be sharpened. Tulving and Lepage speculate that episodic memory is the
'latest arrival on the evolutionary scene', one that gives its possessors the
possibility of 'time travel' (2000: 211, 213). However, a point to grasp here is
that this time travel happens in the now. Right now I am up in my study
traveling back to the 1950s remembering being a boy on vacation in Iowa.
I can hear the inflections of my mother's voice as she described our dead kin
in the photographs. So the fact that people have episodic memories means
that there are really two nows: 'present-now', where what is happening is
roughly represented as it is happening; 'past-now', where what is happening is

a replaying of a representation of what happened. Present-now I am in my study. It is a shameful mess. Past-now is, even as I survey the wreckage of my study, a replay of the representations of those antique photographs and the sounds of my mother. This ability, born of episodic memory, to hold two realities – present-now and past-now – represented at roughly the same time in a person's awareness, is, if not unique to humans, certainly vastly more developed than in other animals.

A key to understanding semantic memory is to recognize that it is not memory of perceptions of sensations themselves, but memory of semantic representations of perceptions of sensations or their abstractions. Semantics is concerned with the organization of signs. These, following Charles Peirce (1958), are of three types. 'Icons' are signs where there is a similarity between the sign and the object. A photograph of Peter is an icon of her. 'Indexes' are signs where there is a causal relationship between the signs and the objects represented. Having to hold on to things, while swaying – just a bit – was an index of Peter's growing alcoholism. Most signs, however, are 'symbols', where the relationship between the sign and the object it represents is arbitrary. The symbol 'mother' represents the object, 'Peter'.

Languages are semantic systems based upon symbols (words or lexemes) and ways of combining these (their syntax).[10] This leads us to an ability to recognize what Tulving and Lepage consider the 'crucial' difference between episodic and semantic memory. The former is 'concerned with remembering past experiences as such', while the latter is 'concerned with acquisition and use of knowledge' of signs associated with these experiences (2000: 214). What is crucial here is that the past is remembered not only as perceptions of sensations of what happened, but equally it is recalled semantically as symbols of what happened back in the distant then. Memory uses semantic memories to make episodic ones. For example, I can remember from my semantic memory that lexemically Peter was a 'woman', a 'mother'. Syntactically, 'Peter was my mother'.

Once I have 'mother' semantically identified, I remember from my episodic memory the time she told me about when the garment workers' union head-quarters in Johannesburg was attacked in 1948 by thugs, out to bust the union. She worked for the union. As the men came rushing up the stairs, she grabbed her belly and pleaded 'I'm pregnant!' Then, fast, she raised back her leg. She was a champion horsewoman, so the leg would have been powerful. Her kick sent the first bunch of toughs downstairs. Semantic memory, then, makes possible much of episodic memory. Let us turn from perceptual to procedural pasts.

'Procedural', also termed 'motor', memory is remembrance of 'skills and other cognitive operations' (ibid.: 151). Perceptual memory is stored representations of what was. Procedural memory is stored representations of what was done about it. Peter died as a result of her alcoholism, a perceptual memory. We buried her, a procedural memory. Procedural memories can combine explicit and implicit components. Peter explicitly followed the script: 'When attacked, defend!' But she did not remember to kick. She just did it. Further, there appears to be a tendency for explicit procedural memories to become implicit. When you are learning a language in school you are explicitly taught its syntax, the rules that arrange words into phrases and sentences. However, once you have mastered the language, syntactical rules have become implicit, and you just chatter away without remembering them. Many memories contain – in the sense of having associated together – both explicit and implicit elements. So, for example, when you see a dog such as Sebastian, you consciously follow the script 'Pet the mangy beast'; though the way you actually do it – smoothing here, avoiding mange there – may be automatic, without any explicit grammar of petting.

Just as wives have their husbands, so perceptual memories have their associations with procedural ones. My 'car' is a perceptual memory; that I 'drive' it is an explicit procedural memory; and how I actually move along – absent-mindedly, sedately – is an implicit procedural memory. Such associations mingle at least three sorts of memories: perceptual memories of worldly sensations; perceptual memories of the semantic sensations associated with worldly sensations; and, finally, memories of procedural scripts associated with the two types of perceptual memories. Consider, for example, that I remember an ancient man from Bémbassa. I have visual and auditory memories of him. He was terribly skinny, drooled a bit, and talked funny. He seemed to me the oldest man in the world. These are worldly perceptual memories. I remember he was called *gada* which, if you recall from the first chapter, literally meant 'whitebeard', but actually was also used to denote a man who was impotent. *Gada* was a semantic memory associated with these sensual memories. And, of course, I remembered that a man who was *gada* was one you did not have to show *hormo* (respect). This was the procedural memory associated with the worldly and semantic perceptual memories.

These perceptual and procedural memory associations are terribly important for people, because they not only tell what is reality, but what to do about it. If people do not get their memories correct, they have problems living their lives. To illustrate, consider yourself a man walking down Broadway having just seen a great Woody Allen movie. You remember that strolling down Broadway is being 'outside' in 'public'. These are memories of semantic sensations associated with your worldly sensations of where you are. However, you are intoxicated, and you forget how to act in public. It happens. Feeling a bit raunchy after the movie you unzip your pants, remove your penis, and start masturbating. The problem here is that the procedural memory, 'Do not masturbate in public', has become dissociated from the perceptual one that you are in public.

Now fly to the Brazilian Amazon. It is your first time there as, in actuality, you have never been further south than Greenwich Village. You find yourself, stone sober, in a jungle clearing in Nambikuara territory, a region described by Lévi-Strauss (1948). A man walks into the clearing. You see him grab something encased in a long woven grass cylinder sticking out in front of his waist. It looks like a condom with hubris. At first you cannot tell what he has grabbed. Then you see it more clearly, and remember, 'That is his prick.' Next you see him agitate his member against one of his thighs. 'Wow', you think, 'He's bopping his baloney in public.' Remembrance of sensations of penises past is a worldly perceptual memory; that of agitating it is a procedural one concerning masturbation.

The only problem is, as Lévi-Strauss would inform you, you have your procedural and perceptual associations all wrong. You are associating as if you were on the Upper West Side, but you are in the Amazon. The man is not naked. The woven condom is a penis sheath, formal attire. The agitation of his penis is not public masturbation. It is a sign of greeting, and of peaceful intention. Thus, association of perceptions of penis agitation with 'masturbation' may make sense on the Upper West Side. But you are in Nambikuara territory. It's a jungle out there, where the proper association is between the perceptual memory 'agitation of penis' with the procedural memory for 'greetings'. The point here is simple. If you cannot make the proper associations between perceptual and procedural memories, you may not be able to distinguish masturbation from greetings, which could contribute to troubles going about your everyday life. What are the brain structures responsible for these memories?

Haha!

It is now that Fuster's work becomes relevant, because he offers an associationist synthesis of recent research concerning the biology of memory.[11] He says that the starting point of this synthesis is recognition 'that memory representations are comprised of widely distributed cortical networks' which 'are probably hierarchically organized, overlapping anatomically, and profusely interconnected' (1998: 1223). In fact, studies appear to indicate a double hierarchy of both procedural and perceptual memories. The 'hierarchy' of explicit perceptual memories 'ranges from the sensorily concrete to the conceptually general' (1997: 453–4). At the bottom of this hierarchy are perceptions from the senses – either from a single sense, like sight alone, or a number of senses like sight and sound. These are uni- or multi-modal perceptual memories. Next up the hierarchy are remembrances that involve a number of perceptual memories of events (episodic memories). Furthest up the hierarchy are memories that in some way conceptualize in less or more abstract manners the event (semantic memories). A simple example illustrates this hierarchy: my memory of the Statue of Liberty (a multi-modal perceptual memory) is associated with my memory of my last trip to New York City (an episodic memory), and with the recollection that the statue (a less abstract semantic memory) is supposed to represent liberty (a more general and abstract semantic memory).

Fuster holds that this memory hierarchy exists as nested neuronal hierarchies within the brain that become 'progressively . . . more widely distributed', as one remembers more general and abstract matters. Specifically, the evidence shows that 'perception and the memory' of something 'share much of the same cortical substrate' (1989: 169). This means that memories of unimodal perceptions are likely to be found in or near the primary sensory areas of the posterior cortex. Multi-modal perceptual memories appear to be found in 'the polysensory association cortex and, in addition, into the limbic structures of the temporal lobe, the hippocampus in particular' (Fuster 1997: 454).

These neural networks 'become broader and more widely dispersed, encroaching into progressively widely dispersed cortical domains', as recollections ascend the memory hierarchy and become more complex episodic and semantic declarative memories' (ibid.: 454). The posterior association cortex in the temporal lobes seems especially important in these perceptual memories. A number of studies indicate that semantic memory is held within broad networks in the posterior association cortex. Specifically, lexical memory seems to be found in modules in the temporal-parietal lobes on the left side of the brain in what is called Wernicke's area (see especially Martin et al. 1996). Conceptual remembrances, the highest level of the perceptual memory hierarchy, appear to have the most widespread cortical distribution throughout the cortex.

Fuster argues that procedural, like perceptual, memory also exhibits a hierarchy that begins with conceptions of how to proceed, and declines thence to specific plans and programs of how to proceed, to particular specific acts that implement plans and programs, and on to, at the lowest level, particular motor movements that constitute acts. The lowest levels of the procedural memory hierarchy are found in the spinal cord, brain stem, and cerebellum, which store repertoires of reflex acts. The cortex of the frontal lobe supports all the other higher levels of procedural memory. The primary motor cortex, the lowest level of procedural memory in the cortex, stores remembrances of elementary motor acts 'defined and determined by the contractions of specific muscles and muscle groups (Fuster 1997: 455). Next up in the hierarchy is the premotor cortex. Studies indicate that neural networks in this region 'encode motor acts and programs defined by goal, sequence or trajectory' (ibid.: 455). The PFC is the highest level of the procedural memory. Here networks remember 'the schemas of goal-directed action, commonly referred to as plans' (ibid.: 455). Memory, then, consists of networks of neurons of varying complexity.

How is long-term memory stored? It is important to recognize here that the storage of information is learning. This arises from contact with external reality that produces sensations that, taken all together, is experience, and 'experience shapes the design of circuits' (Damasio 1994: 112). The process by which experience reshapes synapses, and thereby makes new connections, occurs because every time we sense something – a sight, a sound, an idea – a number of neurons get fired. And sometimes they do not return to their original state. This is true because the same experience provokes the same pattern of neuronal firings, and repeated patterns of firing lead to new synaptic connections in the networks of firing neurons. This is 'Hebbian plasticity', which operates according to the proposition that 'cells that fire together wire together' (LeDoux 1996: 214). Hebbian plasticity began as a purely hypothetical generalization, though empirical research currently supports it (Bliss and Lømo, 1973). Researchers using electron microscopes focusing upon only two neurons have been able to picture the physical changes that occur in synapses when repeatedly triggered, as memories are stored. These images show formation in the synapse of a second contact point between the two neurons linking by firing (Toni and Pouchs 1999).

Many realities are perceived. Few are remembered. The hippocampus functions in the selection of those perceptions that become perceptual (that is, declarative) memory. How this selection occurs is apparently as follows:

> Sensory processing areas of the cortex receive inputs about external events and create perceptual representations of the stimuli. These representations are then shuttled to the surrounding cortical regions, which in turn, send further processed representations to the hippocampus. The hippocampus then communicates back with the surrounding regions, which communicate with the neocortex.
>
> (LeDoux 1996: 193)

Hebbian plasticity appears to start in the sending of cortical neurons only if the hippocampus signals. The hippocampus, then, is a selector ordaining what sensations will, and will not, be remembered. Further, when the hippocampus signals, it acts as an 'associator of discontinuous events', in the sense that certain things are remembered along with other things as occurring in certain places and times (Wallenstein et al. 1998: 317). The hippocampus, then, is a material structure that gives humans a capacity to learn that reality consists of events associated in different spaces and times.

Whether the hippocampus signals to set the cortex to work building memory appears to depend upon whether the information it receives has emotional significance and whether it is related to previously stored information. The hippocampus helps you remember what is emotionally significant for you and what you have remembered before. If you are a taxi driver, your livelihood depends upon your knowing your way around the streets. Remembering places, then, is emotionally important to you, because, if you do not know how to get to where your fare wants to go, she or he may be angry, which is an emotional bummer. So among cabbies this information is more likely to win hippocampal approval for memory storage than different interpretations of Derrida.

The point here, as Fuster puts it, is that 'all memory is . . . *associative*' (1995). It is associative in a double sense. In a first, neurobiological sense, memory is networks which Fuster believes to be hierarchical networks of cortical neurons forged by Hebbian plasticity that associate by their synaptic linkage different representations of episodic, semantic, and procedural pasts. Further, memory is associative in a second sense of the particular content of those representations, a content that is a hodge-podge of what happened to be remembered associated with whatever else that happened to get remembered with it. In my cerebral cortex is a neural circuitry concerning a honeysuckle. This circuitry is synaptically linked to one concerning a tamarind. The honeysuckle network has with it a world of associations – of Sebastian, of my mother and her stories. The tamarind network, too, has its world of earlier associations of Barma and their stories.

But remembrance of things past, so seemingly evanescent – recall of that day in Iowa so long ago – is strands of a material wiring that stores representations of past-nows which are important to individuals both in terms of what they encounter a lot and what (as we are about to see) they feel about what they encounter. It is time to consider emotion.

Emotion

> [H]uman understanding is greatly indebted to the passions.
> (J.-J. Rousseau, *Discourse on the Origins of Inequality*, 1984 [1754])

> [E]motions are states elicited by rewards and punishers.
> (Edmund Rolls, *The Brain and Emotion*, 1999)

Plato in the *Phaedo* condemned emotion as a trickster that befuddled comprehension, and ever since many have believed that understanding is the higher realm of reason, emotion the lower one of passion, and that humans at the mercy of their passions will lack the understanding that comes from reason. However, others like Rousseau have believed that somehow understanding is 'indebted' to emotion. One strand of neuroscientific research into emotion, especially that of Antonio Damasio (1994) and Joseph LeDoux (1996), is Rousseauian because it investigates the debt understanding owes to emotion.[12] These scholars treat emotion as 'a type of information stored in memory' (Kosslyn and Koenig 1992: 438). Emotion is a kind of perceptual information and, like any perception, it helps you to understand reality. This raises the question, what kind of perception is emotion?

Certain researchers, going back to Darwin (1872), suggest that the bodily states of emotion are those most closely related to survival. Fear and anger are information that help you survive. More recent research suggests that emotion does not directly relate to survival but to the reinforcing properties of realities in which people find themselves. Edmund Rolls, prominent in developing this approach, reports emotional 'states' are 'produced by reinforcing stimuli' (Rolls 1999: 65). Emotions are 'elicited by rewards and punishers including changes in rewards and punishments' (ibid.: 60). A stimulus, an event in the external world, is a 'reward', a positive reinforcer, if it is a reality for which an animal will work. It is a 'punisher', a negative reinforcer, if it is a reality that the animal will work to escape or avoid. Positive reinforcers feel somehow 'fine'. Negative reinforcers feel 'not so hot'.

For example, consider what happens walking down Broadway, when you see your worst enemy at 114th Street, who you have reason to believe is seeking to get you fired. This creep is a punisher, and you really feel 'crushed'. Then, a few blocks later, at the entrance to the Labyrinth Bookstore, where you have gone to find the latest on clinical depression, you encounter your new sweetie who, radiating sexual vibes, suggests that the two of you go to see Woody Allen's latest film, *Deconstructing Derrida, the (Upper) West Side Story*. These are terrific positively reinforcing stimuli. Actually, seeing your sweetie is a visual worldly sensation. Hearing yourself say 'Hi sweetie' is an auditory semantic sensation. Feeling aroused by her is an emotional sensation. Each perception tells you more about your reality – that is, it increases your understanding. You grasp, the good times are about to roll! You feel 'fantastic'. Until the creep walks in and warmly hugs your sweetie. It turns out they are best friends, a negative reinforcer. You slouch off feeling crestfallen to the section on psychopathology, but recognizing that emotions can produce sensations about the rewards and punishers in your world. Something of the neurobiology of emotional perceptions needs to be presented.

First, however, emotions should be distinguished from feelings. Emotion refers to states of the nervous system and, beyond that, of other parts of the body, as a result of detecting rewarding or punishing realities. Feeling is a type of sensation that pertains to awareness of those bodily states. Feelings might be imagined as 'rather like colors' (Carter 1998: 82), because they cannot be described in words but, like a color, they suffuse your awareness. The feelings associated with rewards tinge your world in light, pleasant colors. Those associated with punishment produce darker, less pleasant shades. Different emotions and feelings occur in 'different brain networks' (LeDoux 1996: 106). The key networks are those in the earlier described limbic system and certain parts of the cortex. What conjoins thought and feeling is the existence of abundant feedback neuronal pathways that link cortical with limbic system circuits. This circuitry is especially well developed between the PFC, the amygdala, and the hypothalamus. Thus reason and feeling networks are parts of larger, common corticolimbic pathways extending throughout the brain.

The limbic system includes (as noted earlier) the thalamus, hypothalamus, septum, amygdala, and hippocampus. The thalamus provides sensory information to the brain. Some of this flows into the limbic system – importantly, the amygdala. If a person gets emotional, it is because the amygdala signals muscular responses in the face and limbs, autonomic responses in the ANS, neurotransmitter responses in neurotransmitting cells, and a variety of endocrine and chemical responses that result from the hypothalamus responding to the amygdala's signal to it to trigger these responses. The amygdala, then, appears the key organ in the limbic system, 'involved in the appraisal of emotional meaning' (LeDoux 1996: 169).

Additionally, the amygdala appears to be to emotional memory what the hippocampus is to perceptual memory. Research shows it is involved in the 'memory of reward' (Gaffan 1992: 471), because it 'is specialized for' helping people to 'learn' a particular type of liaison, that of 'a repeated stimulus' which 'reliably predicts an event that is of intrinsic value (positive or negative)' (ibid.: 482). It does this by remembering the association between a particular environmental event, the 'stimuli', with its 'reward value' (ibid.: 471). The association, then, is of particular rewarding and punishing external realities with their re-presentation as pleasant or unpleasant emotions. Simply put, the amygdala allows a person to remember 'whether something is good or bad' (Brodal 1998: 560). Weiskrantz (1956) was, perhaps, the first to suggest this role of the amygdala, and Rolls asserts that there is now 'much evidence' supporting it (1999: 101).

However, there is also evidence that certain realities are able to evoke emotions such as anger or fear without any prior history of reinforcement. Unexpected events, for example, may provoke fear. The manner in which this occurs appears to be as follows. An event occurs in reality, perhaps a loud kaboom. This stimulus is transmitted from auditory receptors to the thalamus and along to the amygdala. There it is 'detected' (Damasio 1994: 131). This term is imprecise. First, it is not known whether 'detection' occurs only in the amygdala. Second, it is not clear exactly what goes on in detection. Presumably the signal to the amygdala induces it, in turn, to trigger its efferent connections to body muscles, to the ANS, to neurotransmitting nuclei, to the hypothalamus that ultimately lead to chemical and endocrine responses in the bloodstream. All of which responses are the bodily states of emotion – in this case, most likely fear.

Then there are the emotions, discussed earlier, which depend upon the amygdala's learning the reinforcing properties of different realities. For example, interactions with the police for many young, poor folk are difficult. A poor lad from Bedford Stuyvesant in Brooklyn is far more likely to experience police who bully and beat than would a wealthy young gentleman from Park Avenue. The poor boy's amygdala may well have remembered the cop as a punisher. If this were the case, it means that when a poor boy sees a cop his amygdala will switch on tense muscles, start the ANS, and get the hypothalamus to crank up chemical and endocrinal responses. The kid will feel fear. The rich boy, on the other hand, on encountering his friend the kindly officer, having experienced nothing of the reinforcement history of the poor boy, will experience none of the fear.

Mention should be made of the emotional impact of language. It should be appreciated that symbols – such as words alone or in some narrative – when spoken by someone or printed in a text are external realities. They are just as much stimuli out there as a car's backfire and, because of this, they can provoke emotion. Certain studies find that the retrosplenial cortex is consistently activated by emotionally salient words (Maddock 1999). The precise role of this area in the linguistic coloring of feeling is unclear. However, for poor persons in a rough neighborhood in New York City, where everybody knows of police brutality and corruption, the symbol 'cop' is a real punisher. Say the word, the retrosplenial cortex probably lights up, and colors people's awareness in bad feelings.

What may happen here is that the same stimulus – the aforementioned policeman – that is transmitted from visual receptors to the thalamus and thence on to the amygdala where, on the basis of punishments past, it evoked fear, may also travel on parallel networks. The thalamus will send one signal of the cop's sensation to the amygdala and another signal to the visual cortex. There it will be *re*-presented as the visual image of a cop. This visual image can be transmitted to areas of episodic and semantic memory that further *re*-present the cop as one who is a particular 'bad ass'. Further, these two representations might find their way to the PFC, and the retrosplenial cortex, which would then trigger the amygdala, setting off its bag of emotional tricks; in this case, icy fear of a really 'bad ass' cop.

In summary, there appear to be two types of perceptions: one sensational and the other emotional. The former provides humans with information about reality that can be seen, heard, tasted, and so forth. Feelings, the awareness of emotions, add another dimension to this knowledge. Worldly and semantic sensations tell you if something seen, heard, and tasted is 'big' or 'little', 'noisy' or 'silent', 'sweet' or 'sour'. But this information, while useful, does not tell you what the something really portends for you. Emotions provide this missing information. They prioritize: reality is either a reward or a punisher. A sensation tells you what is. A feeling tells you whether it is good or bad.

Memory is sensational, feeling, and procedural perceptions of past-nows; and remember that present-nows emerge from their association with past-nows. To illustrate how this is the case, let us take a hypothetical example from the film *Attack of the Killer Tomatoes*. *Attack* was a spoof of monster movies, whose chief premise was that there are tomatoes out there that can eat you. Now, imagine that you are ten again, and that you did not 'get' that the movie was a parody. Then consider what might happen if upon arriving home from the film you spied a vast, scarlet shape. What is it? You have a sensational perception of a giant, speedy tomato. You retrieve, from your episodic memory of the film that these tomatoes are not your friends. The emotionally salient semantic sensation 'carnivorous' pops into perception from your semantic memory. You have retrosplenial lift-off. Heartbeat races, blood pressure rises, as feelings of horror flood your consciousness. Past-now constructs present-now. Priorities straight, you run from that tomato. Finally, all this emotion is the operation of specialized neural networks, in particular subcortical and cortical pathways – otherwise put, clumps of neuronal guck – recommending the conclusion that emotion is the operation of material structures. It is time to consider reason and what it puts to work, action.

Reason and action

> [T]he power of judging correctly . . . is properly called Good Sense or Reason.
>
> (René Descartes, *Discourse on Method* 1985 [1649])

What has been explained up to this point is how the brain goes about perceiving reality – which raises the question, what happens to those perceptions? Descartes suggests answers to this question. Even though he is the ultimate target of our arguments, Descartes *was* discerning and, at the very beginning of his *Discourse on Method* (1637) he linked 'Good Sense' with 'Reason'. What seems significant here is the linkage of reason with the senses or, in our terms, perception. One interpretation of this linkage might be that reason for Descartes is 'judging' perceptions to figure out what makes 'Good Sense'. If perceptions are present and past representations of reality, if judging is calculating, then reason is calculating on the basis of these perceptions what makes good sense to do in future reality.

Reasoning involves electrochemical events. Mayer wrote – summarizing findings through the 1970s – that investigations of the 'higher functions' do not yet 'prove that thinking is nothing more than the chemical-electrical activity in a specific portion of the brain' (1983: 34). However, even then there was clearly some electricity generated when people put on their thinking caps. The work of Samuel Sutton (see Sutton et al. 1965) is important here. He pioneered the use of ERPs (event-related potentials) or changes in EEGs associated with specific stimuli. Some of these stimuli were problem-solving tasks involving reasoning. In certain studies he first presented the problem, and then observed the ERPs as people thought about its solution. These show 'an increase in negative activity and then an increase in positive activity' (Mayer 1983: 35). Such inquiries did not demonstrate what was going on in the brain, but they did reveal that, whatever it was, it was electrical. The 'spark' of reason, then, is no metaphorical allusion. How does this spark operate?

Cognitive neuroscience is far from providing a complete answer to this question, though one response is emerging, 'supported by an impressive body of factual material' (Fuster 1989: 157). According to Fuster, 'a superordinate function . . . of the PFC as a whole is the temporal organization of behavior' (ibid.: 157). For action to be so organized, reason must calculate what to do at what times. Parkin (1996: 239) distinguishes two views of PFC involvement in reason; one that regards it as a 'central executive' and another that considers it a 'working memory'. Luria (1966), Stuss and Benson (1987), and Norman and Shallice (1986) articulated the former position. The latter position was that of Goldman-Rakic (1987). My judgment is that the two views are complementary. The central executive position is more concerned with *what* the PFC does, while the working memory approach concentrates upon *how* the PFC does what it does.

The idea of a central executive in the brain is similar to that of a chief executive officer (CEO) in a huge corporation. A corporation has lots of different parts whose activities need to be planned and scheduled to get what it does done. The CEO is the executive in charge of this work. The PFC in this analogy is the brain's CEO. It triggers reasoning to calculate different outcomes. As a result, particular plans of action are chosen, thereby creating an intention. According to Goldman-Rakic, the PFC is able to be such a 'CEO' because it is a working memory. The notion of such a memory is developed further in Chapter 5, but here it might be understood as neural wiring that gives the PFC its executive privileges. As Goldman-Rakic puts it, 'The ultimate function of the neurons in the PFC is to excite or inhibit activity in other parts of the brain' (1992: 115). Specifically, the PFC is the part of the brain that can turn other parts of the brain off and on in order to get things done. This allows it to work on perceptions of current realities, past memories of those realities, and future doings about them. Thus the approach to the PFC advocated here combines the two separate approaches into what might be called an 'executive working memory' view of the brain's most anterior region. There are two sorts of evidence supporting this view.

The first pertains to regional cerebral blood flow (rCBF) studies. There is increased blood flow in regions where reasoning is occurring, and rCBF studies identify these regions. Roland and Friberg (1995), in the mid 1980s in a now classic study, measured people's rCBF as they performed three different feats of mental calculation. The first feat was called '50–3 thinking'. It asked subjects to imagine 50 and then to continuously subtract 3 from the result. The second mental chore was called 'jingle thinking'. It asked subjects to jump every second word in a nine-word circular jingle. The final calculation was termed 'route-finding thinking'. It required subjects to imagine they were at their front door and then to walk alternatively to the left or right each time they reached a corner. The first task, because it involved calculations based upon memory of numbers, might be considered an example of arithmetical reason. The second, because it depended on calculations based upon memory of the sound of words, was a form of auditory reason. The third, because it depended upon visual memory, involved visual reason.

The results of the Roland and Friberg studies were as follows. All the reasoning tasks 'increased' rCBF in the PFC (1995: 574). However, rCBF also increased in other areas of the cortex, with the areas of increase differing with the type of reasoning being performed. Specifically:

The rCBF increased bilaterally in the angular cortex during 50–3 thinking. The rCBF increased in the right mid-temporal cortex exclusively
during jingle thinking. The intermediate and remote visual association
areas, the superior occipital, the posterior inferior temporal, and the
posterior superior parietal cortex increased their rCBF during route-
finding thinking.

(ibid.: 574)

A main finding of the study was that 'Different types of thinking activated
different cortical fields' (ibid.: 574). But always the PFC was in operation
and appeared to trigger other cortical areas to do the sort of calculating
required in the different forms of reasoning. The PFC signaled the angular
cortex for '50–3 thinking', because it was in this region that arithmetical
reasoning occurs. It triggered the mid-temporal cortex, because it is here that
certain forms of auditory memories appear stored that would be necessary for
auditory reasoning. It triggered various parts of the occipital cortex, because
it is here that visual memories are stored which were needed for the visual
reasoning.

More recent PET and fMRI imaging studies – many reviewed in Roland
(1993) and Posner and Raichle (1994) – tend to corroborate the findings
of the Roland and Friberg study. Reasoning occurs in neural networks throughout the cortex. Reasoning involving different senses tends to activate the
areas of the cortex where those senses become perceptions. Always, the PFC
is in operation in all forms of reasoning. A specific neural circuitry in the
left and right intraparietal area is associated with 'knowledge of numbers and
their relations' (Dehaene et al. 1998: 355; see also Butterworth 1999.) More
generally, deductive and probabilistic modules appear to be centered respectively in the associative occipital and parietal and in the left dorsolateral
frontal regions (Goel et al. 1997; Osherson et al. 1998). Figure 3.4 presents a
diagram of the brain indicating where different linguistic and quantitative
modules are believed to be located.

The second sort of evidence that supports an executive working memory
view of the PFC comes from studying what human capabilities are lost following injury to the PFC. These studies, which began with Phineas Gage in the
nineteenth century, showed that PFC injuries produced reduced ability to
plan. Mr Gage was a construction foreman building railroads in northern New
England in the middle of the nineteenth century. A ghastly explosion sent a
crowbar hurtling through his PFC. He survived but, in the words of a doctor
who attended him, became a 'child' who was 'pertinaciously obstinate, yet
capricious and vacillating, devising many plans of future operation, which are
no sooner arranged than they are abandoned' (in Damasio 1994: 8). Mr Gage
had childish emotions that got in the way of regulating his life – that is, of
exhibiting will.

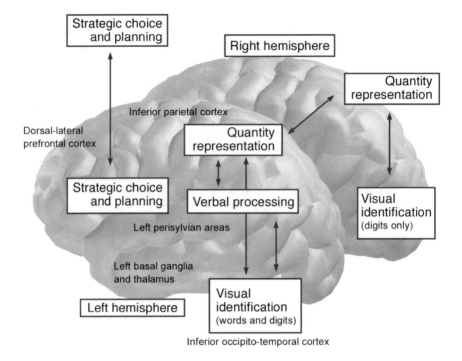

Figure 3.4 Partial and hypothetical diagram of cerebral areas involved in number and verbal processing

Source: Dehaene et al. (1998: 195); *Artist:* A.N. Reyna

A second case history of a young man with a stroke that damaged his PFC is also instructive. The young man

> was able to move about normally enough but seemingly without any desire to speak. On those occasions when he did speak, usually uttering nothing more than a single phrase, his speech was understandable. . . . From this I concluded that the relevant brain areas for speech remained intact but unactivated. . . . It was as if he lacked the inner drive necessary to activate the speech process.
>
> (Restak 1994: 113)

Eventually, the man recovered enough to discuss his previous condition. He said, 'he had retained his desire to speak to others, do things and move about generally, but couldn't "force" himself to get started. It was if he had lost his will' (ibid.: 114). Thus, damaged PFC impaired will – with 'will' meaning the ability to schedule behavior over time, in other words, to act.

The PFC has been treated as an undifferentiated single entity up to the present. However, there are different parts to it that need to be specified. These are the dorsolateral, orbitofrontal, and ventromedial cortices and the subcortical anterior cingulate cortex. There is speculation in what follows because 'little consensus has emerged' about 'the function specializations of these areas' (Duncan and Owen 2000). Novel findings continually revise previous conclusions. Nevertheless, it appears that the dorsolateral cortex performs 'The nuts and bolts of thinking – holding ideas in mind and manipulating them' (R. Carter 1998: 195). It thereby has the job of 'assessing priorities' (Pribram 1997: 360; see additionally MacDonald et al. 2000, and Rowe et al. 2000).

The orbitofrontal cortex seems to perform at least two chores. The first of these is the 'perception of novel relationships' (Krasnegor et al. 1997: 1). It is here that the work of Rolls (1998) has been significant, for he has shown that the orbitofrontal cortex detects when reinforcing stimuli change. These are situations where realities that were formerly rewarding become not so, and where other realities that were formerly punishing become not so. When the orbitofrontal cortex performs this task it is emotionally prioritizing that something new is happening out there in reality that the dorsolateral cortex might want to think about. A second responsibility of the orbitofrontal cortex is to inhibit inappropriate action brought on by immediate emotions. A dentist may provoke some fear in you. However, your orbitofrontal cortex appears to operate in such situations making certain that the fear does not translate into a jab at the good dentist's snout.

The ventromedial cortex apparently 'integrates functions' of the two preceding cortices with other modules in the 'rest of the brain' (Krasnegor et al. 1997: 1). How this occurs is by no means clear. The ventromedial cortex may also be critical in giving meaning to life. The kind of meaning being discussed here needs to be specified. It is not semantic meaning in the sense that this word denotes and connotes that. Rather, it is emotional 'meaning' in the sense that certain thoughts and actions actually feel meaningful – that is, worthwhile. Carter has put the matter as follows: the ventromedial cortex 'incorporates the whole of our being, making sense of our perceptions and binding them into a meaningful whole' (1998: 197).

The precise role of the anterior cingulate cortex (ACC) has recently come into question. It had been allocated the chore of being the PFC's 'command center' (C.S. Carter et al. 1998). This assertion may be too strong. Different parts of the PFC 'command' in different areas. Nevertheless, there remains a sense that it is important in attention, helping people to 'tune in' to certain perceptions (Botvinick et al. 1999). Specifically, the ACC may perform a monitoring function, with it being 'the brain's error detection and correction device' (Bush et al. 2000: 215). It is to be anticipated that future research will bring a clearer idea of what these four different regions of the PFC do, how they are interrelated with themselves and with other regions of the brain.

However, there is at present evidence to warrant the view that operations of these four different cortices are related to each other and, through executive working memory, produce reason and action. One concern needs to be made explicit. There appears to be a contradiction between the domain-specific view of modularity, which views a module as 'insensitive to central cognitive goals', and the ability of the PFC to function as a central executive organizing reason. This apparent contradiction is resolved in the final chapter.

Finally, it is clear that this all wiring – modules, PFC, and so on – is material, and that it conducts electrochemical 'sparks' of reason, sparks which come to produce will, and which are colored with emotional meaning. It is time, finally, to consider consciousness.

Consciousness

> There is no end of hypotheses about consciousness.
> (Gerald Edelman, *Bright Air, Brilliant Fire*, 1992)

> Human consciousness is just about the last surviving mystery. . . . And, as with all the mysteries, there are many who insist . . . that there will never be a demystification of consciousness.
> (Daniel Dennett, *Consciousness Explained*, 1991)

Indeed, there has been 'no end' to speculation concerning consciousness. A goal of this section is to help to dispense with some of the 'mystery' that has surrounded this theorizing. Sensation, be it worldly, semantic, or feeling, makes people aware of perceptions, memory, and emotions. Awareness is consciousness. There is an enormous literature seeking to explain consciousness, some of which argues for a non-corporeal consciousness that splits in two opposing immaterialist and materialist positions.[13] Immaterialist positions tend to dominate in philosophy and the humanities, materialist positions in neuroscience. However, immaterialists recognize that they cannot ignore that the brain plays an enormous role in consciousness. Robert Grant, for example, skeptical of the materiality of consciousness, appreciates 'that my consciousness, which in the human case means self-consciousness or subjectivity, is at least partially determined by (and is certainly dependent on) external electrochemical events in my body and brain' (1997: 3).

Much of the neuroscientific speculation has been materialist, and has sought to identify the places in the brain responsible for consciousness. Penfield placed it in the upper brain stem of the cerebral cortex (1947). Mozzuri and Magoun (1949) put it in the reticular formation, for the neurons there are responsible for the general state of alertness of the brain. O'Keefe (1985), believing that consciousness has to do with memory, argued that the hippocampus played a central role in it. Weiskrantz (1997) examined certain types of injuries to the visual cortex and came to the conclusion that these indicate a strong role for this cortex in consciousness. Paul Churchland (1995) has argued that consciousness arises out of the properties of what he calls 'recurrent' (namely, feedback) neural networks. Specifically, he theorizes that fanlike circuits that run to and from the intra-laminar nucleus of the thalamus and the surface of the cerebral cortex are responsible for consciousness.

There have been theories that assert that there is more than one type of consciousness. Antonio Damasio (1994) originally focused upon the right parietal lobe of the cerebral cortex because lesion studies reveal that this area is essential for a person to have a continuously updated sense of themselves as embodied creatures that exist in time. In his later (1999) discussion of the topic he distinguishes between 'proto-self', 'core', and 'extended' consciousness. He argues that certain brain stem nuclei, the hypothalamus, and the medial parietal cortices are responsible for proto-self consciousness and that regions of the superior colliculi in the tectum, the entire cingulate cortex, the thalamus, and some prefrontal cortices play roles in core and extended consciousnesses (ibid.: 157, 180–1).

Edelman has crafted a theory of consciousness that emphasizes memory. He distinguishes between 'primary consciousness', a state 'of being mentally aware of things in the world', from 'higher-order consciousness', a state that 'involves the recognition by a thinking subject of his or her own acts or affections'. Primary consciousness is about 'images in the present' with no 'sense of a person with a past and future'. Higher-order consciousness involves 'a model of the personal, and of the past and the future as well as the present' (1992: 112).

The regions of the brain involved in primary consciousness, according to Edelman, are the sensory cortex, which represents information from the external world; the hypothalamus and certain other subcortical regions, which represent information from within the body. This information is integrated in the amygdala and the hippocampus and placed into 'categories' by memory stored in association areas of the frontal, temporal, and parietal cortices (ibid.: 120). Higher-order consciousness is possible when the areas of the brain that Edelman believes serve language functions (Broca's and Wernicke's areas) are added to the previous circuitry. These two regions allow for symbolic awareness of what people are aware of in their primary consciousness. This is a 'consciousness of consciousness' (ibid.: 132) – that is, a higher-order consciousness.

There is no consensus among neuroscientists as to which theory of consciousness is preferable, and there is a fidgety tendency to resort to witticisms. Dennett's *Consciousness Explained* (1991), for example, is said to have 'explained . . . away' consciousness (Gazzaniga 1997: 182). It might be helpful in such circumstances to contemplate the decerebrate. When an anesthetic is administered to an animal, the cerebrum seems to be 'put to sleep'. If, next, a transection is made severing the cerebrum from the remainder of the brain and this organ is removed, the animal is said to become a 'decerebrate'. Such an animal does not 'wake up'. Sir Charles Sherrington, the first to make such an operation towards the end of the nineteenth century, reported that the decerebrate lacks 'thoughts, feelings, memory, percepts, conations' and is a 'mindless body' (in Penfield and Roberts 1959: 16). The implication of the preceding is clear. There is a place in the brain, which has a structure, neural networks related to each other by electrochemical energy flows, which when removed from the body takes with it consciousness. Sir Charles's decerebration supports materialists' views. Consciousness is not some mysterious incorporeality. It had been right there in the chunk of the brain that was the cerebrum that Sir Charles had hacked out. But just what it was remains an agnoiological void of obvious significance.

This ends investigation of whether there is an immaterial mind. This inquiry had sought to reduce the 'ambiguity' Mead found in the concept of mind and the 'vagueness' that Kossyln detected in that of thinking. 'Thinking' is states of connected neural networks producing perception, memory, and reason. Sensation and feeling are perceptions that represent past and present reality. Reason calculates using present perceptions, analyzed in terms of past perceptual and procedural memories, to arrive at what to do about future reality. Action implements that future, even though sometimes it may not do what makes good sense. So thinking appears less vague, mind less ambiguous, and Ramón y Cajal vindicated. The brain, as he said it did, minds 'the material course of thought and will'. The ghost busting of the two preceding sections has implications for Cartesian dualism. It is time now to consider these.

'Simply preposterous': Cartesian dualism, mind, subjectivity

One implication of the two previous sections seems clear. It is appropriate to eliminate both the notion of the subjective, in its ontological sense, and the mind, in its Cartesian sense. Let us review the stages of our argument to see why this is so. The argument of Ghost Busters I (pp. 48–9) explained how the objective and subjective were simply locations, places in the topography of reality defined in terms of whether they were internal or external to persons; which meant that something subjective was also at the same time objective, because one person's internal place was external to all other persons. But it was claimed there was a real difference between the subjective and the objective, because the subjective was a place of the conscious mind that was immaterial.

Ghost Busters II (pp. 49–82) addressed this claim in some detail. Different aspects of the Cartesian mind were examined and provided evidence that the mind is material. Perception, memory, emotion, reason, and consciousness were shown to be, in the words of Steven Pinker, pretty much 'the physical states of bits of matter' (1997: 25). Such findings have prompted the following conclusion: 'In light of modern neurophysiological knowledge, the vast majority of scientists and philosophers . . . would regard [Descartes's claim that the mind] "needs no place and depends on no material thing" as simply preposterous' (Cottingham 1986: 119). Some go so far as to declare, 'there is no such thing as the mind' (Gregory 1987: 514).

However, there have been attempts to preserve mind by changing its basic definition. One way that this is done is illustrated by Pinker himself, who asserts, 'the mind is not the brain but what the brain does' (1997: 24). This new understanding of mind is a functional one, for, as Mario Bunge has said, 'the mind is not a thing apart but a set of functions' (in Griffen 1987: 669). A Pinkeresque mind is fundamentally different from its Cartesian alternative. It is not 'a thing apart', an immaterial soul. It is what a material something, the brain, does. What the brain does is to process information. This might be called 'minding'; and just as a storekeeper's job is minding the store, so a brain's function is minding being. By minding – thinking in the sense of the operation of the neural networks involved in perceiving, remembering, and reasoning – a person takes information in the form of representations of the now, retrieves representations of the sensations or feelings of the past that bear upon the now, and calculates representations of future realities. In sum, our evaluation of Descartes's notion of mind has entered into the I-space of the nervous system and finds only a material brain minding the store of reality; or, as Toren recently put it, 'mind' and 'body' are 'aspects of a single phenomenon' (1999: 3).

So the subjective is just as material as the objective, and the objective–subjective ontology collapses. Cartesian dualism turns out to be 'simply preposterous', a three-century gaffe. If this is true, then the insurmountable has been confronted. The ghost is exorcised, and we say goodbye to all that – Cartesian mind, ontological subjectivity, and Cartesian dualism – a hardy dog of an ontology that will not hunt any more following its confrontation with the reality of the brain.

Readers may be exhausted. Ghost busting is hard work! Readers may be motivated to seek a refreshing diversion – a screening of *Attack of the Killer Tomatoes*, a chapter of *Critique of Pure Reason*, which they will need anyway for Chapter 5. But I beg their continued attention for just a moment, because with one ontology down, now it is the time to propose another.

SOCIAL MONISM

> Of course, a typical personality can be viewed as having a structure. But so can a physiology, any organism, all societies, and all cultures, crystals, machines – in fact everything.
>
> (Alfred Kroeber, *Anthropology*, 1948)

Alfred Kroeber, in the above quotation, was in a rebarbative mood, cheerfully sniping at British social anthropologists. Below, I shall use his attack to help explain the need for another type of social anthropology. But in order to make this case we need to consider monism, the 'view that there is but one fundamental reality' (Runes 1970 [1960]: 201). Monism was implied in the very observations that were used to confront Cartesian dualism. The onto-logical subjective *was* objective. Both were *material*. The two were one. So subjective and objective reality is perhaps better imagined as some sort of monism. But of what sort, because there are different varieties of monism among which one has to make a choice? What follows is a rationale for the monism that forms the basis of string being.

Alternative monisms can be built upon different ways of conceptualizing 'oneness'. A first type of monism is that which insists that the 'one' is realities that share something. For example, all life may be said to be carbon based. Such a monism might be said to be a 'similarity monism', because what is is similar. A second sort of monism occurs when reality is, in some way, wired together. The 'one' in such a monism is realities strung together with other realities, and so this monism might be termed a 'strung' monism. A third sort of monism occurs when reality consists of similar, highly strung entities. The monism broached below is of this third sort.

Let us begin with the similarities. Kroeber, whose quotation begins this section, was a fiercely partisan American cultural anthropologist who dis-dained the British social anthropologists' insistence upon structure, dismissing it as 'fashionably attractive' (1948: 325). But, *malgré lui*, he did recognize that crystals, machines, organisms, culture – in fact, 'everything' – had 'structure'. Everything exhibits structure because it is 'ordered relations of parts to a whole' (Firth 1963 [1951]: 30). Now it has been made clear in this chapter that individuals are enormously complex organizations of material structures, those of the nervous system and the remainder of the body. But individuals hang out together to do things. They may do golf, the law, or medicine. These practices have their parts – individuals – and individuals relate to each other in regular ways. So practices have their structures.

It happens that certain practices get organized with other practices, helping each other out to do still other things. Let us call these 'bundled practices'. For example, a health maintenance organization (an HMO), which in the United States provides medical insurance, will have claims, accounting, and legal departments, with each department helping the others out in their practices so that the HMO can do what it does, maximizing profits to its owners. Such organizations of practices have component parts, the practices, which consist of material entities, individuals, and the physical things they use to perform what they do. These component parts relate to each other in regular ways. HMOs have staff meetings where department heads coordinate the different departmental practices.

The point here is that humans as social beings are involved in three spaces that share two similarities. Remember that the term 'space' was defined in the first chapter as abstractions that denote organizations of doing. 'Social being' was the realities of what got done in space. Human spaces are those of the CNS, individuals, and their organizations of practices, and they are similar in that they involve both material and structural realities.

Further, these three spaces are strung together over time. Nervous systems are wired into bodies to make individuals. Individuals and their acts are strung together with other individuals to make practical structures. Similarly, practices are strung together with other practices to make bundled practices. Thus, human reality is an ascending or descending (depending on how you look at it) hierarchy of ever more, or less, complex material structures that are interconnected. This is one sense in which it is appropriate to term this whole a string being. What might this monism be called?

Individuals who do not hang out with others very much are said to be 'loners'. Convivial souls who hang out with everybody are said to be 'social'. The monism under discussion has the CNS hanging out in individuals who hang out in practices that hang out in bundled practices. Consequently, this monism is, in the sense just identified, pretty highly social and so might be called a 'social monism'. Thus anthropologists who investigate it are appropriately referred to as social anthropologists.

At this juncture the two terms – E-space and I-space – will be re-introduced to assist with navigation in the geography of the social monism. These spaces refer to particular social beings at particular times in the social monism. 'E-space' denotes organizations of practices and bundled practices that are external to individuals. 'I-space' is the structuring of organs, especially in the CNS, internal to individuals. E- and I-space are parts of the same thing, a social monism. The preceding gives us a way of theorizing space–time travel.

History is one damn E-space after another; which is to say that string being involves sequences of antecedent and subsequent E-spaces. Further, it is asserted that the operation of the CNS in an antecedent individual's I-space makes possible the subsequent operation of CNSs in I-spaces, that in turn make possible what subsequently happens to individuals and their practices. Thus, within the social monism, E-spaces are what get connected and I-spaces are what do the connecting.

There is disciplinary continuity and change here. The new social anthropology continues the older one's attention to structure, but with a considerably enlarged understanding of the term. The old social anthropologists' structure roughly corresponded to what was termed 'practices' and 'bundled practices' in E-space. The new social anthropologists' structure involves the CNSs of individuals that are parts of the structures of practices that are parts of the structures of the organizations of practice. The older social anthropology was content to portray social structure as a snapshot of E-space at a point in time. No snapshots for the new social anthropology:

it wants to go to the movies. So it analyzes the string being occurring in antecedent and subsequent sequences of E- and I-space in the social monism. Social anthropology, so understood, is the discipline that discovers the states of the spaces of the social monism over time in all the nooks and crannies of human history to explain how human realities get strung together; in other words, to explain string being.

The work of this chapter, ghost busting, is over, and we are left with the conclusion that there must be something, a connector, that strings antecedent with subsequent reality. Otherwise: no connector, no string being. So there is a primordial imperative incumbent upon string-being theory. Find the connector! The following two chapters argue that a cultural neurohermeneutic system does the job of making connections.

Part II
The connector

Chapter 4

Neurohermeneutics

> [T]he cortical substance imparts life, that is sensation, perception, under-
> standing and will; and it imparts . . . the power of acting in agreement with
> will.
>
> (Emmanuel Swedenborg, 1740, in Allman 1998: 28)

This chapter inquires, what is a connection? The answer it provides to this
question is that a neurohermeneutic system is the connector linking antecedent and subsequent E-spaces. Actually, the idea of a neurohermeneutics
was implicit as far back as the Enlightenment when Emmanuel Swedenborg
announced that 'the cortical substance imparts . . . understanding'. However,
the chore of the present chapter is to make this idea explicit and, more than
that, to make it plausible to skeptical readers. The campaign to reduce hostile
skepticism is developed over three sections.

The first section offers an opinion as to the nature of connection by
examining what the philospher David Hume called the 'cement of the
universe', causation. It is suggested that causation is connection. The
particular approach to causality elaborated emphasizes the tying of structural
knots. Central to this approach, metaphorically speaking, is that reality
involves causal strings, composed of events in structures that are knotted
together. The key to understanding causation is to explain how the knots, the
connectors, are tied so that they string being together. Different realities,
different knots; which is to say: the connector operating in a garage-door
opener is different from that in Barma E-space.

The second section starts the search for the connectors of E-space. It is
suggested that hermeneutics is concerned with how humans make connections
between each other; and so the exploration for connectors reviews the genealogy of hermeneutic thought, especially contrasting that of Martin Heidegger
to that of Max Weber. The latter's approach is singled out for its interest in
causality. However, inspection reveals a flaw in Weber's causal hermeneutics.
The third section of the argument addresses this flaw by showing how neural
networks, most importantly in the cortex, constitute a neurohermeneutic

system that performs a neurohermeneutic process. This system is shown to knot together E-spaces so that the social monism is a string being.

KNOTTY CAUSATION

> *Causal processes* are the means by which structure and order are *propagated* . . . from one space-time region of the universe to other times and places.
>
> (Salmon 1998: 298; italics in the original)

Implicit notions of causality are ancient. The Bible, for example, in Genesis, just after Adam and Eve's expulsion from the Garden of Eden, has God demanding of Adam, 'Did you eat from that tree?' To which Adam responds, 'The woman whom you gave to be with me, She handed me the fruit from the tree; and I ate.' Adam, of course, is excusing himself by giving God a causal account of what happened, asserting that the woman's gift of fruit was the cause of his eating – in effect saying, 'She caused the problem.'

Aristotle was the first, at least in the Western tradition, to make explicit what was implicit in accounts like those in the Bible. In his *Physics* he offered a formal definition of the cause; and identified material, formal, efficient, and final causes. The Aristotelian account of causation 'dominated' European and Middle Eastern explanation until the late Middle Ages (Bynum et al. 1981: 26). In the Enlightenment David Hume called causality 'the cement of the universe' (1739: 662); even though he was terribly skeptical of the adequacy of the understanding of causality, both in *A Treatise of Human Nature* (1739) and in *An Inquiry Concerning Human Understanding* (1748). However, Hume's cement metaphor seems inappropriate, because, whatever the universe is, it is in motion – fluid, transforming.

So let us not be causal mobsters who bury being in Humean cement. Rather, let us develop an approach that begins with the recognition that reality is continually doing things. This approach follows from a discussion of the philosopher of science Wesley Salmon's notions of physical causality in the light of Louis Althusser's views about structural causality. Both Salmon and Althusser contribute to an ontological rethinking of causality as involving migrating and changing structures. First, a brief history of understandings of causality is presented to explain why there is a need for an ontological revisionism of the concept. Then this re-visioning is performed.

Hume's skepticism concerning causation subsided in the nineteenth century with the rise of positivism. J.S. Mill, for example, in his *System of Logic* (1843) propounded inductive canons for discovery of causal relations between phenomena. However, the skepticism had returned by the first three decades of the twentieth century with a vengeance, in part due to the rise of statistics and the formulation of atomic and quantum physics. Bertrand Russell, as mentioned in the introduction, argued for the 'complete extrusion' (1953) of causality from intellectual life. Werner Heisenberg, who proposed the Uncertainty Principle in quantum theory (1930), was certain that it rendered the concept of causality implausible. Karl Pearson, one of the developers of statistics, wrote in his *Grammar of Science* (1911) that 'Beyond such discarded fundamentals as "matter" and "force" lies still another fetish amidst the inscrutable arcana of modern science, namely the category of cause and effect' (in Pearl 2000: 340). Such positions concerning causality are termed 'eliminationist'.

The opinion that causality was a fetishism requiring 'extrusion' was fairly commonplace in certain intellectual circles by the mid-twentieth century. I was initiated into a version of it when I took physics and chemistry in the late 1950s during my junior year at a 'progressive' prep school. There the knowledge that causality was dead was 'cool'. It conferred a prestige for science types, just as an esoteric understanding of *Ulysses* did for the literary types. It is possible that the popularity of such eliminationist positions may have helped Geertz feel comfortable with his extrusion of causality from cultural hermeneutics.

Of course, nobody ever told us at the Putney School, up in those leafy Vermont hills, that we were out of date. For by that time there was work in a number of disciplines – especially in philosophy, statistics, and later in the burgeoning field of computer science – that reestablished the importance of causality for understanding reality. Significant among these studies was Ernest Nagel et al.'s *Freedom and Reason* (1951) that argued against Heisenberg that quantum physics did not demonstrate that there were realms of being which were non-causal. Mario Bunge's *Causality* (1959) was important for synthesizing a number of arguments against the various anti-causality positions. Such work has led today to 'a general repudiation of . . . eliminationist approaches' (McKim 1997: 5).[1]

The pro-causation positions have taken three forms; methodological, philosophy of science, and ontological. Methodological positions respond to eliminationist contentions that the methods of the empirical analysis can never validate the occurrence of causation, especially in the non-experimental situations that prevail in the human sciences. One response to this criticism has been to develop methods of causal statistical inference, such as techniques of multiple regression, path analysis, and structural equation modeling. Most recently, powerful computer algorithms based upon mathematical graph theory have been developed to ascertain the validity of causal models (see Glymour 1997; Scheines 1997; Pearl 2000). These methodologists are currently confident, believing, 'In the last decade . . . causality has undergone a major transformation: from a concept shrouded in mystery into a mathematical object with well-defined semantics and well-founded logic' (Pearl 2000: viii).

The philosophers of science have sought to explicate the role of causality in science. Here, perhaps, the boldest innovation has been the formulation of an alternative to the covering law (also known as the deductive nomothetic) model of explanation. This model, presented in its most influential form by Carl Hempel and Paul Oppenheim in 1948 (1965) had been severely criticized by the early 1960s and a search was on for alternative accounts of explanation. Wesley Salmon's *Scientific Explanation and the Causal Structures of the World* (1984) and R.W. Miller's *Fact and Method* (1987) have been important contributions to this project, suggesting that explanation is not about deduction but causality. Miller goes so far as to claim that all explanation is effectively causal.

A point to grasp here is that the philosophers of science and the methodologists had greatly raised the significance of causality for understanding reality by claiming that explanation was in important ways causal and that there are effective methods for discovering it. However, neither the methodologists nor the philosophers of science spent much time worrying about what causality was; which is to say that they were fairly indifferent to its ontology. This, of course, raises the stakes with regard to ontological matters. Below, an opinion is offered as to the *is* of causality.

In order to formulate such an opinion, let us begin with a perfectly adequate definition of causality, but one that does not get down to the ontological nitty-gritty. Bunge defines causality as follows:

> One says that event C *is* the cause of event E if, and only if, the occurrence of C is sufficient for that of E (e.g. severe drought causes crop failure. . .). On the other hand, we say that C is *a* cause of E if, and only if, C is necessary but not sufficient for E (e.g. food scarcity is necessary but not sufficient to raise food prices.
>
> (1996: 31)

There is no problem with this definition if one wants to characterize what causality means in purely logical terms. So it is appropriate to say that severe drought is the cause of crop failure because it is 'sufficient' for it, or that food scarcity is a cause in increased food prices because it is 'necessary' for them. But such a definition does not explicate what it is in reality that happens for something to be sufficient or necessary for something else. The knotty approach to causality crafted below is ontological in this sense.

Causal ontology

Let us begin by specifying where causation occurs. Causality is not something that pertains to abstractions, though abstract concepts, and statements built from such concepts, may refer to causal realities. Abstractions are *re-presentations* of reality but not that reality itself. Assertions that causation is, or is about, only abstractions are declarations that there is no reality to causality, which seems untenable. Whatever causation is, it is something or things.

Detonations of the atomic bomb, a cause, led to – instantaneous for some, slow for others – deaths of hundreds of thousands at Hiroshima. This was no abstraction. It was a tearing and roasting in the real world. Where causation belongs, then, is in reality. It is events leading to other events. 'Events' being things happening in the world and 'happenings' being things put into action (that is, in some way moved over space and time.) It is Adam wheedling, 'She did it!' – an event that is an effect, after God's question, an event that is a cause. Now it is time to explore what causation is in this world.

Causation is the making of 'causal strings', chains of causes and effects. These may appear immensely long, complex, and reticulated, but they all include two parts and a relationship. The two parts are causes and effects. According to Hume, these are identified in terms of their deployment in space and time. Cause and effect are spatiotemporally contiguous, with cause being spatially different from, and temporally prior to, effect. Further, according to Hume, the relationship between these parts is one where they are 'constantly conjoined' (1739: 657), so that every time there is a particular change in the cause there is a particular change in the effect. Constant conjunction ties the knot between cause and effect.

Hume explains constant conjunction by relegating it to the status of a psychological habit of 'the mind to conjoin' (ibid.: 662). Salmon presents Hume's argument as follows: 'Since the effect always follows the cause' in our minds, 'we are primed to anticipate the effect on the next occasion on which the cause presents itself. The relation between cause and effect is . . . habit'; which means that causality as 'habit' is a mental state that 'does not exist in the physical world outside of our own minds' (Salmon 1998: 15). If Hume's understanding of constant conjunction stands, then people are truly hard-headed. This is because they walk around with the cement of the universe in their heads.

Some thinkers, finding Humean causation a bit of a hangover, have attempted to give constant conjunction a material basis independent of the mind. John Trimmer, thinking about the realities studied by physicists and chemists, suggested that the constant conjunction between cause and effects was the result of 'forcing' (1950: 1–3). Mario Bunge suggested that forcing was 'producing' in the sense that a cause produced an effect (1963 [1959]: 46–8). Thinkers interested in causality quickly grasped that the notions of forcing and producing were similar. However, I shall use the former term in preference to the latter. Producing resonates with too many purely economic meanings, whereas forcing conveys more clearly the idea that I want the term to bear of making something occur. Some critics ventured, as did Simon (1957), that forcing was a redundancy because it was another term for constant conjunction. Still others worried, 'we cannot possibly observe or measure such "forcings"' (Blalock 1964 [1961]: 10). These concerns are removed if causation is understood as a forcing reality that allows the antecedents, another reality, and the consequents, still another reality, to exhibit constant conjunction. Forcing, then, is a third kind of reality that wedges itself in between two other realities, cause and effect, to knot effects after causes. What are the properties of a reality that is forcing?

It is at this point that Salmon becomes relevant. He has argued that 'causality is physical – it is an objective part of the structure of our world' (1998: 24). This position has been subjected to criticisms, some of which, like that of Dowe (1992, 1995), seem to be amplifications of Salmon's perspective, while others, like that of Kitcher (1989), seem more dismissive. However, a strength of Salmon's position, which its critics recognize, is that it advances understanding of forcing. It is 'Physical connections' (Salmon 1998: 17). He provides an illustration of what he means by such connections in the following:

> [W]hen I arrive home . . . I press a button on my electronic door opener [cause] to open the door [effect]. First, there is the interaction between my finger and the control device, then an electromagnetic signal transmits a causal influence from the control device to the device that raises the garage door, and, finally, there is an interaction between the signal and that mechanism.
>
> (ibid.: 17–18)

The physical connection, here, is the electromagnetic signal running from door opener to door. The notion of physical connection needs to be related to those of forcing and constant conjunction. Salmon's term 'physical connection' is what others called 'forcing', because it is a material reality that attaches events in another material realm, of the cause, to those in still another, the effect; and in so doing forces by taking events in one realm of being and leading them to those in other realms. In Salmon's example, depressing the door opener always opens the door. They exhibit constant conjunction. Now this is no habit of the mind. There is a reality out there which accounts for constant conjunction. It is the forcing, the electromagnetic signal, that physically connects activities in the door opener to those of the door opening – as surely as a New York City subway on the tracks links the 116th subway stop with the 96th stop, or the flight of a bullet binds the shooter with the shot.

Those who insist that constant conjunction is only perceptual habit ignore the existence of a subway on the tracks or the bullet's trajectory, and would thus stand on the tracks awaiting the train or between the shooter and the shot, putting themselves in harm's way. Hence, Humean insistence upon constant conjunction as purely perceptual habit could be hazardous to your health. Rather, constant conjunction depends upon the existence of 'forcing' realities that exhibit two properties. First, they are material (namely, physical). Second, their materiality is of a type that allows them to attach antecedents with their consequents.

Such an understanding allows a comment upon the ontology of chance. Reality is a concatenation of causal strings. Some of these strings merely co-occur. Such causal strings are said to be 'autonomous'. For example, there are causal strings involving professional baseball and professional football in September and October in the United States. The events of these causal strings consist of games won and lost. They are found in the same space (the United States) at the same time (the fall), but what happens in the race for the World Series in baseball is irrelevant to what happens in the race for the Superbowl in football.

Other causal strings co-occur because there are forcing realities that *regularly* compel this. These causal strings are 'integrated'. For example, every four years, at the same time that the baseball and football races are going on, the Democratic and the Republican parties conduct campaigns for the Presidency of the United States. Each campaign is a causal string of events of what the candidates do to be elected. However, what happens in the campaign of one candidate regularly forces the campaign of the opponent to respond.

Still other causal strings co-occur because there are forcing realities that *irregularly* link them. These are 'chance' causal strings. The performance of a Beethoven symphony is one causal string. A person repeatedly sneezing during its performance is a second, normally autonomous, causal string. An especial sensitivity of the first violinist during the performance, due to a dental emergency, resultant from a history of poor dental hygiene, is a third, normally autonomous causal string. Now when the sneezer hacks especially loudly it may force the violinist to miss a note, something that would not regularly occur. It might be said that the violinist's misplay was pure chance. But I am proposing that there is no such thing as chance. The causal string that resulted in the first violinist's dental distress (an irregular event) was enough to completely distract her already faltering concentration, forcing the mistake. 'Chance' is the occurrence of unusual concatenations of causal strings that may make the forcing realities connecting the strings hard to detect.

A next step in the understanding of causation is the recognition that forcing realities and their antecedent and subsequent realities are structures of structures. To understand why this is the case, we have to get Althusserian. Louis Althusser, especially in *Reading Capital* (Althusser and Balibar 1970), argued that structural causality was a key to understanding the human condition. Further, he insisted that Marx had discovered this causality and that it was an 'immense theoretical revolution' (1972 [1970]: 182). It is important to note that in choosing to work with structural causality I am working with views that have been largely dismissed. E.P. Thompson denounced Althusser's work in terms of expletives such as 'shitty' (1979). André Glucksmann purged structural causality with the airy assertion that it 'actually says nothing of itself, just because it can say everything or anything – it inaugurates no actual type of analysis' (1967: 88).[2] I disagree, and, in explaining why, hope to show that Althusser's understanding of structural causality is consistent with the view that reality for humans is a social monism.

Althusser derived his notion of structural causality from Spinoza's concept of 'immanent cause' (Althusser and Balibar 1972: 187).[3] Something is immanent if it is 'remaining within' or 'indwelling' in something else (*Random House Dictionary*, 1967). For Spinoza, God was a cause immanent in nature. Anger is immanent within the nervous system. For Althusser human reality is that of structure, and causality is immanent within structure because:

> the effects are not outside the structure, are not a pre-existing object, element or space in which the structure arrives *to imprint its mark*: on the contrary, it implies that the structure is immanent in its effects, a cause immanent in its effects in the Spinozist sense of the term, that *the whole existence of the structure consists of its effects*, in short that the structure, which is merely a specific combination of its peculiar elements, is nothing outside its effects.
>
> (Althusser and Balibar 1972: 188–9; emphasis in the original)

Structure for Althusser is conceptualized as 'regions' (ibid.: 182) that are connected structures. This is an ontology where 'a cause is immanent in its effects' in the sense that causes, forcings, and effects are regional structures 'indwelling' in a whole (ibid.: 182); in the case of humans, that of the social monism.

Let us get real: the shooting of the four cops' guns in the Bronx (the cause) killed Amadou Diallo (the effect). Shooting is activities in a particular structural region, the gun, that are physically connected by the bullets' trajectories, to another structural region, Diallo, altering his body from a living to a lifeless form. Causality occurs within structures. Causes and effects are indwelling in regional structures that are physically connected. Diallo's butchery, the effect, was immanent within the structure that was the cops and their guns, the cause, and their bullets' path, the forcing. Causation, then, is forcings occurring within structures of structures; these being *antecedent, forcing,* and *subsequent* structures. So the Diallo example makes clear that Althusser was dead right to claim that causation always involves a situation where 'the structure is immanent in its effects'. It is time to return to consideration of the reality of forcing in order to develop the notion of a structural knot.

Causality, as Salmon put it, is 'the means by which structure and order are *propagated* . . . from one space–time region . . . to other times and places' (1998: 298; emphasis in the original). Propagation is the spreading of something from somewhere to somewhere else. For, example, a rumor can be propagated from one person to another. Something propagated is something moved. A rumor moves from Alice to Bob. What is propagated in causality is events in 'structures or order'. What moves is the events themselves from one region of structure (the cause) to become other events in other regions of structure (the effects). This movement from antecedent to subsequent to antecedent, cause to effect, and on and on, might be thought of as a string – an odd sort of string because there is movement in it, a bit like electricity moving in wiring – but a string, nevertheless, of being. However, for the string to exist the events of the cause must be knotted to those of the effect, posing the question, what is a knot?

A knot is the earlier-discussed forcing structure, for it is this structure that operates to take events in the antecedent cause and transform them into those of the subsequent effect. This is because forcing structures are at some time attached to, in the sense of literally becoming part of, antecedent and subsequent structures; and, during this attachment, events happen in the forcing structure which transmute the events in antecedent structure into those of the subsequent structure. These events during attachment, because of this transformative capacity, are what tie the knot. In the case of the social monism, forcing structures knot antecedent E-spaces with subsequent ones, thereby making string being.

This view of the ontology of causation provides an answer to the question, what is connection? Forcing structures are (1) material structures, (2) attached to antecedent and subsequent structural regions that (3) have transformative capacity. As a result of these three properties forcing structures are those blocks of matter that themselves exhibit causal strings which function to make connections in reality. Consequently, because of its knotting abilities, a forcing structure is aptly termed a connector. Think of this in terms of the causation involved in having children. The antecedent region of structure (the cause) is two healthy people making love. The subsequent region of structure (the effect) is a newborn child. The connector is the reproductive systems of the two parents. The connector, attached to both the cause and the effect, has the transformative capacity to take events that migrate in from the cause (semen and ovum) and transform them (through gestation) into events that migrate out as the effect (the birth of a child). This, then, is a knotty approach to causation.

Now we are in a position to offer an answer to the question, what is a connection? Connection is causation. It is the operation of connectors. Connectors knot reality into causal strings. Find the connectors in the universe and you explain the knotting of events through space and time. Find the connectors in that portion of the universe that is the social monism, and you explain the knotting of E-spaces into complex interconnected strands of string being. I believe a neurohermeneutic system is an important connector operating in the social monism. The next section of this chapter begins the search for this with a discussion of hermeneutics.

HERMENEUTICS

> At the heart of all hermeneutic enterprises is the presupposition that a TEXT, whether legal, religious, historical, or literary, contains a determinate meaning, whose recovery, whether possible or not, is the goal of interpretation.
> (*Columbia Dictionary of Modern Literary and Cultural Criticism*, 1995: 132–3)

> *Hermeneutics* as the art of understanding *does not yet exist* in a general manner, *there are instead only several forms* of specific hermeneutics.
> (Schleiermacher, *Hermeneutics and Criticism*, 1998 [1838]: 5, emphasis in the original)

Friedrich Schleiermacher, whom we shall encounter below as one of the founders of hermeneutics, might – and then again, might not – have been disappointed with this section. His goal was to reduce the '*several forms*' of hermeneutics to a common theory. This section shows that there is yet another form of hermeneutics but one to which the earlier hermeneutics may all belong. A further goal of the present section is to show that the *Columbia Dictionary* had got it wrong. The quotation from it asserts that the object of 'all' hermeneutical analysis is the 'TEXT'. Now text is a contested term, with one of the terms of the contest being the scope of what it denotes. Broader definitions, to which some postmodernists are partial, have text referring to 'all phenomena, all events' (Rosenau 1992: xiv). Derrida famously put it, 'Il n'y a pas hors de texte.' Narrow definitions restrict the term to written documents, as did Schleiermacher (1836). Centrist versions, flavored by semiotics, especially that of Barthes (1975), treat it as any discourse involving signs that produce meaning. I shall argue below that some hermeneutics, Weber's, has *not* been concerned with analyzing texts, that this hermeneutics has been interested in causality, and that it leads to a neurohermeneutics. A brief introduction to hermeneutics gets us into this argument.

Hermeneutics, the theory of interpretation, has understanding as its unifying notion. Understanding has been achieved when the meaning of the text has been interpreted. In such hermeneutics the ball game is this: figure out the meaning and you have made the interpretation. Meaning will be discussed at some length later in the chapter. However, whatever it may be, it is information about now, bearing upon the future, based upon the past. Consider, for example, that you are sitting in a pleasant room, reading Geertz's *The Interpretation of Cultures*, across from the most attractive person you have ever dreamed of seeing. Imagine your surprise when that delightful creature squeezes closed an eyelid. She, or he, does it looking directly at you two more times. You think, 'What does this mean – blink or wink?' And then you have got it, you know the meaning, a wink – *une* wink *séductrice* – and you have made the interpretation. Your loins stir.

This interpretation is about now, because the winking is transpiring right there before your eyes. But how was it that you were able to make this interpretation? You had grasped the difference between a wink and a blink in the past, through close study of Professor Geertz. And, of course, this interpretation of the now, based upon the past, has implications for the future; witness the preparation for action in your organs of procreation. The point here is that hermeneutics is of interest because it prepares people for their future by telling them about a now based upon their past. The making of an interpretation instantly connects past, present, and future. A problem, however, is that there have been different hermeneutics, so that it is important to stop a moment and search for one that is more compatible with causal analysis.

Twentieth-century hermeneutics might be imagined as a single path that diverged in two very different directions. One turning, I believe, is unpromising because it violates the principle of Occam's razor. The other is more promising because it points the way to a causal hermeneutics that can be useful in explanations of why and how events occur in the social monism. However, both derive from a premodern problematic, struggling for modern acceptability. Before, there was the Baconian scientist seeking to validate the truths of nature, there was Hermes whom the Barma of Chad might have termed a *malawaya*. Hermes was a Greek god. A *malawaya* was a 'master of gossip'. Hermes scuttled about, master gossip-like, magically interpreting the secrets of the supernatural world of the gods to ordinary folk. Premodern hermeneutics flourished in antiquity and medieval times when the prevailing worldview insisted that there were two realities, one of the natural world and another of the supernatural. Hermeneutics was the exegesis of sacred texts to reveal supernatural mysteries to ordinary folk. Priests, priestesses, shamans, seers, and the odd necromancer obliged as the Hermeses who did the interpreting; not on the basis of any observation of what went on in nature, but on the basis of understanding the words of gods as told in their texts. This was because nature in such premodern mentalities was the works of gods; so that it behoved master-gossips like Hermes to forget the natural, contemplate the supernatural.

Modern hermeneutics has been a largely German enterprise that began to flourish during the early nineteenth century. This hermeneutics has largely dropped the earlier preoccupation with the supernatural though, ironically, it grew out of a huge debate, the German Reformation, concerning the proper interpretation of the supernatural. The year 1520 was critical. Three years earlier, in 1517, Martin Luther had protested the sale of 'Go-to-Heaven' cards, called indulgences, sold under the auspices of a papal monopoly. Luther's protest was immensely popular so, to put a stop to the meddlesome monk, Pope Leo X issued a 1520 bull giving Luther sixty days to recant or be branded a heretic. Luther responded by writing a number of tracts defending his position. In one of these, 'To the Christian Nobility of the German Nation', he gets to the heart of his debate with Catholicism, and it is a hermeneutic heart. He says the Romanists (that is, Catholics) claim 'that only the pope may interpret Scriptures' but that they 'cannot produce a single letter (of Scripture) to maintain that the interpretation of scripture . . . belongs to the Pope alone'. This being the case, Luther thundered, 'we must compel the Romanists to follow not their interpretation but the better one' (Luther 1970: 11, 20); which raised the hermeneutic question, just how does a Hermes make a 'better one'? Here the response was simple. Better interpretations did not depend on any Pope but on 'learning' (ibid.: 21, 25). When the Pope's sixty days were up, Luther sent a letter from Wittenberg to a friend announcing, 'Greetings. On December 10, 1520 . . . all the following papal books were burned. . . . This is the news here' (ibid.: iv).

So the news from Wittenberg was that the Reformation was a debate over interpretation; with Protestant rebel Hermeses contesting the right of the Catholic Hermeses to interpret scriptural texts. However, in this war of the Hermeses, once German Protestants had challenged the authority of the Catholic hierarchy to interpret scripture, they urgently needed a better 'learning' to make their interpretation credible. This meant that there emerged in Protestant places, especially Germany, a tradition which sought to develop better methods of biblical interpretation. Eventually, thinkers within this tradition began to ask a broader question: how does one do better interpretations in general? Responses to this question in the seventeenth and eighteenth centuries pointed the way to modern hermeneutics.[4]

Johann Dannhauer, a Strasbourg theologian, began the chore of transforming hermeneutics into something more than a tool for scriptural exegesis in the early seventeenth century in *Idea boni interpretis* (1630), where he explicitly sought to identify the criteria employed by a *'boni'* (good) interpreter. Friedrich Schleiermacher, a Prussian army chaplain's son, broadened Dannhauer's approach, especially in *Hermeneutics and Criticism* (posthumously published in 1838, though written considerably earlier) into a general theory of hermeneutics applicable to all texts. Although Schleiermacher's approach allowed the interpretation of secular texts as well as those dealing with the supernatural, he kept a tie with premodern hermeneutics by emphasizing that interpretation was not a science, because 'Understanding is an art' (1998 [1811]: 229). Further, he said, 'Art is that for which there admittedly are rules, but the combinatory application of these rules cannot in turn be rule-bound' (ibid.: 229). This is another way of saying, it is all a mystery and you more or less magically pull off interpretation.

J.G. Droysen (1858) and Wilhelm Dilthey (1883, 1894, 1900) adopted and expanded upon Schleiermacher's ideas, proposing hermeneutics as the basis for understanding in all the intellectual disciplines that study humanity. Dilthey, as we shall see, was especially influential in proposing hermeneutics as an alternative to scientific enterprise. Max Weber, especially in *Economy and Society* (1913), took another turn down the path of hermeneutics by seeking to make it acceptable to a world dominated by science. Weber tried to show, if analysts used hermeneutic techniques, how they could better achieve a stronger science, especially regarding causal analyses. Heidegger a decade or so later returned to a non-scientific hermeneutics with a vengeance. Here, then, are our two, non-scientific and scientific turnings in twentieth-century hermeneutics. Let us look a bit more closely at Heidegger.

Heidegger believed, 'man is rather "thrown" from being into the truth of Being, so that ek-sisting is this fashion he might guard the truth of Being, in order that beings might appear in the light of Being as the beings they are'. Clearly, 'Being' and 'being' are important to Heidegger. Further, he believed that philosophers had ignored Being in favor of being since ancient Greek philosophy, which was unfortunate, because 'the advent of beings lies in the destiny of Being' (1996 [1972/1927]: 286). Luckily, Heidegger assured everybody, he was an expert in Being.

Now being was easy to understand. It was honeysuckles and tamarinds – things that exist in the world, realities. Being with a small 'b' was studied by science, though by 1929 Heidegger in 'What is Metaphysics?' was revealing what he believed were grave inadequacies in science. Being with a capital 'B' was another concept, far more difficult to grasp. As Heidegger grew older, especially after 1945, at least one commentator says that he emphasized 'the ineffability of Being' (Wolin 1991: 11). For example, in the famous 1946 'Letter on Humanism' he wrote:

> Yet Being – what is Being? It is It itself. The thinking that is to come must learn to experience that and to say it. 'Being' – that is not God and not a cosmic ground. Being is farther than all beings and is yet nearer to man than every being, be it a rock, a beast, a work of art, a machine, be it an angel or God. Yet the near remains the farthest from man.
>
> (Heidegger 1996: 287)

Let us scrutinize this quotation. Its first two sentences intone, almost in a chant: Being is It which is It; which tells you nothing because you are never told what 'It' is. The next few lines inform that Being is not 'God' or 'cosmic ground', which narrows matters down, though the assertion that Being is both 'nearest' and 'farthest' is perplexing. The point is that the quotation announces it will explain Being and does not. This, in conjunction with the melodramatic tone of the quotation, 'Being – what is being? It is It itself', certainly leaves readers feeling that Being is ineffable.

The ineffability is intended. Heidegger wanted to be a mystic. Caputo, a reader generally sympathetic to Heidegger, documented that, following 'What is Metaphysics?' there were strong similarities between Heidegger's work and that of the fourteenth century Dominican mystic Meister Eckhart (Caputo 1978). Such mysticism, Caputo claimed, allowed Heidegger to 'leap beyond the realm of giving reasons in order to take up a non-conceptual, non-discursive, non-representational kind of "thinking"' (ibid.: 4). This is because

'Being', with a big B according to Heidegger, is 'no product of thinking' (1953: 356).

Certain commentators, attempting to explicate the meaning of quotations like the one just examined, do attempt to think about Being. For example, Caputo informs readers, 'Being means the appearing (*Erscheinen*) of what appears, the shining gleam (*Scheinen*) of beauty (*Schönheit*)' (1992: 276). LeMay and Pitts, trying to explain Heidegger to beginners, allow that It is a 'difficult idea' but they believe it 'can be . . . understood through a comparison of Being with light'. This exercise is helpful because, 'just as one never actually sees light, but rather things lit by light, one never directly experiences Being, but rather beings which exist through Being' (1994: 34). Frankly, Being as like 'light' or the 'shining gleam' of 'beauty' still seems ineffable; and the problem with the ineffable is that it is indescribable, so that the words used to describe it must be mumbo-jumbo. A magical tradition of premodern Hermes flitted on in Heidegger.

One point seems clear in this ineffability. There is a Heideggerian dualism. This consists of being that can be studied by an inadequate science, and Being which, Heidegger promised, if you learned his hermeneutics, presented in *Being and Time* (1927) and other publications, would put you in the forefront of the Hermeneutic Circle interpreting Being; provided that you recognized, as Bleicher put it, that 'the "as-structure of understanding" is based upon the *fore-structure* of understanding' (1993 [1980]: 259).

This dualism further ties Heidegger with premodern seers, because it recreates their belief in two realms that need to be known about; only this time these are not the natural and the supernatural. They are being and Being. It further crowns Heidegger as the King of the Hermeses because his hermeneutic provides the key to understanding Being, which leads to 'the advent of beings'. So who needs to fiddle with an impotent science of beings anyway? Heidegger certainly did not. During the Third Reich, he joined Hitler and, as a member of the Nazi party, participated in implementing the Hitlerian design for beings.[5]

Heidegger's invention of Being seems a violation of Occam's razor. This methodological maxim attributed to William of Occam 'asserts entities that should not be multiplied beyond necessity' because, as William put it ' "It is vain to do by many what could be done by fewer" ' (Fetzer and Almeder 1993: 100). The addition of Being to being seems just as fallacious as the burdening of the natural with the supernatural. There simply is no reality other than reality, suggesting that being is being and Being is Mumbo-Jumbo. Further, perhaps, Heideggerian violations of Occam's razor have their own specific, unfortunate consequences. This is because, just as ancient and medieval Hermeses gossiped about the supernatural at the expense of knowing the natural, so Heidegger interpreted Being at the expense of being.

Heidegger's collaborators may suggest that I misinterpret his notion of Being, insisting that he did not mean by it a separate epistemic realm.

My response to this is that Heidegger's texts, like the Bible, offer fruitful fishing grounds that can turn up all sorts of fishy interpretations. However, one fact seems indisputable. He urged followers to concentrate upon understanding Being. This has its opportunity cost. It takes a long time to know Being, as any Heideggerian will tell you. Time spent interpreting Being is time lost knowing being. This had to have made Heidegger less knowledgeable about Hitlerian designs. The philosopher K. Jaspers, a German contemporary of Heidegger, believed this to be the case, when he stated in 1945 that 'Heidegger certainly did not see through all the real powers and goals of the National Socialist leaders' (in Wolin 1991: 3). So perhaps the kindest excuse one can give for Heidegger's embrace of Nazism is that his hermeneutics made him less knowledgeable about what was happening around him; for example, to Jewish beings. I can muster little enthusiasm for such a hermeneutic.

So it is time to backtrack, at least in time, to the end of the nineteenth century to appreciate what led up to Weber's turning. In order to grasp Weber's position one needs to recall those of Droysen and Dilthey. Droysen, according to von Wright, 'appears to have been the first to introduce' a distinction between two types of knowledge which he called explanation (*erklären*) and understanding (*verstehen*) (1971: 5). Dilthey 'sharpened the distinction' (Martindale 1960: 377). According to Dilthey, there were two fundamentally different ways of knowing which might be thought of as two adjacent, but different, flower-beds of *Naturwissenschaften* (natural sciences) and *Geisteswissenschaften* (human studies). Gardeners in the former bed used the tools of science to achieve explanation, while those in the latter bed used those of hermeneutics to achieve understanding. The goal of explanation is the flowering of causal laws; that of understanding is 'grasping meaning' (Rickman 1962: 39).

Just exactly what is in bloom when one grasps meaning is unclear. One dictionary of semiotics reports the concept of meaning to be 'problematic' (Bouissac 1998: 99). Another finds it 'the source of no slight confusion' (Colapietro 1993: 48). Given the preceding, some wags judge it to be 'extremely difficult' to say anything 'meaningful' about 'meaning' (Greimas 1990: 3). However, perhaps two 'translation' and 'intentionality' traditions can be distinguished. Semiotically, from the vantage of Saussure (1916), the meaning of something is what is signified. Of course, as the title of a recent work by Tallis indicates, it is *Not Saussure* (1988), what is signified by signification, though it appears that the research derived from Saussure treats meaning as a purely linguistic phenomenon. Greimas, for example, defines signification as 'transposition of one level of language into a different language'; so that 'meaning' becomes 'simply this possibility of *transcoding*' (1990: 7). Here the meaning of a text is its translation. But Dilthey had not read Saussure. He was not a linguist, and he believed it was a 'mind-affected world' (1962: 67). This was the case he reasoned, because 'In history we read of productive labour, settlements, wars, foundations of states . . . but what moves us, above all in these accounts is what . . . can only be experienced inwardly; it is inherent in the outer events which originate from it and which, in turn, react on it' (ibid.: 69). The crucial assertion in this quotation is that the external events of history – wars, and so on – 'originate from' events 'experienced inwardly'. A person's 'will' is the internal force that 'moves' people because it gives 'life its value, its goal and its meaning' (ibid.: 69). The will achieves 'development and form' according to meanings that reside in the mind. But what is meaning?

An answer to this question depends on apprehending how Dilthey conceived the individual. For him an 'individual . . . is . . . a point where systems intersect; systems which . . . possess an independent existence and development of their own through the content, the value, the purpose, which is realized in them' (ibid.: 78). Dilthey believes, 'Every organized unit . . . acquires a knowledge of itself' (ibid.: 78). This knowledge is from the 'systems' that 'intersect' with individuals. These systems are 'standpoints for valuation' or 'cultural systems', and it is 'they' that 'have meaning' (ibid.: 78, 79). Meaning, thus, for Dilthey was an attribute of the 'standpoints for valuation' associated with 'organized units'. The notion of 'organized units' seems to be Dilthey's general term for groups. So what he is saying is, first, that an individual within a group acquires that group's 'cultural system' which specifies life's meaning and, then, that these meanings allow the individual to have 'purpose' to inform their wills. Now intentionality 'is that property of many mental states and events by which they are directed at or about or of objects and states of affairs in the world' (Searle 1983: 1), which suggests that Dilthey's is an intentionality approach to meaning involving the mind's use of cultural systems to create understanding that is the basis of will. Meaning is not translation. It is intention. Dilthey's hermeneutics, then, is understanding of intentional meaning.

Dilthey clearly specifies that his hermeneutics does not involve causal analyses, though he believes such inquiries can be made and, in fact, should be made, but by psychologists (1962: 69, 70). Rather, his hermeneutics would investigate meaning in the manner of 'literary history and criticism', utilizing the methods of literary critics when dissecting a poem, and such techniques, he believed, 'are only concerned with what the pattern of words refers to, not – and this is decisive – with the processes in the poet's mind but with a structure created by these processes yet separable from them' (ibid.: 7). Here Dilthey is espousing the tradition that views hermeneutics as the analysis of the meaning of texts. What people do and say are their texts; and the flower of Dilthey's meaning is the intentionality of these texts that is interpretable from 'outward expressions' of 'inner states' of 'mental life' (ibid.: 75).

Malgré lui, Dilthey pointed the way to a causal hermeneutics. After all, he maintained that there are 'mental processes' in a 'mind-affected world'. Now the word 'affect' means 'to act on; to produce an effect' (*Random House Dictionary* 1967: 24); and it is causes that produce effects, so – even though

Dilthey's preference was for a non-causal hermeneutics – he recognized that mind and world were in a cause-and-effect relationship; which brings us to Weber and mono- and multiple cropping.

I have worked at times among a group called 'development experts'. One of the things I learned doing this work was that there was 'monocropping', where you planted only one crop in a plot; and 'multicropping', where you planted more than one. The experts all agreed that monocropping was more rational because you made more money at it. Modern farmers did it. Multicropping was less rational because you made less money at it. Traditional African farmers did it. Then, certain dissident experts began to notice that, under the conditions in which Africans farmed, multicropped fields were often more productive than monocropped ones. The hermeneutists' insistence that scholars do either natural sciences or human studies imposed a monocropping. Scientists, in their garden, cultivated only the white rose of causal law, while hermeneutists, in their plot, farmed only flaming poppies of meaning. Now Weber – originator of the traditionalist/rationalist dichotomy – will turn out to have been something of a traditionalist himself, at least in the sense of being an intellectual multicropper.

Weber called his intellectual garden 'interpretive sociology'. He believed this sociology put researchers:

> in a position to go beyond merely demonstrating functional relationships and uniformities. We can accomplish something that is never attainable in the natural sciences, namely the subjective understanding of the action of the component individuals. The natural sciences on the other hand cannot do this, being limited to the formulation of causal uniformities.
> (1968a [1913]: 15)

A point to grasp here is that Weber's hermeneutics is conceived to allow scholars to 'go beyond' and create knowledge that before was 'never attainable'. Going 'beyond', achieving the 'never attainable' – these are strong phrases. Weber believed he was creating a super-science, and this super-science was a causal hermeneutics; one that multicropped the flowers of intentional meaning and causality in the same flowerbeds by *both* interpreting the meaning of something *and* placing this meaning within causal processes. How he did this is described below in terms of the knotty causality sketched in the previous section.

Interpretive sociology 'is a science concerning itself with the interpretive understanding of social action and thereby with causal explanation of its course and consequences' (ibid.: 4). The object of the analysis here is 'social action'; that is, of how individual actions relate to the actions of other individuals. The analyst seeks 'interpretive understanding' of such action to achieve 'a causal explanation of its course'. 'Action' is behavior to which 'the acting individual attaches a subjective meaning' (ibid.: 4).

The meaning of meaning in Weber resembles that in Dilthey. Meaningful action is 'subjectively understandable' (ibid.: 5); that is, it has 'an intended purpose' (ibid.: 7). Weber distinguishes a type of understanding that he calls 'explanatory'. This is understanding in which one knows the 'motive' behind the individual's action; with it recognized that 'A motive is a complex of subjective meaning which seems to the actor himself or to the observer an adequate ground for the conduct in question' (ibid.: 8). The notion of 'motive' is the key to Weber's causality. This is because, 'A correct causal interpretation is arrived at when the overt action and the motives have both been correctly apprehended and at the same time their relationship has become meaningfully comprehensible' (ibid.: 12).

What Weber is asserting here is that there are causal processes in which individuals are the causes and their actions are the effects. Further, he insists that in the natural sciences scientists would observe 'uniformities' between these causes and effects. Weber's uniformities are Hume's constant conjunction. First a pitcher pitches, second a batter swings. There are uniformities between the individuals and their actions. The action of 'hitting' is constantly conjoined to 'pitching'.

Now the reason Weber believes he can cultivate flowers of knowledge 'never attainable' before is because he believes he has found, to use the term of the previous section, the connector between cause and effect. Discovery of this leads Weber to believe he knows what forces the constant conjunction between individuals and their actions. Motives are the connectors. Batters bat because they are motivated to do so; that is, these motivations give meaning to their lives.

To summarize Weber, two sorts of related investigations occur when cultivating the garden of interpretive sociology. The first of these is that of the natural scientist, and involves the establishment of 'statistical uniformities' between different individuals and their actions. Then, the second line of inquiry, that of the hermeneutist, reveals what are the meanings that motivate and so function as the connector between antecedent actions (the causes) and subsequent actions (the effects). So the Weberian garden of interpretive sociology really does multicrop, conjoining flaming poppies of meaning with the white rose of causality. Finally, the goal of this analysis is not to interpret the meaning of a text. Far from it, Weber would have dismissed Derrida's principle, 'Il n'y a pas hors de texte' as irrelevant. The goal of interpretive sociology is to discover how motivations, with meanings immanent in them, force connections between causes with effects. In such analysis, 'Il n'y pas de texte!'

The preceding may sound compelling; but things may not be so rosy, at least from the vantage of introducing a knotty causality into the garden of Weberian super-science. The problem is that Weber gives meaning and motives no physical basis. There is no account of how an immaterial motive actually goes about forcing very material action. The analyst may interpret what the meaning of an action was, but they do not know how or why meaning forced action because they do not know what it is. Thus Weber's causality fails to provide a material basis for his connector between cause and effect. We know that it is a mind-affected world. This Dilthey told us. We know that it is a mind-affected world because motives force action. This Weber told us. But neither Weber, or for that matter any other hermeneutist, gives us any idea what the connector is between individuals, their meanings, and their actions. This means, if we want to cultivate Weber's garden of a super-science, we had better start looking for the connector – the material structural reality that interprets meaning, thereby knotting antecedent regions of structure and their consequents. This brings us to neurohermeneutics, a theory of interpretation that achieves Schleiermacher's goal of explaining the different forms of hermeneutics 'in a general manner'.

NEUROHERMENEUTICS

Neurohermeneutics is Weberian in a double sense. First, it seeks, as did Weber, 'interpretive understanding' of what happens when people act. Second, this understanding is – as Weber would want – part of a 'causal explanation'. However, the problem with Weber's hermeneutics was the connector. Motives were a phlogiston – a something supposed to do something that was nothing, and nothing cannot do something. Our connector is a something. It is a physical structure of neurons that knots events in antecedent E-spaces (the causes) with those in subsequent E-spaces (the effects). As such, it is the subway tracks connecting past with future in the string being of social monism.

However, before proceeding, it is important to argue that this hermeneutics is not a repudiation of all earlier hermeneutics. To the contrary, it is to the enormous credit of the lineage of hermeneutists from Dilthey and Weber to Edmund Husserl, Paul Ricoeur, and Hans-Georg Gadamer to have brought to the attention of thinkers that interpretation matters. People do figure things out in their heads and, on the basis of these interpretations, they do come to have certain intentions, which they act upon. Now, many of the more 'positivist' social thinkers who dominated in the nineteenth and first half of the twentieth century – for example, the unilinear evolutionists and the neo-classical economists – ignored interpretation. This meant that the hermeneutists had discovered something of an agnoiological hole. But, there is something in that hole, the brain, and, as demonstrated in the previous chapter, it performs the functions of the mind, including interpreting what to do. So, to refuse to investigate how the brain makes interpretations violates agnoiological sensibility by deliberately choosing not to know something that you need to know to know more and get out of a hole. It is for this reason that it seems appropriate to formulate a neurohermeneutics. Let us turn to Swedenborg, whose quotation began this chapter.

Swedenborg (1688–1772) is not remembered for his biological researches. He was a Swedish cosmologist and a theologian who, after the discovery of the principles of Newtonian mechanics, spent much of his life speculating about the movement of stars. However, at the height of the Enlightenment he anticipated a neurohermeneutics because he recognized that the cortex 'imparts . . . understanding and will; and . . . the power of acting in agreement with will'. If Swedenborg's 'understanding' is appreciated to result from interpretation and if it is, further, recognized that people intend what they 'will', then the CNS, but especially the cortex, is involved in interpretation, and what you figure out 'imparts' action. So it turns out that the idea of a neurohermeneutic system is two centuries old. Below readers acquire the ABCs of neurohermeneutics.

Jacques-Pierre in love and the ABCs of getting connected

The brain, the individual it is in, and other individuals external to the first individual are different structures, but they are at some point, for some period, physically hooked up to each other. This is obviously the case with an individual into which the brain has been lashed by millions upon millions of neuronal connections. However, the claim that different individuals are physically connected to each other appears problematic; because it seems to assert that people are in some way Siamese twins, something clearly untrue. However, the assertion becomes more plausible when we amplify it to suggest that the physical unions are not permanent but temporary – made, broken off, and remade. How this works is illustrated by using a hypothetical pair, Gwyn and Jacques-Pierre, to illustrate the biology of getting connected, via the making of an immodest proposal.

People hear speech. Speech is different sounds. For example, Gwyn says, 'I like you', to Jacques-Pierre, a down-and-out dramatist, who has been working on a comedy, *Jacques-Pierre in Love*. Now, the sound of being liked is material. It is periodic variations in air pressure. Air pressure is the closeness of air molecules to each other. Pressure is compressed when the molecules are densely packed. Pressure is rarefied when they are less densely packed. Sound waves are the frequency of alternations of compressed and rarefied patches of air molecules. Speech is the production of sound waves that carry messages. Let us trace out what happens when two individuals speak. Electrochemical impulses bearing information are directed from the motor cortex of one individual to the muscles in that individual's mouth. There the muscles turn the electrochemical messages into sound waves. These are directed to the sense organs in the ear of another individual, or individuals, where for a brief instant the air molecules in the sound waves strike the auditory receptors in the cochlea of the second individual's ear. Then sensory neurons translate the sound waves with their information from the first individual into stimuli, another form of electrochemical information that is transmitted first to the medial genticulate nucleus of the thalamus, where it is relayed to the primary auditory cortex of the second individual. Thus, the two individuals, the structures Gwyn and Jacques-Pierre, are physically connected to each other when air molecules of the sound waves from Gwyn attach to Jacques-Pierre's sensory organs.

Now consider vision. People move or write. Light waves reflect off movement or writing. They are reflected as photons with different frequencies of the emission of electromagnetic energy. The frequencies of electromagnetic energy involve different rates of flow of electrons. Different frequencies of electromagnetic energy carry messages from the physical objects off which they have reflected. Vision is the reception of photons bearing information. Let us contemplate a man seeing something a woman does in order better to visualize what is happening here.

When Gwyn moves or writes, electrochemical information is directed from her motor cortex to her muscles. Perhaps, holding a copy of *Geertz for Dummies*, she winks and writes a quick note, 'You are nice.' The wink and the writing become photons whose electrons travel to Jacques-Pierre's eye, where they strike photoreceptors in his retina. There they are transduced from electromagnetic to electrochemical energy, stimuli, whose information is transmitted along the neurons in the optic nerve to the lateral genticulate nucleus of the thalamus and then on to the visual and other parts of the cortex, allowing Jacques-Pierre to interpret, 'Wowie! A wink plus "You are nice"!' Thus, with vision, as with hearing, two individuals are physically connected to each other.

Jacques-Pierre 'gets' (that is, interprets) the message. As a result, he intends and feels 'love' about this Gwyn. He will get it on with her, and to do so his brain sends certain electrochemical information to the muscles in his mouth, tongue, and throat. These contract and relax in such a manner as to send out a stream of air molecules bearing the information, 'Hey Gwyn, sweetie pie, we could be great together, ya wanna do it? Doggie style or missionary position, your choice!' Jacques-Pierre, a man of action, translates intention and feeling into this speech, discursive action, a singularily vulgar and immodest proposal.

The case of Gwyn and Jacques-Pierre getting connected, though hypothetical, has served to illustrate something not hypothetical: the actuality of the material connections between people as they make interpretations, conceive intentions, and act. It remains to be suggested that these exhibit a knotty causality. Remember, for investigators to suspect that they have such causality on their hands they must establish (1) constant conjunction made by (2) a connector between causes and effects. The Gwyn–Jacques-Pierre episode reveals a constant conjunction in a three-part sequence. At time A a person sees or hears something. Jacques-Pierre sees and hears Gwyn. This leads, at time B, to his interpreting what he saw or heard. Jacques-Pierre 'gets' what Gwyn said and wrote, and contemplates certain thoughts and feelings about what has been figured out. He gets a 'love' for Gwyn. Finally, at time C, he acts on his love. Jacques-Pierre blurts out, 'ya wanna?' This is, indeed, a naughty causality.

The As, Bs, and Cs that Gwyn and Jacques-Pierre are involved in are a constant conjunction that occurs in all reasonably neurologically sound, interacting humans. A: first there is the arrival of stimuli, followed, B, by the interpretation of stimuli and the formation of intentions and feelings about these, followed, C, by action. The constant conjunction being asserted here means that if A, then B; if B, then C. The rationale supporting this claim is that stimuli cannot be interpreted and made into intentions and emotion by the brain unless they have previously arrived, which means no B unless A. Finally, acts cannot occur unless the brain has created intentions and feelings about these – electrochemical energies bearing information to the body about what to do – which means no C unless B.

These As, Bs, and Cs are antecedent events (causes) in an E-space in the case of the As and subsequent events (effects) in the case of the Cs. In the Gwyn and Jacques-Pierre example they are Gwyn's wink and note in the antecedent E-space and Jacques-Pierre's proposal in the subsequent E-space. As such causes are constantly conjoined to effects. As are conjoined with Cs because of Bs. B is the connector, the neurohermeneutic system whose particulars are now detailed.

Loosely speaking, this connector is the entire CNS. However, its nature can be more precisely specified. Connectors are supposed to be material. The CNS is material. It is neurons. Connectors are supposed to be structures. Neurons in the CNS exhibit synaptic linkage between each other into the modules, circuits, pathways, and so on which are the structures of the structure of the CNS. Remember, it was suggested in the previous chapter that there were in the order of a trillion linkages in the CNS, which made it not only a structure, but the most complex one for its size in the known universe. Connectors are supposed to attach events in antecedent regions of reality with subsequent ones.

We learned in the previous chapter how there were afferent pathways which ran roughly from receptors to the thalamus and on in parallel circuits into the sensory cortex and limbic system. These pathways, as we have just seen with Gwyn and Jacques-Pierre, literally attach a person to the realities surrounding them. This means that everything that happens in the CNS is subsequent to the original attachment. Hence, afferent pathways are the devices in the CNS that attach to antecedent regions of reality, and so they might be called antecedent attachment devices (AADs).

Additionally, it was learned in the previous chapter that there are efferent pathways which leave from the PFC for the pre-motor and motor cortex, thence on to the basal ganglia and cerebellum, and, finally, down the spinal cord to the different organs of the body, like the muscles, that attach to, and affect, external reality. But these effects on reality, like Jacques-Pierre's immodest proposal, are subsequent to the antecedent reality, Gwyn's wink. So the efferent neural pathways that attach to muscles that make actions that effect realities attach to subsequent realities, and may be said to be subsequent attachment devices (SADs).

Finally, we know from the previous chapter that the AAD brings information in the form of depolarization patterns from the antecedent reality into the diverse and profusely linked circuits of the sensory cortex, the PFC, and the limbic system. These circuits operate to 'reason' about this antecedent reality. They do so by representing it as emotional and sensual, current and past perceptions and by calculating emotionally and intentionally how to proceed given such perceptions. Jacques-Pierre perceives a wink. He calculates, 'She likes me,' and feels real good about it. Thus, this neural threesome – sensory cortex, PFC, and limbic system – takes information about antecedent reality and transforms it into information about how to proceed vis-à-vis a subsequent reality; which information it sends on, apparently through the anterior cingulate cortex, to the SAD. This trinity of neural networks transforms information about antecedent realities into information about subsequent ones, so it is a transforming device (a TD). Thus, the CNS has connected material structures that operate as AADs, TDs, and SADs, which means that it satisfies all the conditions of a connector. It is a something, a material chunk of structure with antecedent attachment, transforming, and subsequent attachment devices. Such a something ties knots, splicing events from antecedent spaces to those in subsequent spaces.

CONCLUSION

This chapter has sought in a preliminary fashion to identify what *it* is that allows individuals to figure out – that is, interpret – their worlds. The first section of the chapter got us out of the 'cement' of Humean causality by arguing an alternative, knotty approach to structural causality which makes discovery of connectors tying antecedent with subsequent realities the chief analytic chore of those interested in making causal connections. The next section of the chapter reviewed certain aspects of hermeneutics, suggesting that Weber had envisioned a causal hermeneutics with the capacity of explaining how individuals tied antecedent with subsequent reality. Unfortunately, Weber's hermeneutics were flawed. So the preceding section of the chapter has proposed that different linked structures in the CNS bring stimuli bearing information of reality to certain brain structures that interpret these stimuli; that these interpreted stimuli then move on to other brain structures that form intentions and emotions based upon these interpretations; and, finally, that these are moved on to other brain structures that activate muscles to perform action. So Swedenborg appears to have been pointed in the right direction. 'Cortical substance' by imparting 'understanding, . . . will; and . . .

the power of acting' through the AAD, TD, and SAD in the CNS is the connector.

Neuroscientists tend to label as 'systems' linked structures in the CNS that perform some function, or set of functions. For example, there is a belief that there are limbic and motor control systems. Thus, just as the brain has linked neurons that function in emotion, so it also has neurons linked to each other that function in the representing of, and acting upon, reality. 'Interpretation' is the operation of neurons to represent, and act upon, reality. The organizations of neurons that do this are the 'neurohermeneutic system'. The system will be said to perform a 'neurohermeneutic process', involving a knotty causality that leads from the reception of stimuli to the inception of action. 'Neurohermeneutics', then, is the study of this system and its processes.

A virtue of this approach is that it both enlarges the scope of hermeneutics and contributes to explaining, as Schleiermacher had wanted, what is 'general' about the several forms of hermeneutics. Hermeneutics is no longer merely the interpretation of texts. Rather, it is about how humans interact with reality. What is common to the different forms of hermeneutics is that they all make interpretations. Most hermeneutists who know about the United States would interpret a wink as a 'come-on'. But these same hermeneutists would be content to make their interpretation and not to explain what reality it was that made them make their interpretation. This is like stopping the train before it gets to the station. Certainly, it is important to interpret what people do, and it is to the credit of the hermeneutists to have insisted that this was the case. But their very certainty makes an approximately true response to the question, what *is* interpretation, even more important.

The response to this question is a theoretical hypothesis – and like all such hypotheses it is in search of fuller validation – to the effect that *all interpretation is the operation of a neurohermeneutic system functioning as a connector, stringing antecedent to subsequent E-space in the social monism.* To make this clearer, let us return to Martin Luther's response to the papal bullying. The events from Pope Leo's threat, an antecedent E-space, were ushered by sensory receptors into Luther's neurohermeneutic system, out of which came neuronal signals that went to his muscles that became his diatribes against Catholicism, a subsequent E-space. To deny that the antecedent papal threat, the cause, migrated into Luther's neurohermeneutic system is to deny reality. Luther officially received the Pope's bull on October 10, 1520. He heard it. He read it. To deny that Luther interpreted this threat in his neurohermeneutic system is to deny reality further. Where else could it be interpreted? The other parts of the body do not do interpretation. To deny that his neurohermeneutic interpretation was the basis of his subsequent anti-Catholic polemics, the effect, is to still further deny reality. Luther took his interpretation of the Pope's demand and poured it out in texts like 'To the Christian Nobility of the German Nation'. So an antecedent was strung to a subsequent being, beginning that particular string (of) being known as the Reformation.

However, it would be wrong to assert that Luther's anti-Catholic vitriol was only in response to the Pope. Other Catholic officials attacked him. Important here was Mazzolini, who became the Grand Inquisitor and Censor of Books in 1515. Luther was clear in his 'Babylonian Captivity of the Church', written just after his piece appealing to the German aristocracy, that he was responding to these attacks as well as those of the Pope (Luther 1970: 124). The point here is that there were a number of antecedent causes, all of which were Catholic attacks upon him, which migrated into his neurohermeneutic system. Clearly, they went through his AAD to his TD, where they were transformed into his own counter-attacks – that is, SAD turned into the different tracts that became a basis for Protestantism.

It might be argued that interpretation takes places somewhere else than in a neurohermeneutic system. For example, Erik Erikson had tried to explain Luther's actions psychoanalytically (1962). The problem here is that the various concepts in psychoanalysis – ego, id, repression, and so forth – are supposed to refer to biological realities of the nervous system. Hence, psychoanalysis presupposes a neurohermeneutics. However, psychoanalysts or other scientists have never found egos and ids. Hence, psychoanalysis is a failed neurohermeneutics. This suggests that the shoe is on the other foot. There *is* a neurohermeneutic system. It *does* make interpretations, though understanding of how this is the case is still limited. Thus, those who would deny the importance of a neurohermeneutic system must discover a reality that, on the basis of the evidence, is a better interpreter than it.

Certain final points need to be stressed. There are connectors and there are connectors. Salmon's garage-door opener can do one thing, and one thing alone: it opens garage doors. The human neurohermeneutic system can do a vast number of things. Think of all the things it did to write the hundreds of pages that Luther wrote against Rome. Further, the neurohermeneutic systems of different people connected to the same E-space can do different things. Napoleon and Wellington, as we shall see in the next chapter, both facing Waterloo did the opposite thing. Napoleon attacked, Wellington defended. Finally, other approaches have treated hermeneutics causally (see especially Davidson 1963; Child 1994). However, these approaches have tended to leave culture out. Similarly, the neuroscientists, who have begun to consider the role of the brain in cognition, also tend to leave culture out. The following chapter puts culture – and the 'golden arrow' of desire – in, offering a cultural neurohermeneutics that explains why neurohermeneutic systems are not garage-door openers and why different people in the same E-space, with the same neurohermeneutic systems, do different things leading to different E-spaces.

Chapter 5

A neurohermeneutic theory of culture

> Bring me my bow of burning gold!
> Bring me my arrows of desire!
>
> (William Blake, Jerusalem)

The old poet demands his bow and arrows. This chapter brings them. Let me explain how. The previous chapter argued the plausibility of a neuro-hermeneutics. But the devil is in the details. The present chapter adds details, especially those pertaining to the role of culture in the neurohermeneutic process. The chapter's argument begins in a fine revolutionary mettle explicating a revolution in the revolution. Specifically, it demonstrates that Boas's notion of culture revolutionized what Kant had believed to be revolutionary in his hermeneutics in a way that advances the view that any neurohermeneutics should be a cultural neurohermeneutics. However, this raises the question, what is culture?

The second section responds to this question. It examines previous debates in cultural analysis including those of definition, of the utility of cultural essentialism, and of culture's ontological whereabouts. It resolves these debates in a manner that recommends a 'two-cultures' approach that suggests that culture operates in two material realities. The first of these realities is said to be within the brain and a place of neuronal culture. The second of these is said to be beyond the brain in E-space and a place of discursive culture. Neuronal culture is said to be a thing of 'shreds and patches', and it is these that operate in the neurohermeneutic system.

The third section – integrating elements of the Kantian hermeneutic, the shreds-and-patches approach to culture, and certain aspects of the neuro-scientist, J.M. Fuster's understanding of memory – theorizes that the neuro-hermeneutic system works through an interpretive hierarchy utilizing cultural memories of past realities to represent present realities in ways that form desires about future realities. Because neurohermeneutics 'runs' on culture, it may be said to be a *cultural* neurohermeneutics. Cultural neurohermeneutics, then, is a golden bow that looses arrows of desire; and culture is part of the archer's prowess which helps guide those arrows to their target. Finally, the chapter is brought to a swift conclusion with a modest proposal that is the core of a neurohermeneutic theory of culture. The structures of the neuro-hermeneutic system are what Lévi-Strauss called the 'fundamental structures of the . . . mind'.

A (BOASIAN) REVOLUTION IN THE (KANTIAN) REVOLUTION

> Thoughts without content are empty; intuitions without concepts, blind.
> (I. Kant, *Critique of Pure Reason*, 1991 [1781]: 63)

Franz Boas is reported to have read Kant's *Critique of Pure Reason* (1781) while his ship was frozen into Baffin Island during that winter of 1883, which recommends the philosopher to those with anthropological imaginations. Though Boas never explicitly sought to relate his position to that of Kant, I shall argue below that *Doctoraluk*'s views revolutionize, in the sense of making more powerful, what Kant had thought to be revolutionary in his own thought. The approach to Kant will be through the work of Edward Hundert.

Hundert, in *Philosophy, Psychiatry and Neuroscience* (1989), authored a position which, while it does not label itself neurohermeneutic, offered a neuro-biological basis for understanding interpretation. However, Hundert recognized that his approach relied upon certain aspects of the *Critique of Pure Reason*. Here Kant had asserted that knowledge, among other things, resulted from the operation of different faculties of the mind; especially sensibility, understanding, and desire. Kant, unlike Swedenborg, did not tie the mind to any 'cortical substance'. Hundert sought to be Kant's Swedenborg by specifying the neuro-anatomy implied in Kant's faculties of sensibility and understanding.

The term 'faculty' may be confusing here, especially for academics who are likely to think of it as those other poor fools with whom they work. But Kant used the term to refer to non-learned cognitive abilities; and, to the extent that Kant's faculties are innate, they resemble the domain-specific modules. As Hundert explained Kant, the faculty of sensibility was concerned with 'the *sensory* aspects of experience (e.g. colours, shapes, odors . . . etc.)'; while the faculty of understanding was involved with 'the *intellectual* aspects of experience (e.g. beliefs, expectations, plans)' (ibid.: 21; emphasis in the original). Kant believed that the two faculties were a 'united operation' (1991 [1781]: 63), because the only way the faculty of understanding received what he termed 'sensations', or 'intuitions', was through the faculty of sensibility. However, once understanding had been 'united' with sensations, its function, as Hundert explains it, was to '*make sense* of that data by organizing it into a coherent experience of the world' (1989: 21; emphasis in the original).

What Hundert calls the 'organizing' of data into a 'coherent experience' is its interpretation. This means that Kant was something of a hermeneutist. Of course, the neuroscientific question is, how does the neurohermeneutic system carry out the work of this interpretation?

It is in response to this question concerning the faculty of understanding that Hundert makes his contribution. He 'divided the brain into "input", "central", and "output" systems' (ibid.: 201). Input systems are the areas that perform the tasks, as described in Chapter 3, of sensing and perceiving. Output systems are those areas that, upon receipt of information from the central system, perform the tasks of putting the body into action. They are the motor cortex and associated regions of the brain. However, it is the central system which is critical, because this, according to Hundert, is Kant's faculty of understanding where 'the meaning of information' is established (ibid.: 201). Hundert locates the central system in the associational cortex. Here is where interpretation takes place.

So Hundert, seeking to give a biological basis to Kant's faculty of understanding, advances Swedenborg by proposing a specific area in the cortex that performs the chore of interpreting. He provides 'anatomical, functional, and neurochemical' evidence (ibid.: 197) in support of his view. However, there are concerns. Hundert does not clearly explain what goes on in the associational cortex during interpretation. Certainly the associational cortex is involved in interpretation but this is a vast place, one that might be likened to the brain's Amazon rain forest. This means that it is critical to explain how the different neural topographies in this jungle work, and it further needs to be made clear that interpretation is not a purely cortical affair. Thus, Hundert validated the plausibility of the view that interpretation involves a neurohermeneutic system, though he provided few details of how this might be the case.

One way to begin to specify these is to note that Hundert ignored what Kant believed was revolutionary in his approach. Kant claimed that his was a transcendental philosophy. A 'transcendental' is that which is necessary for, or a condition of, something. Liquid water and sufficient cold are transcendentals of ice. He further insisted in the *Critique of Pure Reason* that a priori ideas were transcendentals necessary for knowledge produced by the faculty of understanding. Such ideas were not memories of past experience. In fact, they had nothing to do with experience. They were prior to, that is, a priori, experience. A priori ideas were not so much actual ideas, such as the idea of a 'Sebastian' or a 'honeysuckle'. Rather, they were *abilities to think categorically*, to have ideas that classified things into categories such as those of 'Sebastians' or 'honeysuckles'. Specifically, such ideas classified sensations into ideas based upon certain categories.

Kant believed there were four a priori categories: those of quantity, quality, relation, and modality, each divided into subcategories (1991: 79–85). Empirical knowledge was arrived at as follows. First, the faculty of sensibility interpreted what a person senses as intuitions or sensations and then passes these on to the faculty of understanding. Next, this faculty interprets the sensations by using the a priori categories to classify them into such-and-such a thought. For example, the faculty of sensibility might interpret what it sees as sensations of things in the air. These, then, might be re-interpreted by the faculty of understanding as of the quantity 'two', of the quality 'birds', in the modality of 'flying', in the relationship of 'above' and 'below' each other.

Recent studies of animal cognition support Kant's position to the extent that they show that the capacity for categorical thought is enormously developed in humans compared to other species and that this capability is part of their neurological organs.[1] However, studies in developmental neuroscience indicate that environmental factors play a role in the development of neural circuitry. For example, there has been research that showed that animals raised in 'enriched' environments exhibit increased dendritic branching (Holloway 1966; Volkmar and Greenough 1972; Juraska 1984). Such branching is the number of dendritic connections one neuron makes with others. Animals living in environments that are enriched in terms of the number of stimuli they experience have neurons that make more connections. It is unknown exactly what, and how important, is the environment's role in the development of the neural networks involved in categorical thought. The studies just discussed find that neural circuitry may not be acquired solely through the genes, which implies that there may be no such thing as pure a priori thought.[2] However, the brain does develop under normal conditions neurological structures with certain capacities for categorical thought. These capabilities are *already there* when a person receives external stimuli and begins to think about them. So it is these pre-existing circuits and their capacities that might be thought of as a priori.

Kant was elated with this transcendental approach, claiming that it was a Copernican Revolution in the understanding of knowledge. He believed that this was so because in the past Empiricists, such as Hume, argued that knowledge derived entirely from experience; while Rationalists, like Leibniz, believed it depended solely upon the way reason thought about experience. Kant believed that his revolution showed how both experience and reason were necessary. The faculty of sensibility took the information of the senses and made them into the sensations or intuitions. The faculty of understanding took the sensations and, on the basis of a priori categories, classified them into different 'thoughts' about the sensation.

Kant was on to something here. Certainly, you cannot make an interpretation of 'birds' unless you have the ability to think of being in terms of qualities. Similarly, you cannot interpret that there are 'two' birds unless you have some ability to think quantitatively. The suggestion being made here is that the a priori ability to think categorically is, in Kant's terms, a transcendental of culture. You cannot interpret something unless you can classify it. Recognition that categorical thought is critical in the interpretation of reality is the Kantian revolution. However, as is often the case, the revolution was incomplete.

This is because the mere fact that humans can think categorically does not get you very far, for as Kant himself had insisted in the quotation which began this section, 'thought' without 'content' is 'empty'. The ability to think categorically allows you to think categorically. It does not provide you with those categories, the 'content', of your thought. Forget any other categorical imperatives you may have heard about, the real categorical imperative is: *you cannot think categorically unless you have specific categories*. What was incomplete in the Kantian revolution was that there was no account of what might provide the 'content' of the different categories. It is here that the Eskimos' *Doctoraluk*, Boas, becomes relevant.

There was a recognition in certain areas of nineteenth-century social theory that humans learned, in Comte's terms, 'fundamental opinions' (1853) or, in the terms of Durkheim and Mauss, 'collective representations' (1903). These recognitions crystallized, as Sahlins observed into Boas's notion that culture was the learned 'categorization of experience' (Sahlins 1976a: 71). Boas believed, reflecting his Kantian inclination, that 'classification of experiences' was 'a fundamental trait of human thought' (1938: 189). But Boas's categorizations, unlike Kant's, were learned and remembered.

Specifically, as a result of his different ethnographic encounters, Boas realized that different peoples learned different 'principles of classification' (ibid.: 191). Perhaps acknowledging the nostalgia of a season frozen in ice, he often used, Eskimo examples of categorization. For example, he noted that in English there was but one word, 'snow', which categorized the frozen stuff that blankets winter worlds; while 'in Eskimo' there is 'one word expressing, "snow on the ground"; another one, "snow falling"; a third one, "drifting snow"; a fourth one, "a snow drift"' (ibid.: 191). Boas did not have a fixed nomenclature for words as the Eskimo had for snow. Sometimes he said they were parts of language. At other times he called them 'customary' or 'traditional' expressions. Currently, as Sahlins has pointed out, such terms would all be understood as elements of Eskimo 'culture' (1976a: 70).

The difference between a Kantian a priori category and a Boasian one might be illustrated as follows. If an Eskimo woman saw drifting snow and applied to it the Eskimo word for such snow, she would be classifying it into a particular Eskimo cultural category. However, the ability to calculate in such a manner, to take one idea and place it within another, would be an example of a priori categorical thought. Boasian culture was the missing 'content' for a priori thought to think with. No longer was categorical 'thought' without 'content' and hence 'empty'. Kantian a priori categories might be imagined as a 'hardwiring' built into the brain, while Boasian culture might be envisioned as the 'programs' that provide the specific content of the categories. So the Boasian revolution was a recognition that culture 'programs' the Kantian 'hardware' in the brain.[3] Taken together, cultural 'programs' plus Kantian 'hardware' equal the cultural neurohermeneutic system. But at this moment we know little about culture and so, in order to better understand this system, we take up the topic of culture in the section below.

TWO CULTURES

> [T]here is no such thing as human nature independent of culture.
>
> (C. Geertz, *The Interpretation of Cultures*, 1973: 490)

> History has left us no generally consensual definition of culture, nor could any completely satisfactory definition be given.
>
> (J.P. Surber, *Culture and Critique*, 1998: 4)

A prevailing mood with regard to understanding culture is illustrated by the above quotation from Surber. The mood is bleak. Surber says, do not even hope to define the term. I have little use for such pessimism. This section of the chapter offers an approach to culture based upon a recognition that the social monism is composed of both E- and I-spaces. It is an approach, which, for once is in agreement with Geertz, and shows why he is correct in asserting that human nature is dependent upon culture. Indeed, I go further. The nature of humans *is* cultural.

Back in the 1950s, the British novelist C.P. Snow talked of two – scientific and humanist – cultures. The account of culture advanced here is also talks of two cultures, but these cultures are far different from those of Snow. There is 'neuronal culture' within a person, within the structures of the neuro-hermeneutic system in I-space, and there is 'discursive culture' external to a person, part of the structures of E-space. The discussion below seeks first to establish the utility of the neuronal versus discursive cultural distinction, and second to document differences between the two cultures, showing how, if one conceptualizes neuronal culture as a thing of 'shreds and patches', one can be in a better position to account for how culture operates in an individual's neurohermeneutic system.

Neuronal and discursive culture

It is well known that 'anthropology brings with it a professional tendency to privilege the cultural' (Appadurai 1996: 11). So it is expected that anthropologists will be cultural boosters. One consequence of this boosterism is that anthropologists, with certain notable exceptions (such as Deacon 1997), have slighted the role of the brain in culture. Conversely, neuroscientists have returned the favor. A survey of the cognitive neuroscience literature indicates that neuroscientists, with one exception (Gazzaniga 1985), are uncultured in the sense that culture plays no part in their explications. In order to grasp the role of culture in the brain, especially in neurohermeneutics, it is important to step back to make a choice pertaining to broad versus narrow definitions of culture; to distinguish 'perceptual' from 'procedural' culture; and to specify the nature of cultural construction. Consideration of these matters will lead us to a recognition that there are two – neuronal and discursive – cultures; with both sorts of cultures relevant to what happens in the neurohermeneutic system.

Narrow versus broad definitions

Let us begin by considering a debate between those who have favored broad as opposed to narrow definitions of culture.[4] E.B. Tylor, of course, propounded the broader conception of culture as 'that complex whole which includes knowledge, beliefs, art, morals, law, custom, and any other capabilities and habits acquired by man as a member of society' (1958 [1871]: 1). This definition of culture is vast. Culture is not only what people know and how they act, it is additionally 'any other' thing humans have from socialization. Implicit in Tylorian culture is a recognition that it is something learned and shared. You are not born with culture. Genes do not cause it. You acquire it by learning it by being a member of society. Further, other members have it also, so culture is shared.

A narrower, 'culture-lite' view became prominent in the 1960s that stripped all the 'any other' adhesions from culture. This means that culture, though it is still learned and shared, no longer pertains to behaviors or actions. There are Geertzian and cognitive anthropological variants of this narrower view. Geertz insisted that culture was 'historically transmitted patterns of meanings embodied in symbols' (1973: 87). Steven Tyler, prior to a postmodern phase, when still speaking for cognitive anthropology, said, 'A culture consists of many semantic domains organized around numerous features of meaning' (1969: 360) that are 'the organizing principles underlying behavior' (ibid.: 357).

Geertz's and Tyler's narrow definitions are two peas in a semiotic pod. Geertzian culture is 'patterns of meaning'. Tylerian culture is 'semantic domains'. Now a semantic domain is a pattern of meaning and meanings are signs making categorizations. Cultural signs can bear intentional and trans-lational meanings. 'Translational' meaning is what a cultural sign denotes in terms of other cultural signs. 'Intentional' meaning refers to what a cultural sign intends in terms of being, with its being understood that intention can refer both to realities denoted by the sign and how to proceed vis-à-vis those realities. What the Barma cultural sign '*kuin*' intends is that region of reality that gave birth to you. Translationally a '*kuin*' is a 'mother'. The procedure of adding something to something else is intended by the cultural sign '+', which translates as 'addition'. What is intended in Trobriand culture by an '*mwali*' is a chunk of reality that includes leaves and shells in a circle that fits on your biceps. Translated, it is an 'armband'. Thus a narrow definition of culture might be shared, learned organizations of signs with intentional and trans-lational meaning.

There has been a debate over the relative merits of the two definitions of culture. Offer one in a paper presented at a scholarly meeting and someone in the audience is likely to pop up, like a jack-in-the-box, and scold you for not using the other. This being acknowledged, I shall work with the narrower definition. It makes escape possible from the tautological bathos that culture causes culture that arises with a broad definition of culture; and it does so in a manner that helps to demonstrate the role of neuronal culture in the causing of human action. It is time to formulate a concept of cultural construction.

Cultural construction

This formulation is accomplished by connecting culture and memory, which is done by recalling the concept of information. Information, it will be recol-lected from Chapter 3, is representations of what is and/or what to do about it. Some information is cultural in the sense that it is shared by members of a population. Americans whose brains have not been rendered dysfunctional by alcohol or drugs share the information that there are 'mothers' and 'lovers'; and that you do not sleep with the former while you do with the latter. Now memory is stored information. Stored information not only includes sensations – sights, sound, smells, and so on – but the cultural signs associated with these. The word 'associated' needs to be clarified. Here it means that specific sights, sounds, smells, and so forth, sensations in Kant's terms, are remembered and represented as themselves with additionally specific cultural signs from a person's semantic memory. This means that the representation of the sen-sations that are a rose – scents, colors, thorns – is remembered in association with a specific cultural category, the sign of the 'rose'. Now, for the most part, all explicit memories of sensations have their cultural associations, which is to assert that human memory is fundamentally cultural memory.

Consider, for example the Trobriand culture bearing upon Kula exchanges. Those circular things that Trobriand brains represented as having leaves and shells are associated with the cultural sign 'mwali', one of whose translational meanings is 'armbands' and another is 'vagu'a', or 'valuable'. Moving from the sunny tropics to the mean streets of New York, and what might go on in the minds of police there, consider that the cultural sign associated with the sensation of a blur in bed is a 'mother' – do not 'touch' her. Further, consider the cops' memories in the Diallo case of the sensation of a dark blur in the hallway is 'black', 'male'; 'fuck him over!' Trobriand islanders and New York City cop memories, then, are crowded with representations of sensations and their associated cultural signs. It is as if humans are into compulsively 'playing it again' – first as sensation, next as associated sign or signs.

Now is the time to introduce a concept of cultural construction. Constructivist approaches are extremely widespread, with many social theorists, like Bourdieu, declaring their positions to be constructivist.[5] None of these constructivisms is explicitly neurobiological. The present one is. Specifically, it proposes that neural memory networks operate when somebody constructs something.

Remember from Chapter 3 that 'Our memories are networks of inter-connected cortical neurons, formed by association, that contain our experiences in their connectional structure' (Fuster 1997: 451). Further, remember that these memories are episodic and semantic. Now semantic memory is words in a language, but words – for those who have learned the language and shared translational and intentional meanings – are cultural signs. This reiterates what was just learned: semantic memory is actually cultural memory. Episodic memory in this light becomes the cultural signs attached to the sensations that result from the episodes of a person's life. If, for example, you are reading Dante's *Divine Comedy* about Beatrice while watching scenes on the television of refugees, then one episode of your episodic memory will include sensations of Beatrice and the suffering of refugees associated with the cultural signs 'Beatrice' and 'refugee suffering'.

Why memory is associative is explained by D.O. Hebb's principle of 'synchronous convergence' whereby 'two cells or systems . . . that are repeatedly active at the same time will tend to become "associated", so that activity in one facilitates activity in the other' (Hebb 1949: 70).[6] Your memory of Beatrice is within a set of episodic and semantic cortical neurons. Your memory of refugees is within another set of such neurons. Because the two cortical networks were laid down at the same time – that is, are synchronous – they become 'interconnected cortical neurons'; which is to say that they and their representations are associated. So when you think of heavenly Beatrice, grim refugees pop up in your mind. Additionally, 'Each new memory is the expansion of old ones; it simply adds associations to pre-existing nets' (Fuster 1997: 452). You are still reading Dante some time after seeing the refugees on the television, when it brings to you images of the African killed by the New York City police. So images of refugees and murdered Africans are part of your remembrance of past Beatrices. The occurrence of this synchronous convergence is 'well documented' (ibid.: 451) in the cortices of a number of mammals, including humans (see, for example, Stent 1973; Singer 1993).

Given the preceding, provisionally cultural construction is association of sensations with cultural signs in a person's episodic and cultural memories. For example, when I see the honeysuckle it is associated with the sensation of Sebastian and the cultural sign 'dog'; and the honeysuckle brings back many other associations. There is that of the tree out behind the village of Bémbassa and the cultural sign 'tamarind'; and the tamarind brings back the sensation of Amina and the cultural sign 'beautiful'.

Associated with sensation and sign is emotion, because a portion of all stored memory is emotional. This is because the amygdala ensures that different semantic and episodic memories have different emotions associated, often implicitly, with them. 'Honeysuckle', 'dog', 'tamarind', and 'Amina' each have feelings associated with them. The honeysuckle has been a soothing place of shade and light. Sebastian the dog, who gave a deep affection, and on occasion flies and mange, to each member of the family, died last winter. We buried him, furiously attacking the frozen ground with pick axes, to give him a grave near the honeysuckle. There is now a feeling of sadness associated with the 'dog'. The 'tamarind', of course, was the precursor of the honeysuckle, a secret world of shade and light, and the occasional cooing of a dove, that gave peace. Amina is a complex set of emotions. She aroused sexual feelings in me, though I never tried to act on these. At the same time her sheer beauty gave pleasure, the sort of pleasure that beauty gives. So when I remember Amina I feel pleasure, with the faintest rise of eroticism. So the cultural construction of honeysuckle is associated with different feelings of pleasure tinged with a bit of sadness.

Finally, to round off this discussion of cultural construction, it should be clear that people live in a real world but it is one that they have culturally constructed. There is E-space out there. But from the vantage point of an individual, that world is 'culturally constructed' by the operation of episodic, cultural, and emotional memories that associate remembrances of sensation, cultural sign, and emotion. This brings us to perceptual and procedural culture.

Perceptual and procedural culture

A distinction can be made explicit between two sorts of 'perceptual' and 'procedural' cultural memories. These are respectively representations of being and procedures scripting actions on the stage of being. Examples of the first sort of information are 'dogs', 'ghosts', or 'consciousness'. This is information that re-presents sensations of what is a dog, ghost, or consciousness, and so might be said to be 'perceptual'. Such information may concern realities that are either external or internal to individuals. 'Dogs' are always external. 'Ghosts' are usually external. 'Consciousness' is always internal. Certain perceptual cultural signs may not directly pertain to internal or external realities, but such information almost invariably has been, or is, useful for negotiating such realities. 'Zero' is such a message.

The signs in perceptual culture, because of their categorical nature are related to each other according to, as Boas recognized, certain 'principles of classification'. 'Related' here means that the signs occupy categories that may be classified with regard to other categories. For example, a 'dog' is a 'pet' that is an 'animal'; while a 'wolf' is not a 'pet' though it is an 'animal'. The signs 'dog' and 'wolf' are related in that both fall within the category 'animal', and unrelated in that they are not both within the category 'pet'. There are a number of terms that might be given to categorical organizations of signs – 'folk taxonomy', 'cultural model', or 'paradigm' come to mind. However, perhaps a useful term is 'schema'.[7]

The notion of 'schema' is especially attractive because most organizations of signs are open in the sense that they have the capacity to generate novel signs to refer to new realities. Roy D'Andrade has specified that an attribute of schemas is that they are 'highly *schematic*' leaving 'unspecified a number of "slots" which can be filled in by context or by additional information' (1995: 123). For example, recently some persons have begun to domesticate wolves. Thus, the wolf is beginning to fit into a new category in the *animal* schema of a 'pet' because of a new reality emerging about them. Perceptual culture thus includes perceptual signs that are elements in perceptual schemas.

A second sort of cultural memory involves information scripting 'what to do about what is'. Individual bits of such plans will be called procedural signs. Related procedural signs will be said to be procedural schemas. The sign 'hunt' is of importance in procedural culture pertaining to wolves. Other signs like 'stalking' and 'charging' that are related to the hunt are part of a *hunting* procedural schema. Sometimes the scripts in procedural culture are simple and clear. 'Bikes' are to be ridden, '*mwali*' to be exchanged for a '*soulava*' (necklace). At other times the procedures are complex and open. 'Democracy' and 'freedom' are to be 'defended' – but how?

Norms and values pertain to procedural culture. A 'norm' is a cultural assertion about what a person should do about what is. A 'value' is a cultural assertion about whether it is good or bad what a person does about what is. Values are important because they appear to tie procedural culture with emotion. This is because, it will be recalled from Chapter 3, the amygdala sorts and remembers the emotionally good and bad. Something highly valued is likely to be remembered pleasantly; something not valued, unpleasantly. For example, perceptual culture classifies some form of sexual behavior with kin as incest in all populations. The norm is that one should not commit incest, and this norm is associated with the value that it is terribly wicked to do so. Many people report feelings of disgust at the very idea of incest.

Perceptual schemas may, or may not, have spatiotemporal dimensions. The perceptual cultural signs 'past', 'present', and 'future', critical to the US *historical* schema, certainly have a temporal aspect to them. Those of 'doll', 'ball', and 'squirt gun', part of a *toy* schema, lack such a dimension. However, procedural schemas tend to have a spatiotemporal aspect to them. You proceed in some order. At time$_a$ you do this in space$_a$; at time$_b$ you do that in space$_b$. The procedure for the *Kula* schema is: first in time in one place, exchange an *mwali* for a *soulava* and, second in time in another place, exchange that *soulava* for another *mwali*.

It is important to recognize that perceptual and procedural cultural memories are culturally constructed together. Indeed, the same sign may bear both perceptual and procedural meanings. Dorothy Holland and Debra Skinner, who investigated what they call the US college woman's *romance* schema, provide an example that illustrates this point. In this schema:

> A male earns the admiration and affection of a female by treating her well. Intimacy is a result of this process. The female allows herself to be emotionally closer, perhaps as a friend, perhaps as a lover, perhaps as a fiancée, to those attractive males who make a sufficient effort to win her. . . .
>
> Normally prestigious males are attracted to establish close relations with prestigious females, and vice versa. Sometimes, however, a male can succeed in winning the affection of a female whose prestige is higher than his own. However, the more attractive she is, the more he must compensate for his lack of prestige by spectacular efforts to treat her well.
>
> (1987: 101–2)

The perceptual cultural signs needed to proceed in the world of romance include, among others, 'male', 'female', 'lover', and 'prestige'. The sign 'lover' has both perceptual and procedural meanings. Perceptually, a lover is a person. Procedurally, you sleep with the person. A basic procedural move for a man in this schema is to 'treat her well if he intends to become her lover'. A related procedural move is 'the higher her prestige, the better you have to treat her'.

The point here is that perceptual cultural signs in schemas tell a person what exists in E-space – lovers and prestige. Procedural cultural signs in those schemas tell that person what to do with what exists. The association of particular perceptual and procedural signs with particular sensations is the cultural construction of reality. It tells you what is, and what to do about it. You want a low prestige lover, take her to McDonald's. You want a higher prestige one, take her to the best restaurant in town, give her flowers, and do not forget the champagne.[8]

Finally, an obvious but important point, when signs from the perceptual and procedural schemas of people get strung together they create units of information vaster than is the case when the individual signs stand alone. For example, the perceptual sign 'lion' provides a fierce bit of information. But it really does not tell you very much. The addition of the procedural sign 'attacks' increases the information to 'Lion attacks'. This certainly gets your attention. Who is attacked, when? And the addition of two more perceptual signs 'you' and 'now' tells you exactly what you need to know: 'Lion attacks you now'. A question occurs, as you flee the imaginary lion, fully cognizant of the importance of these grander units of information: how does one conceptualize them? In order to answer this question it is necessary finally to give our cultural approach some status.

Varieties of neuronal and discursive culture

The type of 'status' of interest here is not that of the Smiths keeping up with the Joneses. I am interested in ontological status. Where in being does culture belong? This question can be answered by re-running a debate between Geertz and certain cognitive anthropologists over the ontological status of culture. The answer to the question we arrive at will lead us to recognize that there is 'neuronal' and 'discursive' culture in the social monism. Cognitive anthropologists firmly located 'the stuff of culture in the mind' (D'Andrade 1995: 182), though they were not all that explicit as to where the mind might be located. Geertz was appalled, insisting 'Culture is public because meaning is' (1973: 12). Both sides to the debate seem correct; though, in explaining how this is the case, I shall alter some of the terms of the argument. 'Black' and 'man' are perceptual signs in contemporary US culture. When a policeman remembers, 'That guy is black', this is what D'Andrade would call 'in his mind'. But when the cop yells to his partner, 'That guy is black', then his brain has transformed internal electrochemical events in neural networks into external, 'public' sound waves whose particular configurations bear information.

The preceding has implications for those who say, 'Cultures . . . are not material phenomena' (Tyler 1969: 3). Of course they are, and they come in two material forms: either as internal brain activities in I-space, or as transformations of those into some external physical forms, usually speech or writing in E-space. It is in this sense that *both* Geertz *and* his opponents were correct. The material basis of internal culture is the neuronal networks of memory. Hence, such culture is aptly termed 'neuronal'. The material basis of external culture is the photons of light waves or the molecules of sound waves of speech or writing. Hence, such culture might be usefully termed 'discursive'.

Now it is possible to specify different units of information. A bit of neuronal culture will be said to be a 'cultural sign'; one of discursive culture will be said to be a 'cultural lexeme'. When talking of schemas stored in people's 'minds', we shall presume them to be stored in neural memory networks. So they will be termed 'neuronal schemas'. Similarly, when speaking of schemas contained in spoken or written texts, they will be termed 'discursive schema'. The different signs in different schemas may be strung together by reason, as defined in Chapter 3, to make larger units of information. These are either thoughts or texts. 'Thoughts' rely upon neuronal culture and will be said to be the operation of neural circuitry producing collections of signs associated with sensations, produced by some process of calculation. 'Texts' in discursive culture will be said to be the externalization of those collections of signs in speech or writing.

Simple and clear procedural neuronal thoughts will be termed 'recipes'. When a recipe is spoken or written down, it becomes a discursive text and will be called an 'administrative procedure'. The Ten Commandments, when committed to memory, are important procedural recipes in Judeo-Christian neuronal culture. Those same commandments when boomed out by clerics or displayed as texts have become administrative procedures in discursive culture.

More complex thoughts of procedural neuronal culture, those involving a number of recipes, will be said to be a 'strategy'. A strategy that has gone public and is spoken or written is an 'ideology'. Mercantilism, liberalism, nationalism, democracy, Nazism have been important ideologies in the modern world. When these have been set to memory, they have been strategies of neuronal culture that have guided human practice. Strategies, or ideologies, that appear to the individuals who hold them to 'go without saying' because they are 'obviously true' might be said, following the discussion in Chapter 2 of Gramsci and the Comaroffs, to be 'hegemonic'.

Are thoughts about how the stock market works a recipe in the United States underwritten by a neo-classical economic strategy? Similarly, among early twentieth-century Cheyenne of the northern plains in the American West, is remembering the steps of the Sun Dance a recipe underwritten by a strategy that Llewellyn and Hoebel called the 'Cheyenne Way' (1941)? Such questions pose the problem of how one distinguishes between recipes/administrative procedures versus strategies/ideologies. One way of answering this question is to judge that, if thoughts or texts are so broad in scope as to have their recipes and administrative procedures that implement them, then they are strategies and ideologies.

Thus, thinking in terms of neuronal culture, thoughts about the stock market and the Sun Dance are recipes that help implement the capitalist and Cheyenne ways: namely, strategies. Similarly, thinking in terms of neuronal culture, the taking of more than one wife was a recipe for the implementation of the strategy of nineteenth-century Mormonism. Thinking in terms of discursive culture, the Ten Commandments are an administrative procedure that helps to implement Judeo-Christian ideology. Some strategies/ideologies are so broad as to have sub-strategies/ideologies. Liberalism, for example, contains recipes and administrative procedures both about politics – democracy should be instituted – and economics – capitalism should be instituted. What has been learned so far about culture?

Three matters seem consequential. First, there *are* two cultures out there, materially different and occupying different spaces, that alternate back and forth between each other. No sooner does a cop recognize in his neuronal culture 'That guy is black', than he yells out this information to his partners, 'That guy is black'. Things that change their forms are said to be metamorphic. So it is in this sense that a property of culture is its ability to metamorphose. Sometimes it is out there, in the E-space of discourse. At other times it is in there, in the I-space of culture-bearing neurons.

Second, Geertz claimed that 'there is no such thing as human nature independent of culture' (1973: 490). The fact of neuronal culture supports Geertz's claim. Culture is part of human nature because, when discursive culture enters into neural networks in the cortex, it becomes part of them. It is not known exactly how and what happens to the network, but it is known that something happens. So, it is in this sense that it is appropriate to say that culture is embodied and becomes a part of the brain. If human nature is how people are naturally – that is, biologically – then they are naturally cultural animals that soon after birth come to have enormous capacities, at least compared to other animals, of thinking categorically using cultural schemas. Thus neuroscientists who omit culture and the anthropologists who ignore the brain miss something fundamental in human nature.

Third – and this is why the Boasian revolution in the Kantian revolution is so important – humans do have the faculty of a priori categorical thought. Let us call such creatures, in honor of the person who discovered them, Kantopithecus. But Kantopithecus is an animal, who in Kant's own terms is running on 'empty'. It can think big, but has nothing to think about. What you think about is reality, but Kantopithecus has no real world inside them to think about. It was Boas who put reality inside humans because he had people remember perceptual and procedural neuronal cultural schemas, and these schemas said this is that in reality: marry it, or bury it, or maybe eat it. Such people were no longer running on empty, they had cultural content to put in the gas tanks of their a priori faculties. Let us call this new human *Homo sapiens kantoboasensis*. This creature had made a revolutionary leap. It now had specific categories that told it what was going on in the world. But, and this is the crucial third point, neuronal culture has to be put into the creature. This implies that there must be a discursive culture that is learned to become a neuronal culture that allows *Homo sapiens kantoboasensis* to act on a world they have embodied. It is time to critique cultural essentialism.

'Shreds and patches'

The recognition that throughout people's lives new signs may become associated with old sensations, or new sensations with old signs, will help us replace an essentialist view of culture with a more realistic 'shreds-and-patches' approach. Essentialism is an old set of doctrines in philosophy stretching back to Plato and Aristotle. 'Perhaps the most important' form of essentialism, first associated with Aristotle, 'maintains that some objects . . . have essences; that is they have, essentially or necessarily, certain properties, without which they could not exist or be the things they are' (Flew 1979: 104).[9] Some users of the term 'culture', especially from disciplines other than anthropology, write as if populations have their abiding essences: sets of cultural signs and schemas that are unchanging and shared by all members of a population. For example, the political scientist Samuel Huntington says that civilizations, which he equates with cultures, 'are the most enduring of human associations, "realities of the extreme *longue durée*". Their "unique and particular essence" is "their long historical continuity. Civilization is in fact the longest story of all." Empires rise and fall, governments come and go, civilizations remain' (1996: 43). For such scholars, the existence of such essences means that there is a US culture or a Truk culture, and so on.[10] How valid is such essentialism?

I do not have much truck with it because it is not an accurate predictor of what people actually do. If there is but one cultural essence in a people, then all individuals should share in it; and because of this sharing what they do should be in conformity with the diktats of the essence. Prohibition of murder, incest, and adultery are ancient and at the heart of US procedural culture. However, some Americans murder, some do not; some perform incest, others refrain. President Clinton, raised a Baptist, may have had a conscience that nagged, 'It is not approved US cultural procedure to practice adultery in the form of oral sex with a female subordinate barely out of her teens.' However, she flipped up her dress, flashed her thong, and he sacrificed something of the essence of US culture on the altar of her genital orifice in the Oval Office. The point of such observations is that they indicate that people who should share the same essential culture, and might be expected to do similar things, do wildly different things; which makes one wonder about the utility of essentialism. I shall argue below that it is flawed, because culture, from the vantage point of neuronal culture, continually changes and is only partially shared.

Let us begin this argument by reviewing what has been established. First, 'all memory is essentially *associative*' (Fuster 1995: 11; emphasis in the original). This means that neuronal cultural memories are associative. Further, for each sign in an individual's neuronal culture, some of the meanings are shared and some are not. Specifically, the signs of a person's neuronal culture share basic meanings with other persons while having different locational and individual contingent meanings. The notions of basic and contingent meanings require explanation.

The 'basics' of cultural signs are the translational and intentional attributes of a reality or an abstraction whose perception will result in the categorization of it as an instance of that sign. 'Categorization' means putting something in a category. For example, among Abu Krider, a basic intentional meaning of a *fil* (an elephant) was that it had an enormously long nose. The basics of translational meaning are the signs that represent the attributes of the intentional meaning. A *fil* has a '*mukhar kabir belhen*' (a 'very large nose'). Cultural basics are not cultural essences. They can, and do, change. This is why dictionaries report multiple meanings for terms. Further, the basics of cultural signs can, and do, have their ambiguities. The basics, for example, of the US procedural cultural sign 'sex' at the end of the second millennium had it as 'either stimulation of any sexual organs' or 'the insertion of penis within vagina'; with the former view of sex including vastly more actions than the latter. For example, on the basis of the first view, Queen Elizabeth I, remembered as the Virgin Queen who did not do it, and President Clinton, remembered as the lusty devil who denied he did it, both basically did it. However, on the basis of the second view, Elizabeth died a virgin, even though Sir Robert Dudley, the Earl of Leicester, played lively with her privates; and Slick Willie never did it, not-withstanding Monica's ministrations.

However, even with ambiguities, the basics are usually clear enough for people to 'get' what most things are in their lives. For example, in the United States if an object is seen to be red, to have a V8, four steel belted radials, and a 300 horse power engine, it is basically a 'car'. The fact that it has a fiery color and a big engine means to many, especially young men, that it is a 'hot' car, which does not change its basics – it's a car. The 'basics' of procedural culture are the primary ways of acting vis-à-vis a particular bit of perceptual culture. Cars are basically to be 'driven' and not 'buried in'. So people in the United States pretty much remember to drive their 'car', and only rarely do they get buried in the old Chevy. So it appears that people considerably share cultural basics. Nevertheless, even though US citizens know their 'cops', 'cars', and 'sex', they know these differently, and these differences need elucidation.

This leads us to cultural contingents. People who are members of the same groups or positions will share *both* the basics of cultural signs *as well as* additional cultural meanings contingent upon their common social location. 'Contingent' meanings of signs are those that are dependent upon people's social position or individual histories. Contingent meanings may be inten-tional or translational. 'Locational contingents' are meanings of a cultural sign shared by persons occupying the same location; with a 'location' defined as an objectively identifiable – in terms of organization, functions, and resources – place in a population. For example, everybody in New York City knows the basics of the sign 'cop'. However, many lower-class New Yorkers share locational culture memories of the police, based upon fear, that differ from those of the upper class who, because of their elevated location in society, find them deferential.

So cultural signs in a population have basics, widely shared throughout the population, and locational contingents, shared among those occupying the same location. A translational meaning of 'victory' in the United States is basically 'winning'; but winning has contradictory contingents for those located in society as prosecutors versus those located as defendants. 'Winning' for the prosecutor is having the defendant 'found guilty'; while for the defen-dant, it is being 'found innocent'. A 'good day's work' for a factory owner involves 'profits'. A 'good day's work' for the assembly-line workers is 'time and a half'.

The immodest proposal of Jacques-Pierre might be explained in terms of the locational culture involving courting. He and Gwyn meet in New York City singles bars. The locational components of the procedural culture of courting in such bars differ remarkably from those described by Jane Austen for the early-nineteenth-century English gentry in their bucolic country estates. What you did, among other things, in those manors was to display the 'manners' of a 'gentleman' or 'gentlewoman'. Potential mates acted out for each other delicate rituals that showed that they had the valued 'manners'. It took time to show you had the right sense and sensibility. It would have been 'ill-mannered' for Mr Darcy of *Pride and Prejudice* to importune Elizabeth with 'Ya wanna do it doggie style, honey?' However, a key procedural value in a single's bar is *'carpe diem'* ('seize the day'); and seize it with pizzazz. So a gentleman's manners in a singles bar can be blunt and flamboyant. Jacques-Pierre's immodest proposal seems thinkable in such a location. It might have caused Elizabeth to faint, but Gwyn would probably merely have shrugged 'Not tonight, lover-boy, I got to walk the dog'.

It also happens that persons in the same social locations may share cultural signs whose basics are not shared by other persons in other locations in the population. For example, among the Abu Krider, religious specialists (*imams*) who belong to the Tijaniya sect have tucked away in memory networks signs from Tijaniya theology whose basics are simply unknown to ordinary Abu Krider. Similarly, Trobriand *tolimegwa* (magicians) share basics of perceptual and procedural culture about magic that is unknown to other Trobrianders. Finally, algebraic topologists have locked away in their cultural memories signs of topological spaces that are not shared with hockey players. Much of locational culture is procedural. It is how to do what those in your location do: how to be an *imam*, a *tolimegwa*, or a topologist.

The term 'locational culture' will be reserved both for the locational contingents of signs and for signs whose basics are restricted to those persons occupying the same locations. The cognitive anthropologists of the 1960s anticipated the concept of locational culture by appreciating that there was 'intracultural variation'; a recognition that was itself prepared for by the earlier realization that there were subcultures. It was believed that intracultural variation occurred when people were in a 'different class . . . and/or in different situations or contexts' (Tyler 1969: 4). The problem, however, was that when cognitive anthropologists did their different formal and componential analyses they disregarded the culture found in different 'contexts'.[11] This is to say that they recognized but ignored that there was locational culture. Ignorance is not bliss.

There are many reasons why this is the case. One of these is that the more complex a population is in terms of the number of its locations, the more important will be its locational culture. For example, a man named Twi, from the foraging Ju/huwansi of the Kalahari, a society with few social positions, would basically occupy the locations of male, elder, in such-and-such a family, of such-and-such a band. On the other hand, a woman named Alotta Ricota, from New Jersey in the advanced capitalist United States could easily occupy the locations of being a middle-class, Catholic female, of the Ricota family, from Italy; an alumna of Fordham University who became a computer programer, a Republican, and a member of the Knights of Columbus; who, for her kids, became a soccer mom and a member of the PTA; and also, to reduce the stress and weight of her life, took up martial arts and Weight Watchers. For Twi there would be signs contingent upon only four social locations; while for Alotta there would be a lot more signs contingent upon her thirteen social locations. A general point is being suggested here. Real estate salespeople confide, 'Location is everything!' As in real estate, so in the analysis of shared culture: location means a lot. Specifically, there appears to be a positive relationship between numbers of shared social locations and shared cultural memories. Those occupying more similar locations will have more common cultural memories.

This does not mean that an individual's locational culture is fixed for their lifetime. There can be the addition of entirely new signs with completely new basic meanings when people move into new locations. Consider, for example, the case of a fine arts major who enters an accounting degree program. Before, she knew nothing about financial management; now, she knows a lot. The changes in this case are not to the contingencies of cultural representations that are already in her memory. Rather, they involve the addition of whole new cultural schemas pertaining to finance with numerous new signs with new basic meanings. Before she may have known the basics of being 'painterly'; now she knows the basics of 'investment'. Further, when different locations change, the basics of a sign may remain the same, though its contingencies may alter. For example, after the US stock market crashed in 1929, the basics of 'investment' remained unchanged, though its contingencies became 'bearish'. Such examples undermine the notion of fixed, locational cultural signs in an individual's neuronal culture. Let us move from the discussion of locational to that of individual contingents.

Even though each person leads a life that has certain episodes that are similar to those of other persons in the same locations, those episodes are never *exactly* the same. Additionally, each person has some episodes that are utterly unique. This means that the events that get associated with the basics of cultural signs in the different vignettes of episodic memory will be different. Consider 'sex', whose basic procedural cultural recipes, with some previously noted ambiguity, every adult shares.

Now each sexual episode brings its own associations. This means that for an individual, their cultural memories of sex are changing. As a boy of seventeen, I remember sex in an apple orchard on a Vermont hillside in May. There was the glorious smell of apple blossoms and her puckered nipples, 'darling buds of May'. Later, there was doing it out in the bush, where Ahmet had run for it, and the elephants still lurked. Here, I worried that I might perform *coitus* [crushingly] *interruptus*; life fluids spurting crazily due to the rhythm of a puritanical pachyderm's stomp. So what is 'sex'? The basics stayed the same but the 'individual' contingents varied.

Readers must now formally distinguish individual from locational contingents. The latter are meanings associated with signs due to a person's placement within a population. The former are meanings that get associated with signs because the hippocampus and the amygdala 'clicked' and stored some idiosyncratic perceptual and emotional happenings in a person's life with the basics of that sign. Sex was the darling buds of May in high school. Later, elephants got mixed up in it. As my sexual episodes increased, so did my episodic memory, associating the basics with more individual contingents.

Other people have had different sexual experiences than I have had and, like mine, theirs varied throughout their lifetimes. The case of a woman comes to mind. At the same age that I was in the apple orchard, she too enjoyed pleasant dalliances. However, when she went away to university she was dragged off a path into some woods. She fought. She was beaten, then raped. Consequently, her associations of intercourse are different from mine. I remember apple blossoms. She remembers the feel and the sound of punches hitting – first the blow hit flesh and then, almost instantly, collided with bone. Though we both know the basics, the contingencies are different. Are these different contingencies locational or individual? Certainly, because she is a woman, she has to be wary in a way that I do not. So, perhaps, a certain caution towards sex is a locational contingent that distinguishes US women from their male counterparts. However, the exact feel of how the punches landed – first in soft flesh and then striking bone – seems unique. So there is no immutable, essential cultural sign 'sex'.

Consequently, there are three sorts of shared and unshared meanings for any cultural sign: *the basics, plus locational and individual contingents*. My friend and I both remember the basics. Our gender locational contingents are different. I do not fear that somebody will jump out of the woods and rape me. Our individual contingents are different: apple blossoms versus hard blows striking. Thus the signs and contingents of neuronal culture change throughout an individual's life, and at least some of them are particular to the individual. The former aspect of contingents is termed their 'mobility'. The latter aspect is their 'particularity'. Essentialist cultural approaches are of questionable worth because they ignore the mobility and particularity of an individual's neuronal culture.

How, then, might the mobility and particularity of neuronal culture be conceptualized? Finally, we get to the 'shreds and patches' promised in this section. Robert Lowie had said in his *Primitive Society* that culture was a thing of 'shreds and patches' (1920: 441). He was derided for this declaration at the time. But perhaps the old image can be dusted off and used to help our needs. It might be imagined that the basics and locational contingents of an individual's culture are the 'shreds'. Individual contingents associated with these are the 'patches'. Thus, a person's neuronal culture is a singular, changing patchwork quilt of cultural meaning; a thing of shreds and patches of that which is a person's idiosyncratic life tucked away in expanding neural networks of cortical tissue. Critically, this means that people in a population do not acquire a culture that is identical for all of them. In this sense there is no Kwakiutl culture, or US culture, or any other culture for that matter. Rather, there are as many shreds and patches of culture as there are individuals, and these cultures are, as Christina Toren puts it, 'constructed anew by each person over time' (1990: 8).

To illustrate the preceding point, consider the case of the Emperor and the Duke, Napoleon and Wellington, who shared the location of being commanders-in-chief, and who consequently shared numerous procedural shreds of how to give 'battle'. But beyond these, the patches of their individual contingents varied. Napoleon attacked in battle after battle and won devastating victories at Lodi, Marengo, Austerlitz, Jena, Friedland, and Tilsit, that made him Emperor of continental Europe. The individual contingents in Napoleon's memory with 'battle' were attack. He expressed this when he said, towards the end of his life, 'The issue of a battle is the result of a single instant. . . . The adversaries come into each other's presence . . . they fight; the decisive moment appears; a psychological spark makes the decision' (in Herold 1955: 223). This 'spark' might be understood as Napoleon's way of conceiving an individual contingent associated with the basics of battle. What was this 'spark'? Early in his military career, after experiencing success with offensive tactics, he stated, 'It is axiomatic . . . that the side which remains behind its fortified line is always defeated' (ibid.: 217). So on June 18, 1815, at a small village on the outskirts of Brussels, the 'spark' came. The Emperor attacked.

His opponent was Lord Arthur Wellesley, the Duke of Wellington. Now the Duke had led a sporting life executing a variety of animal species in the killing grounds of Great Britain; then moving on to 'wogs' in India; and, finally, to 'frogs' in the Iberian peninsula, whence he had driven all French forces by 1813. Of course, all this 'wog' and 'frog' killing brought the Duke to the Emperor's attention, prompting him to remark, 'there is this difference between him and myself' (ibid.: 209). What was this *différence*?

When Wellington commanded in the Peninsula campaigns (1808–13) his troops were usually outnumbered (Aldington 1943: 124). Different episodes of battle taught him that, if his soldiers were not to be annihilated, they had better assume the defense. A 'Wellingtonian' battle placed British troops behind the crest of a rise, sheltered from direct exposure to French artillery and musketry. Then the French would charge and re-charge. When their charges had weakened, the British lines volleyed and charged. So the *différence* was one of patches, of individual contingencies of how they gave battle. Napoleon attacked. Wellington defended.

And this is exactly what happened that June 18, 1815. Each gave battle according to the 'spark' of their individual contingencies. Wellington drew his troops into squares at the top of a rise. Napoleon began attacking these about mid-morning. At one point, 'Forty squadrons of the Emperor's finest cavalry . . . attacked'; and thereafter, 'Time after time' they 'charged'. However, at the end of all this, 'the greatest cavalry action of the Napoleonic wars', the 'squares still stood' (ibid.: 239). Finally, towards dusk, 'The Duke called "Stand up,

Guards".' They did, 'gave . . . a devastating volley . . . and then charged' (ibid.: 241). Napoleon had met his Waterloo. The 'general' point illustrated by the preceding is that an individual's neuronal culture is full of contingencies – some locational, other individual – and these patchy details can be the making of history.[12]

In sum, there are two cultures – one discursive, the other neuronal. Neuronal perceptual and procedural signs and schemas are things of shreds and patches that operate in Kantian faculties to make thoughts. These 'thoughts', it remains to be shown, are the result of the operation of an interpretive hierarchy at the core of the neurohermeneutic system. By understanding this hierarchy we can complete the account of the neurohermeneutic system, and thereby present the golden arrow that is the connector between E-spaces. Thus the chapter's analysis has progressed to a point where a return to the neurohermeneutic process is required in order to show how culture functions at different levels of interpretation.

AN INTERPRETIVE HIERARCHY

> Hierarchy: 1. any system of persons or things ranked one above another.
> (*Random House Dictionary*, 1967: 669)

An interpretive hierarchy ranks increasing or decreasing involvement of the neurohermeneutic system in the interpreting of reality as well as increasing or decreasing complexity of the interpretation of this reality. As the above makes clear, hierarchy has its rank, ascending or descending, in some order. A quantitative hierarchy from one to ten ranks increasing or decreasing numbers.   This interpretive hierarchy will begin with interpretations that resemble nervous twitches and end with those of the deepest desires. Kant's and Fuster's positions provide a rationale for such a hierarchy. Let us explore this rationale, beginning with Kant.

Kant, it will be recalled, had said that the human mind enjoyed faculties of sensibility, understanding, and desire. Sensibility provides the mind with the raw data of the senses ('intuitions' in Kant's terminology); while 'Understanding "makes sense" of the data by organizing sensibility's intuitions under various *concepts*' (Hundert 1989: 22; emphasis in the original), thereby creating thoughts about reality. Kant was insistent. The two faculties were interdependent: 'these two powers or capacities cannot exchange their functions. The understanding can intuit nothing, the sense can think nothing. Only through their union can knowledge arise' (Kant 1991 [1781]: 62–3). Such a view of mind implies a hierarchy of interpretations. The mind interprets reality as various 'sensations' at a lower level and then the mind re-interprets these to create 'thoughts' about them at a higher level.

Kant also suggests a further, still higher level of interpretation in the *Critique of Practical Reason* (1788), which considered the faculty of desire. Kant said in *Practical Reason* that 'Life is the faculty of a being by which it acts according to the laws of the faculty of desire. The faculty of desire is the faculty such a being has of causing, through its ideas, the reality of the object of these ideas' (1956 [1788]: 9). 'Life' might here be understood as Kant's way of speaking of what an individual does, that is, that individual's actions. Kant is clear, actions result 'according' to the faculty of desire. This is because this faculty gives individuals the ability 'of causing . . . the reality of the objects' of their desire. At this point 'practical reason' comes into the analysis. Such reasoning establishes 'ideas' about the objects of actions and desires and how to achieve them. Now the preceding suggests a third level of interpretation. First, the faculty of sensibility represents what is. Next, the faculty of understanding re-represents what is by associating it with some sign, or signs, thereby creating a cultural construction that assigns the reality to some category. Finally, the faculty of desire makes calculations upon this cultural construction based upon procedural recipes of the signs that compose it to arrive at desires, establishing what to do about what is represented.

Kant, however, as earlier indicated, provides no clue as to the neurobiology of such an interpretive hierarchy. Fuster does. Remember, he argued for neural hierarchies of perceptual and procedural memory. These, it will be recalled, went from less to more complex memories that were based upon increasingly large neural networks, which processed increasingly large amounts of information about reality. Interpretation, it will be recalled, was operations of the CNS to represent reality by remembering and calculating about the past; which implies that interpretive hierarchies can be established based upon the type of memory utilized to represent present realities. Put in its simplest terms, for any particular reality, what is proposed is this: different memories, different interpretations; greater memories, more complex interpretations; more complex interpretations, larger areas of neuroanatomy engaged in the neurohermeneutic process. The different levels of this hierarchy are sketched below.

A human neurohermeneutic process appears to operate at four levels of interpretation. Readers may be confounded at the claim that there are *four* levels. Kant seemed to suggest only three. However, I argue for four levels because I think he forgot something. Kant's different types of interpretation come about because of representations of physical properties of reality. First you had sensation, next understanding, and finally desire. However, sometimes humans take notice of, and act upon, reality *even before it gets represented* as sensation. Such actions, because they transpire without the guidance of sensation, understanding, or desire seem to happen automatically, and their occurrence is a rationale for a fourth level of interpretation.

Thus the four levels of the interpretive hierarchy are those of automatic response, sensation, lifeworld and, finally, desire. 'Automatic' interpretations do not involve neuronal cultural memories. Nor do they involve any considerable participation of sensory cortical neural networks. 'Sensational' interpretations also do not involve neuronal cultural memory. They do depend upon the operation of sensory cortical networks that represent the physical properties of stimuli. 'Lifeworld' interpretations – the term is borrowed from Husserl, for reasons explained below – involve remembrance of neuronal cultural signs associated with sensations of stimuli, and thus involve the operation of extensive cortical neural networks, especially in the sensory and associative regions of the posterior and frontal cortex. Interpretations of 'desire' result from the calculation of intention and of emotion concerning intention, and involve extensive neuronal cultural memories analyzed in the anatomical structures of working memory, 'the blackboard of the mind' (Just and Carpenter, in Goldman-Rakic 1992: 111), which involve the entire brain, but especially the prefrontal cortex. A more complete elaboration of the different levels of this interpretive hierarchy follows.

Automatic response

Once, while walking in a parking lot next to a library, lost in thought, something happened – and, before I knew what it was, I jumped a mile! When I returned to earth, I recognized that the car of a student racing for a scarce parking space had been bearing down on me. The student – grinning, amused that he had launched a professor – called out, 'You OK?' I responded, 'Yeah, you surprised me.' People usually attribute such actions to being 'taken off guard', or 'being unaware', or just plain 'surprised', as I had said. Categorization of such actions as being based upon 'unawareness' is recognition that there are certain interpretations of what is happening in the world that people make without being cognizant that they will make them. People who act in this manner act automatically. There was a movement and – zowie, kaboom! – before there was any sensation of it, I had jumped a mile.

An 'automatic response' interpretation has been made when an individual has re-presented the properties of a stimulus but not to the level of being aware of them. This form of interpretation appears, in the instance under discussion, to involve the reception of stimuli of the present world, a car's motion, and their transmission along the optic nerve to the lateral geniculate nucleus (LGN) of the thalamus. There this information goes along two neural pathways, one of which produces involuntary action. One circuit goes to the amygdala, the other to the sensory cortex. However, the stimuli along the thalamic-amygdala pathway arrive prior to those taking the scenic route in the thalamic-cortical pathway. So before the sensory cortex can function and re-present 'car', the amygdala had swung into operation sending information to various parts of my autonomic nervous system (ANC) and leg muscles to get scared and jump. Zowie, kaboom, I automatically jumped a mile.

Such automatic interpretation involves subcortical neural pathways that take a 'direct thalamo-amygdala path' but because this 'pathway bypasses the cortex, it is unable to benefit from cortical processing, which means that the amygdala has only 'a crude representation of the stimulus' (LeDoux 1996: 164). Otherwise put, automatic interpretations occur involuntarily, without there being consciousness of what provoked them.

My guess, and it is only a guess, is that Amadou Diallo may have been killed as a result of such an automatic interpretation. The four New York City cops who 'smoked' (that is, shot) him forty or so times knew they were after a 'black' 'male' 'rapist'. They believed such a person was 'dangerous'. They hunted him at night in darkened places that would have heightened the danger. This would have meant that their cortico-amygdala pathways operated as they prowled. Specifically, to transmit representations of 'danger' from the cortex to the amygdala, whence the amygdala would have transmitted information to other parts of the body, especially the ANC, to be aware of the danger. The ANC would have turned on emotions of aggressiveness, alertness, and fear. In short, as the cops stalked they would have been 'twitchy', primed to kill. They came upon someone hidden in the darkness of a doorway. Someone moved, perhaps quickly, in the dark. The cops detected the movement. In an instant it became the stimulus of movement, transmitted to the thalamus, transmitted to the amygdala, which reacted – zowie, kaboom! So before they even knew what was up, they interpreted the stimulus automatically, blowing Amadou away.

A final point should be made. Clearly, there are other sorts of automatic response interpretations beside the one just described. The most obvious of these are different forms of reflex. The stimulus that provokes the response in reflexes is transmitted to the spinal cord, which itself operates to initiate the various muscle movements that constitute the reflex. It is unknown what all the forms of automatic reflex are. This is a gap of significance, especially for those who assert that the sources of human behavior are largely unconscious. It is time to consider a second level of interpretation, that which represents a world of sensation.

Sensational

The second level of interpretation roughly corresponds to Kant's faculty of sensibility. His sensibility was the 'sensation' of the physical properties of a car without the recognition, 'car!' A 'sensational interpretation' has been made when an individual has re-presented the properties of a stimulus in their brain – what it looks, smells, and sounds like. The succession of such interpretations as individuals go about their daily affairs creates a particular re-presentation of reality; a world of sensations – that is, a 'sensational-world'. (A word on nomenclature: sensational re-presentations will be placed between slashes, their cultural signs between quotation marks. Thus a 'dog' is a sign of the sensation /dog/.)

Just how much adults make purely sensational interpretations is unclear. There is certainly a tendency when you see a /snake/ immediately to associate it with a 'snake'; and when you have done this you are at another, third life-world level of interpretation (discussed in the following section). However, there is also a disposition to sense things without having their name explicitly in your awareness. For example, Handel's *Messiah* goes on for hours, and as you listen to it, you may not be continually attentive to the fact that it is 'music'; though it is equally true that at any time you could retrieve into your awareness the fact that you are enjoying fine 'music' rather than listening to a 'speech'. A similar case might be made about visual sensation. For the longest time you just stare at a canvas with /a dark background, pinwheels of color in a turbulent night sky/. Then it hits you – 'painting', 'Van Gogh', '*Starry Night*'.

For much of daily life, you go about sensing things and, as needed, you give these their cultural representation. For example, as I walk on a /cool sunny day/ there are /towering things sticking up out of the ground branching wildly at the top/. Then there is this thing of /roughly spherical things piled on top of each other that forms a horizontal line cutting through the other things/ sticking out of the ground. The transition between sensational – and lifeworlds is easy and almost instantaneous. As I tramp along enjoying the /sunny day/, I become awake to a glorious 'spring'. Next as I stumble towards the /spherical things/ I alert myself to watch out for the old 'stone wall'. Then, tramping on, the 'stone wall' fades from consciousness to be replaced by awareness of an 'apple tree', which has its own array of associated contingents. This slipping into and out of sensational- and lifeworld appears to be one's 'stream of consciousness'.

Considering only sensational interpretation, it would appear that the flow of the neurohermeneutic process that leads to sensational-worlds begins at receptors, with the reception of sound waves or other stimuli bearing information of present realities. These transmit this information along different nerves to different parts of the thalamus. There it is further relayed to the amygdala and the sensory cortex. Sensational interpretation is concerned with what happens to the information that goes from the thalamus to the sensory cortex.

Initially there is a unimodal representing of sensory stimuli in the primary sensory areas. 'Unimodal' here means that only a single sense – such as sight or sound – is represented; with hearing being processed in the primary auditory area of the temporal lobe, vision in the primary visual area of the occipital lobe, smell in the primary olfactory area of the frontal lobe, and taste and touch in the primary somatosensory area of the parietal lobe. Then this uni-modal information is transmitted to activate networks in 'polymodal' association areas, where sights are given sounds, smells, tastes, and so on. These appear located in 'polysensory' convergence zones, at least some of which are in the prefrontal cortex. (Discussion of unimodal, polymodal, and polysensory areas in the association cortex can be found in Fuster 1989: 194.) Activation of the convergence zones seems to give a sensational world its most complete representation in terms of its physical properties.

So, to illustrate: out there is a shaggy creature making noise. The electro-chemical signals of it flow to the visual cortex in the occipital lobe and the auditory cortex in the temporal lobe, where the sights and sounds of it are given unimodal representation. Then these signals flow to networks in the polysensory convergence zones where unimodal become polymodal represen-tations and the sights and sounds of being are represented together. A /dog/ comes to occupy the person's sensational world. It is time to consider the third level of interpretation.

Lifeworld

The third level of interpretation roughly corresponds to Kant's faculty of understanding. However, there can be ambiguity over what constitutes this ability. Understanding, according to a prevailing interpretation of Kant, 'organizes' sensation (Hundert 1989: 22). Of course, the ambiguity lies in the word 'organizes'. There are many ways in which sensation might be organized. However, two of these seem to correspond to what goes on in people's brains and will be said to be the third and fourth levels of interpretation. Let us begin with the third level.

Kant's faculty of sensibility was the ability to take stimuli bearing infor-mation of reality and to represent them as sensation: the physical properties of a /car/ without the attachment of the word 'car'. However, it will be recalled from the section on reflexes that, as soon as I was on the ground, I perceived that the /car/ was a 'car'. Once individuals have made the association – moving object, a 'car' – which is the classification of a present sensation with a perceptual sign stored in neuronal cultural memory, then they have re-interpreted their sensational world and are at a third level of interpretation.

This level of interpretation occurs when signals of sensational worlds go beyond sensory areas to retrieve cultural memories that have been associated with sensations. Sahlins introduced the term 'scanning', it will be recalled from Chapter 2, in his discussion of How Natives Think. 'Scanning' is now given a neurobiological twist, being defined as operations of the neuro-hermeneutic process where signals of a current sensation appear to 'scan' neuronal cultural networks, selecting memories associated with that sensation. Precisely what neurobiologically occurs during these operations is unclear. The preceding also suggests that a distinction should be made here between the part of the memory neural network holding representations of sensations and the part holding cultural representations of the sensations. The former part of the network will be called 'sensational', the latter part 'meaningful'.

Now, sensational memories appear to be stored in neural networks close to the areas in the sensory cortex where sensations of them are first represented. This means that memories of sound are stored in the auditory cortex, of sights in the visual cortex, and so on. Lexical items – that is, words – which are cultural signs, appear stored in the posterior third of the superior temporal gyrus (Wernicke's area). This means that the visual signal of a /car/ might be scanned across cultural memories throughout the cortex to connect a /car/ with a 'car'.

An individual has doubly interpreted when these different, interconnected parts of a memory neural network have been activated; first in the sense of representing the physical properties of reality and second in the sense of culturally representing the physical representation. Reality is 'organized' during this re-interpretation in the sense that it is given meaning. The phrase 'given meaning' refers to that part of the neurohermeneutic process where the shreds and patches of neuronal cultural memory are activated and retrieve the basics and contingents of signs associated with particular sensations.

Metaphorically, it might be imagined that the difference between these two types of interpretation resembles the difference between silent movies and talkies. In silent movies, without any script at the bottom of the screen or any music to help you, things just go on. It is not so clear what they mean. They are herky-jerky flickers on a screen. But in talkies, the words give meaning to things, and so the images take on added life. In Edmund Husserl's terms, this third level of interpretation provides people with what they feel is their 'only real world, the one that is actually given through perception, that is ever experienced and experienceable – our everyday life-world' (1970: 49). Outside my window there are 'trees' and a 'stone wall'. It is 'spring', a 'splendid May' day – with those glorious buds of May. These cultural signs with their individual contingents come at the third level of interpretation and bestow meaning; and meaning gives life, that is, it creates lifeworlds. It is time to go to a fourth level of interpretation, that of desire.

Desire

You, a history professor, are at home in your Park Slope, Brooklyn house that you bought back in the 1960s; when you could still get them cheap because the 'negroes', soon to be 'blacks' and soon to be moved to Bedford Stuyvesant, were still there. It is a starry night – you checked, because you are sensitive. You are reading *Cat on a Hot Tin Roof* and listening to the Hallelujah Chorus of Handel's *Messiah* at the same time, cranked up loud. Your lifeworld is 'hot', full of 'hallelujahs', 'night', and 'stars'; and perhaps 'night' and 'stars' are associated in your memory with Van Gogh's painting *Starry Night*. All in all, as lifeworlds go, pretty swell. Sure beats Bed Sty. Your telephone rings. Your department chair, Stella Paforma, regrets to inform you that your department has been eliminated as part of an exercise in resource allocation. History is history. The jerks in leisure management are going to grow – 'BIG TIME'! Reflexively, you cry out, 'Stella!'

However, immediately your neurohermeneutic process proceeds onto higher levels of the interpretive hierarchy. You scan the stimuli that are the chair's discourse. Your lifeworld alters. 'Hallelujah' is replaced by 'resource allocation', 'stars' by 'leisure management'. Now, you figure out what to do about this new lifeworld, and when you do, you are exercising what Kant would have called your faculty of desire. In rage and fear you figure, 'Gotta get a new job'. This combination of a plan, 'Get job', plus a spritzer of emotion, rage/fear, is desire. It is the fourth level of interpretation. Lifeworlds organize sensations by giving them meaning. Desires organize lifeworlds by providing understanding of what to do about them. Desire is discussed below at some length. However, prior to this discussion, permit a brief aside to make clear how it is *not* conceptualized.

A 'deleuz-ional' approach

There has been an appreciable psychoanalytic tradition, stemming from Sigmund Freud and Jacques Lacan, which, according to Deleuze and Guattari, insists that 'there is only desire and the social, and nothing else' (1977: 29). The tradition plays no part in the approach offered below. Freud's approach to desire is only as useful as his general theory of psychoanalysis. This has been subjected to numerous tests of validation, both in clinical and non-clinical settings, whose findings indicate a validation track record resembling that of Ptolemy's theory of the solar system. The conclusion of these is, 'psychoanalysis rests on no solid evidence' (Crews 1986: 25). It is 'pseudo science' (Cioffi 1970: 471).[13]

This brings us to Lacanian desire, a cocktail of Freud, Hegel, Heidegger, and structural linguistics. Speaking of desire, Lacan reminds his readers that:

> If the desire of the mother *is* the phallus, the child wishes to be the phallus in order to satisfy that desire. Thus the division immanent in desire is already felt to be experienced in the desire of the Other, in that it is already opposed to the fact that the subject is content to present to the Other what in reality he may *have* that corresponds to this phallus, for what he has is worth no more than what he does not have, as far as his demand for love is concerned because that demand requires that he be the phallus.
>
> (Lacan 1977: 289; emphasis in original)

Clearly, the phallus is important in desire, stirring some readers to inquire, what is this phallus? A question to which Lacan gives the following response: 'I shall be using the phallus as an algorithm, so if I am to help you to grasp this use of the term I shall have to rely on the echoes of the experience that we share' (1977: 288). I am sorry, I simply cannot grasp Lacan's phallus. Why?

Alan Sheridan, a translator of Lacan into English, remarks at the beginning of a glossary of Lacan's major terms, 'The short glossary below is not intended to provide adequate definition of concepts. To do so would be quite alien to the nature of Lacan's works' (1977: vii). A second translator and commentator upon his thought makes the point that Lacan showed a 'constitutional predisposition to ambiguity' (Wilden 1981: viii). Both translators are sympathetic to Lacan. However, both say devastating things about him. Wilden indicates there is 'ambiguity' in Lacan's views. Both explain that this permeates his thought because it is 'alien' to him to provide 'adequate definition'. Ambiguity is 'constitutional'.

Now it is folly to make ambiguity 'constitutional' in theory for the reason that something that is ambiguous is uncertain, which means that it is unclear what the theory is about. Perhaps, this is the reason one follower of Lacan said, 'To attempt to sum up his thought seems as impertinent an undertaking as to try to translate certain poems' (Boutonier 1951: 355). However, even though it is impertinent to grasp Lacan's phallus or to 'sum up' his theory of desire, his thought might be abstracted as: speaking obscurely, while carrying a big dick. Thus, psychoanalytic theory is to be praised for recognizing the importance of desire.[14] However, the specifics of its views seem *deleuz*-ional, which returns us to the neurohermeneutics of desire. Let us explore a neurobiological approach to desire.

The neurobiology of desire

Desires involve intentions. The term 'intention' has a long genealogy. It was especially important for Edmund Husserl (1962 [1931]). Remember, Kant had said that 'Life' is acting 'according to the laws of . . . desire'. You get a life by having intentions. Intentions are desire's 'laws'. They are plans or goals concerning future action based upon present lifeworlds and past procedural recipes and strategies stored in neuronal cultural memory. (Intentions will be noted in the text by placing them in double slashes. Thus, the historian whose Park Slope lifeworld was threatened as a result of the chair's information, formed the intention of //getting a job//.)

However, Kant seems to have forgotten something. His actors get a life by acting 'according' to their intentions formulated purely as a result of practical reasoning. Kantian desire is unfeeling, and this appears wrong because, when you intend something, there always seems to be some emotion associated with it. This point has been made with most vigor by Damasio (1994). The evidence that supports this view is the existence of feedback circuits between the prefrontal cortex, the limbic system, and the various modules of reasoning in different areas throughout the cerebral cortex. These are areas of the brain that produce reason, emotion, and their coordination. Because of the existence of such circuits it seems plausible to assert that people's intentions come with an emotion wallop and that it is these two, in conjunction, which constitute desire.

Different thinkers at different times have suggested that people's actions are primarily guided not by desire but by 'will', 'purpose', 'goals', 'motives' (in the case of Weber), or for that matter even 'passions'. The term 'will', especially, has a reputable lineage, playing important roles in the work of thinkers as varied as Hume, Schopenhauer, Dilthey, and Nietzsche. However, I shall not use the term because of connotations it has in everyday speech. Here it is the 'faculty of conscious and especially deliberative action' (*Random House Dictionary* 1967: 1634). As the preceding makes clear, this usage of will does not involve emotion, and people's actions involve feeling because, when stimuli flow into the brain, they cannot avoid the structures producing affect. So action does not result from any purely unfeeling triumph of the will. Terms like 'motive', 'purpose', and 'goal' seem equally void of emotional significance, so they seem equally unhelpful for signifying the chief instigator of action.[15] If humans act with feeling, then the term that designates what produces action should indicate this. Desire, like a cheap perfume, reeks of emotion.

Hume classified desire as one of the passions (1739: 277), which raises the question, why not assert that it is passion in general, rather than a specific passion, desire, that drives people to do their deeds. However, just as concepts such as will, purpose, and goal founder on the side of being too unemotional, so passion errs on that of being overly affective. The term 'passion' pretty much means pure emotion, uncut by any reason. Yet even the heart has its reasons; which is to say, there is no emotion without its rationale. Strikingly, then, humans are driven by desire – impassioned reason or reasoned passion. Desires, then, are a fourth level of interpretation, where persons neuro-hermeneutically interpret their lifeworlds to formulate intentional and emotional re-presentations of what to do. When individuals possess such re-presentations they might be said to achieve understanding of the meaning of their worlds.

It might be asked whether emotion or intention is more important in desire. Because the neurobiology of the relationship between emotion and reason is only just beginning, this question does not appear answerable at present, though the following speculation may be of assistance. Some desires seem dominated by emotion. For example, if you are a peasant in some Latin American country whose daughter is butchered by a paramilitary group, then your desire to //get revenge// may become a raging passion. On the other hand, you wake up in the morning, sleepy, and lurch off to brush your teeth. There is not a lot of emotion in your desire to //brush teeth//, though you feel you should do it.

There is a position, championed by Rolls (1999) that helps us to confront this question. Rolls considers emotion in terms of reinforcement history. Specifically, positively rewarding reinforcement history is emotionally pleasant, while negatively rewarding reinforcement history is emotionally unpleasant. This means that different realities, understood here as reinforcement histories, can create different emotions and different emotions can select different intentions. The crux of this view is that emotion *both* selects and motivates intentions. Consider first events in the world that have been positively rewarding. Such a reality provokes pleasant feelings. Intentions are selected to maintain those feelings, and their maintenance motivates implementation of the intention. However, a reality that has been negatively rewarding induces unpleasant feelings, and intentions are selected that reduce or avoid the negative rewards, and implementation of these intentions motivates by eliminating unpleasant feelings. Thus the appropriate question to raise when considering desire is not whether emotion or intention is more important, but what are the roles of the two; and, in the position just presented, emotions select and motivate intentions which are procedures to achieve rewarding and avoid unrewarding realities.

For example, in the United States the reality of having 'pots' of money is positively rewarding. There are BMWs, grand estates in the countryside; gracious apartments on Park Avenue; getaways in Provence, Tuscany, and Neustadt; blonde trophy wives with taut bodies; muscular boy toys with slender hips; deferential servants, furs, designer clothing, booze galore, other drugs, art, restaurants, and so on. Such a reality is one somebody with a good job can feel good about. They intend to have it. So they spend time figuring out – that is, reasoning – how to get it. They figure out how to get higher-paying jobs. They figure out how to invest in the market. They figure out where to get places where real estate is appreciating. They feel good about these 'get rich' schemes that are the great American desire of //making it//. This poses the question, how does the neurohermeneutic system produce desires?

Working memory, as discussed in Chapter 3, appears to answer to this question. Remember that 'working memory' was first proposed in the 1970s because neuroscientists recognized that what went on in short-term memory was not just remembering things that had recently happened, but involved 'thinking and reasoning' (LeDoux 1996: 270). Working memory might be envisioned as the blackboard of the brain 'working' on its present lifeworld to figure out what to do about it.

Baddeley's model of such memory hypothesized that it 'comprises a central "attentional control system" supplemented by two principle slave systems, one of which, the "articulatory loop" is responsible for the active retention of speech based information, whereas the other "visual-spatial sketchpad" is capable of setting up and manipulating visual images' (1988: 178). According to Baddeley, 'the heart of the . . . model' is in the attentional control system and 'is the central executive' which 'is assumed to integrate information from the slave systems and from long-term memory, and to play an important role in planning and controlling behavior' (ibid.: 178).

Some explanation is required to clarify how this model, with its unfortunate terminology of 'slave systems', delivers desire. Working memory may be thought of as being comprised of three systems, one of which controls the activities of the other two. The latter systems are the 'slaves'. The former system exhibits 'executive control'. Further, there is, as Kosslyn and Koenig put it, 'an interplay between information that is stored temporarily', presenting some portion of a lifeworld, and 'a larger body of stored knowledge', from memory (1992: 406).

The central executive controls these two bodies of information. Smith and Jonides (1999) discuss what is meant by executive control, but emphasize that there is considerable debate concerning this term. Control, however, certainly involves directing the operation of the slave systems in the 'blackboard' of the working memory to plan and control action. This would involve the brain 'performing mental arithmetic, reading, problem-solving and reasoning in general' (Kosslyn and Koenig 1992: 406). Thus, the central executive retrieves remembered information into awareness to calculate plans. Such calculation is precisely what Kant, in *The Critique of Practical Reason*, would have called practical reason and which Baddeley calls working memory. Here, then, is a memory worked over to make plans: what you plan is what you intend, and intentions are the basis of desire.

Another New York City police action illustrates how working memory might operate. On August 9, 1997, a Haitian, Abner Louima, beaten and bloodied by the police, was taken into the 70th Precinct station house in Brooklyn. Officer Volpe, and one other cop, who brought him in, had unfinished business. They marched Louima into a toilet. There Officer Volpe further beat Louima; reaming a broken broom handle up his anus, and then shoving the handle covered with Louima's own feces and blood into his mouth. This caused injuries to Louima's rectum and bladder necessitating three operations and two months' hospitalization. It was all a case of mistaken identity. Volpe thought Louima had punched him during a fracas outside a nightclub and had become 'enraged' (*New York Times*, May 12, 1999: A22). However, Louima had not punched the officer. Volpe reported in court testimony that he was 'mad' at Louima because of the punch and that he 'intended to humiliate him' (*Washington Post*, May 28, 1999: A35) by sticking the shit-covered broomstick in his face. So Volpe's desire involved an intention to //humiliate// driven by a feeling of rage. However, the desire I am interested in is not that of Officer Volpe but of Officer Turetsky, who was in the station house when Volpe performed broom-handle sodomy.

Let me explain why. New York City police, as do other police forces throughout the United States, have a 'code of silence'. This is a part of their locational procedural culture, one shared with criminal organizations. Specifically, it is taboo to provide information to legal authorities concerning illegal actions of colleagues. Cops do not 'rat' on cops. However, two days after the Louima incident, Officer Turetsky ratted and provided evidence against Volpe, breaking a taboo of his culture. Why should he desire to act in such a manner?

Officer Turetsky's desire will turn out to not be culturally deviant but, in order to explain why, let us think in terms of his working memory. Under questioning about the incident, Turetsky's central executive retrieved from his long-term memory into his working memory an image of 'Officer Volpe moments after the alleged assault, swinging a broken broomstick as if it were a sword' (*New York Times*, May 15, 1999: A13). His 'speech-based articulatory loop' retrieved the memory that Volpe 'did not speak' as he came by waving the stick. Officer Turetsky said, 'I thought that this was very unusual' because Volpe was 'very outgoing, and usually liked to be the center of attention' (ibid.: May 13, 1999: A29). Thus, Officer Turetsky's working memory placed Volpe at the scene of the attack, with the weapon, acting suspiciously.

But, perhaps, it was something else in Officer Turetsky's long-term memory, there because of an aspect of his locational culture, that led him to break the code of silence. According to his rabbi, Officer Turetsky 'believes in the Talmud's message'. Now, according to this same rabbi, the Talmud makes 'integrity' the 'prerequisite to justice'. Further, the rabbi mentioned, concerning Officer Turetsky, 'I've discussed these beliefs with him, and he always struck me as someone who takes these values seriously' (*New York Times*, May 15, 1999: A13).

These 'values' are locational contingents in the neuronal culture of Officer Turetsky and are concerned with 'justice'. The officer's religious location seems to have added to his knowledge of the meaning of justice, because he was a Jew who had 'discussed' this cultural representation with his rabbi. Perhaps, the basic procedural meaning of 'justice' – that Turetsky might have shared with Volpe, of Italian, or with Louima, of Haitian, backgrounds – was to //do right//. However, Officer Turetsky's rabbi says that for a Jewish person to //do right// in this situation they must act with 'integrity' – which meant telling what actually happened that night. 'Integrity', then, was a locational procedural contingent, which his rabbi says he took 'seriously'.

There may well have been another cultural sign operative in Officer Turetsky's case, that of 'well-being'. Here we are dealing with a basic meaning, shared by many in the United States, that is part of an *individualism* schema in US culture. The procedural basics of 'well-being' are to 'watch out for number one'. Otherwise put, this means that an individual acts to help another only if so doing helps 'number one'. This means that protecting a corrupt cop by not ratting only goes so far. If not ratting gets 'number one' in trouble, forget it; why 'shit your pants'? Now the Louima incident was being investigated not only by the New York City Police Department but also by the FBI, which meant that if you hid information, you ran the risk of being federally indicted for obstruction of justice. Turetsky was one of those investigated. Perhaps, as he was being questioned, his working memory retrieved the procedural culture of 'well-being' that told him that he would most definitely 'shit his pants' if he persisted in the code of silence, thereby compromising the interests of 'number one'.

There is no evidence of what actually went on in Officer Turetsky's working memory as he worked over the memory of that evening. So one can only speculate on his desire to defy the code of silence. However, the following seems plausible: his central executive retrieved a sensational-world of that August evening which interpreted Officer Volpe's actions in the station house. This sensational-world included a /waving stick/ and /not talking/ and was re-interpreted to provide a lifeworld that represented Volpe as 'acting suspiciously'. Then, on the basis of this lifeworld, Officer Turetsky's working memory calculated what he desired. From his long-term cultural memory, the central executive retrieved the message that his 'integrity' and 'well-being' depended on his reporting these actions. When this occurred, Officer Turetsky had arrived at a fourth level of interpretation. He understood his desire. Guided by the pleasant emotions of achieving integrity and maintaining well-being, he intended to //rat//. What neurobiology operates during working memory to represent such desires?

Remember that Chapter 3 reported that the prefrontal cortex (PFC) operates 'in . . . working memory' (LeDoux 1996: 273), and, because it does, it is 'sometimes referred to as "the organ of civilization" . . . where Plans can be retained temporarily when they are being formed, or transformed, or executed' (Miller et al. 1960: 207). Remember further that the PFC included the dorso-lateral, the orbitolateral, and the ventromedial cortex in association with the anterior cingulate cortex. Now if the 'Plans' of the previous quotation are understood to come with their feelings, then the PFC is the neurobiological structure where desire is formulated. Because of these neuronal pathways, especially with those to the amygdala, it 'selects behavior patterns on the basis of reinforcement history' (ibid.: 145).

Remember, finally, it is not known exactly how these different parts of the PFC 'work' during working memory. However, taken together they exhibit executive control. It is possible that the dorsolateral PFC, which does the 'nuts-and-bolts' job of thinking, signals the operation of various probabilistic, deductive, and other calculations in their respective areas of the cerebral cortex to establish the plans that are intentions. It may be that the anterior cingulated cortex, as the brain's 'error detector' device, monitors how these intentions are being implemented. It could be that the orbitofrontal PFC, with extensive feedback links to the limbic system, signals the emotional content of these intentions, making certain that they seek 'good' and avoid 'bad' rewards.

Possibly the ventromedial prefrontal cortex integrates 'the functions' of the orbitofrontal and dorsolateral cortices with 'the rest of the brain' (Pribram 1997: 360). The preceding should be seen as speculation – nevertheless speculation encouraged by current findings.

So, in summary, what is known and unknown about desire? It is known that people act upon their desires. It is strongly suspected that these desires are formed during working memory through the operation of the PFC. It is equally known that it is unknown how the different structures in the PFC 'work'. This means, in agnoiological terms developed in Chapter 2, that there is a crucial gap in the knowledge of the neurohermeneutic process that operates at the level of desire. Nevertheless, the following vignettes continuing the stories of Musa Kabir and Ahmet, begun in the first chapter, illustrate how working memory might create desire. Let us begin with Musa.

Two vignettes

Remember that Musa Kabir and I conducted research together among the Abu Krider? We were an odd couple, wandering from village to village until we came to the one with *masass*.

Here his entire temperament altered. He was debonair and a bachelor, and normally at dusk it was goodbye Steve, hello young ladies, and perhaps some *niknik* ('intercourse'). But at Goz ed-Debib, Musa suddenly became nervous and fearful. He set up his cot in the same compound that I was in, and did not leave to enjoy the pleasures of the night. Rather, piously, he contemplated the meaning of ancient *Time* magazines. I could see nothing different about this village. Indeed, there was a charm to it – low mudbrick buildings, with the most elegant architecture I had seen in Chad, were laid out along the banks of the Logone River. Large herons would glide through the golden light of dusk to their nests in huge cotton trees that stood sentinel at each end of the village. Finally, at a loss to account for the change in Musa, I asked him, '*Shenu?*' ['What's up?']. He whispered, '*Masass!*'

This, it turned out, was a form of sorcery where the sorcerer was supposed to kill you and then, after you were buried, go with other sorcerers to exhume your body and consume it in a feast of necrophagic cannibalism. The category *masass* was a part of Musa's perceptual neuronal culture. The village we were in, according to him, was full of people who practiced *masass*. Now you could tell if a person was going to practice it on you if they were nice and looked at you. People were being terribly nice to Musa. All this knowledge about *masass* was stored in Musa's neuronal culture. None of it was stored in mine. So when I glanced at the people in the village and they stared back, they looked like ordinary people. But when Musa looked at those same folk and they returned his gaze, he saw something else. Where I saw 'ordinary people', his brain had taken the same sensory stimuli and retrieved cultural memories of *masass* and that 'those practicing *masass* who are nice to you will eat you'.

His working memory had made an interpretation of this lifeworld. It was one of monsters seeking to kill and consume his body in a necrophagic orgy. His amygdala and orbitolateral cortex might have chimed in at this point with a feeling of horror. His PFC retrieved the procedural cultural memories that pertained to addressing *masass*. He remembered a recipe involving a medicine for protecting himself against the sorcerers and was soon consuming it. But the basic procedural recipe for protection against *masass* was to get away from the practitioners. If they could not smile and be nice to you, then they could not get you. Perhaps, his PFC signaled to parts of the brain doing calculations and found that if we left the village, the feeling of horror would be gone, along with the negatively reinforcing stimuli. Musa now understood what to do about his lifeworld. He formed the intention of //leaving//. He expressed the desire, 'Steve, nemshu keské keské' ('Steve, let's split'). We did.

Let us return to the story of Ahmet and Amina, also begun in the introduction. Their story might be told in the form of a causal string, and I shall conjecture about how two of the knots on this string were tied. Remember that Amina was beautiful and that Ahmet was a bit of a loser, a diffident young man who peddled minute quantities from his turned-over box. Their story starts with the events just before Amina left Ahmet. I do not know precisely what occurred at this time as I was in the capital buying supplies. However, Amina had seemed more sequestered than other young women of her age in Bémbassa. She was also ill prior to leaving Ahmet. So she may have left because she felt overly constrained by him Alternatively, she may have left because of her health, and a belief, reported to me, that Ahmet made her 'luck disappear' (nasip goto). I do not know exactly what precipitated her leaving Ahmet, crossing the river, and returning to her father. However, there is a starting E-space1, events just prior to her departure that was followed by a subsequent E-space2, her departure.

The next events in the story were those of Ahmet's breakdown. Remember, this came in the form of his racing naked in an elephant-infested, burning bush. This event should be recognized to be that in E-space3 of this causal chain. In E-space1 events went on that seem a cause of those in E-space2, Amina's departure, which itself became events that acted as a cause of events in E-space3, Ahmet's breakdown. The events in the second E-space that actually provoked the breakdown are unobserved because I was still away.

However, I returned to Bémbassa just after the breakdown and went, as soon as possible, to see him. Earlier, older men and women had consulted with each other and decided that a satega was needed. A satega was the generic term they used for a 'ritual'. The particular ritual they were performing was one that was believed capable of exorcising shetani from his body. Shetan is a widespread term among different Muslim ethnic groups in Chad. Some folk used it to mean 'devils'. This seemed to be a more learned use of the term. Ordinary Barma seemed to understand it in a slightly more disembodied sense, as 'malevolent entities'. The villagers had decided that the satega they would perform was one that had the ability to make the shetani leave Ahmet's body. The curing ritual, then, was the major event of the fourth E-space.

When I saw Ahmet at this time the curing ritual was in progress. As I approached his house, mallams (Islamic ritual specialists) were sitting near his door. They were chanting. At least some of what they chanted came from Koranic verse; though other parts seem to come from somewhere else, perhaps purely Barma religious belief. Once past the chanters, inside the house, my eyes were blinded by the abrupt transition from brilliant sunlight to deep shade. However, it soon became clear that Ahmet was on his side on a mat. Sitting around him were old women (*mobelo*). They did not chant; they gossiped in familiar, cheerful fashion. Every once in a while an old hand reached out casually and patted some part of Ahmet's body.

This was scrunched up in a fetal position. He did not seem to be talking. At the time I thought he looked catatonic, but he could well have just been deeply humiliated and staggered, too terribly depressed to bother to talk. But he must have been able to feel and hear. Closest to him, at the very margins of his body, were the grannies with their patting hands and familiar banter. This seemed at the time almost to reconstruct the protected and secure intimacy of infancy. Then, from outside, Ahmet could hear the solemn chanting. He would have known that these were words with *dono* (power), because they were sacred ones with the ability to make him better. Indeed, after a brief time, Ahmet was better. Looking wan, without Amina, who never returned, he was back to peddling behind his overturned cardboard box. The events of the curing ritual would have been the fifth, and final, E-space in our causal string, and this story has a happy ending.

The progression of five E-spaces is a temporally ordered sequence: E-space1, pre-departure events; E-space2, the departure; E-space3, the breakdown; E-space4, the curing ritual; and, finally, E-space5, the cure. Events in the different E-spaces of this causal string are, what was termed in the introduction, string being, with events in antecedent spaces strung to those on subsequent ones. I can speculate upon what knotted the last three E-spaces together.

Let us begin with the knotting of E-space3 to E-space4. People from Bémbassa told me over and over again that Ahmet was '*mardan ngollo*' ('big sick') and that this was a '*shokul hanna shetani*' (a 'thing of *shetani*'). These people saw a broken-down Ahmet. These sights formed a sensational world interpretation of him. They then used their PFC to interpret such a sensational world by categorizing it in terms of their perceptual neuronal culture. Ahmet's problem was one of a person who was sick because he had been attacked by *shetani*. Villagers' association of these cultural symbols with their sensational-world interpretation of Ahmet created a higher lifeworld interpretation of him.

With this lifeworld interpretation in their memory, their PFC retrieved from their procedural neuronal culture what to do if a person was in Ahmet's situation. This retrieved the memory that you give a *satega*. So they formed the intention of giving a *satega*, which was something that they felt *pusa* ('good') about. When this occurred it meant that those in Ahmet's community had reached the highest level of the interpretive hierarchy. They had interpreted their desire, and what they wanted was //a satega//.

Why the curing ritual worked is unclear, though perhaps two events in it were crucial. The first was the laying on of hands by the nattering grannies.

The second was the chanting of the powerful words. As a result of these, Ahmet's own cultural neurohermeneutic system may have operated in the following fashion. When people lay their hands on you, either in a massage, or something more intimate, it produces a pleasant feeling of relaxation. It is likely that the grannies' laying on of hands altered the emotional feelings in Ahmet's sensational world. He would have felt soothed. It should be emphasized that the curing ritual went on for days, which means that the soothing effects of the grannies was prolonged. So it can be conjectured that after a while Ahmet felt better in his sensational world.

All the time during the laying on of hands, Ahmet would have heard the *mallam*'s chanting. Reaching his ears would be sound waves which would be transduced into electrochemical signals that would eventually arrive at his PFC, which could retrieve perceptual neuronal cultural memories that the chanting has a supernatural power to cure. Ahmet might well have made a lifeworld interpretation to the effect that '*Allah* is helping me'. His working memory might then have scanned his procedural culture to find out what you do in such a lifeworld. He would have found a procedural strategy, 'Live your life according to the Koran.' This might have produced a desire, one he already felt good about, because of the grannies' hands, of going on with his life; and, indeed, Ahmet did go on with his life. Let us proceed to generalize a bit on the relationship between cultural neurohermeneutics and causation on the basis of these illustrations.

Cultural neurohermeneutics and causation

Before addressing the role of cultural neurohermeneutics in connecting space across time, it is helpful to review what has been said about the interpretive hierarchy. First, it should be recognized that as one travels up the hierarchy there is increasing brain involvement. Automatic interpretations occur without great involvement of the cerebral cortex, for the most part. Sensational interpretations take place in the posterior lobe of the cerebral cortex in the different sensory cortices. Lifeworld interpretations occur in the sensory and associational cortices throughout the frontal and posterior lobes as well as in the limbic system, which is largely subcortically located. Finally, the interpretation of desire heavily involves the PFC plus all of the brain regions mentioned above.

The question might be posed, how confident is one of the existence of *this* hierarchy? Let us begin at the bottom. Certainly, humans exhibit automatic responses such as those described in the text. However, humans undoubtedly exhibit other automatic responses and a total inventory of what these are, and what portions of the brain are involved in them, is currently unknown. The preceding, however, in no way invalidates the judgment that there is a level of automatic response with little cortical involvement. It is simply not possible to evaluate the importance of these types of responses.

Equally certainly, people form physical representations of the realities they encounter and associate these with emotional and cultural memories. So people do appear to have sensational- and lifeworlds. However, the question could be raised, are these two sorts of interpretations truly separate? Is it not the case that immediately upon having sensations of a reality, a person culturally and emotionally knows that reality? Such an observation suggests that there are no sensational-worlds independent of lifeworlds.

This question is usefully addressed neurobiologically, and the biological answer to it involves knowing whether the circuits that provide the cultural and emotional associations of sensations operate after other circuits have created the sensations. It would appear that this is the case with regard to cultural associations, because first the stimuli of a reality are transmitted to the appropriate sensory cortices and, second, on to the association cortices, where they are given a cultural representation. First, you see a /dog/ in the primary visual cortex of the occipital region. Second, the signals of this representation are relayed forward to the association cortex where 'dog' is stored in neuronal culture.

However, the situation is less clear with emotional representations. Though there is extensive feedback between the limbic system and other parts of the cerebral cortex, it is also the case that limbic system circuits operate in parallel to those in the cerebral cortex. This means that it is possible that persons could have emotional representations of a stimulus, if the parallel circuits of the limbic system work more quickly than the cerebral cortex, prior to cultural representations of them. The exact structure and functioning of the circuitry linking sensation, emotion, and cultural representation is unknown, so in terms of neurobiology it is unclear how well emotion fits the proposed interpretive hierarchy. Though it does seem to be the case that by the time a sensation has been culturally constructed people often have their feelings about it.

Lastly, how plausible is a level of the interpretation of desire? Certainly humans plan and, arguably, those plans have emotional associations. This suggests a level of interpretation where people figure out what they desire. There may be some who insist that planning can be a matter of calculation, with no emotional strings attached. It does seem that the degree to which there are emotional commitments to desires varies. Many Americans are pretty emotional about 'making it', whatever 'it' might be. Fewer work up the same degree of feelings about flossing. However, assertions positing utterly no emotional associations with intention seem implausible. Such a position asks that the parts of the PFC involved in emotion turn off with regard to intentions. There is evidence to the contrary that this does not occur. Given the preceding, it seems that some sort of interpretive hierarchy such as that proposed earlier is plausible.

A final question needs to be addressed concerning the interpretive hierarchy. This is whether operation is always initiated by an immediate external stimulus. The answer to this question would appear to be in the negative. It is possible for a person, in the absence of immediate stimulation from E-space, to retrieve sensational memories and, with them, their cultural and emotional associations, and to thereby place a lifeworld in the I-space of their working memory. Further, it is possible for the PFC to calculate something with regard to this lifeworld, which, of course, is to formulate a desire. A few weeks back, in the tranquility of a library, with my eyes closed, my mind conjured the image of my sister in Venezuela, a lifeworld, and a pleasant one. So, then I planned how to get there (such as make reservations, check about shots, and so on) to implement the desire to //get there//. Now there was no immediate stimulus that prompted this interpretation of desire, though my wife had been reminding me for weeks, 'Steve, Steve, we've got to visit Venezuela'. This suggests that there may be few desires that come purely out of internal I-space operations of the neurohermeneutic system.

So it appears that there is a neurohermeneutic system performing a neurohermeneutic process that includes running an interpretive hierarchy. This system is something material; gelatinous globs of neural tissue. These globs are touched by – in the sense of being bombarded by photons of light or molecular waves of sound – events in reality, transducing them into stimuli. Realities transduced into signals are then shipped off to the brain, where they are represented a number of times in different ways ultimately to make desire, whose signals are transmitted to the body's muscles to make action, which action does something to the first reality, making a second reality. This process is entirely material. Material realities in the first reality connect with the neurohermeneutic system that, in turn, connects with the second reality, which is equally material. A first reality is an antecedent E-space; a following reality is a subsequent E-space; and the neurohermeneutic system is a connector, physically binding antecedent realities in one time and space with their subsequents, making possible space–time travel.

Remember, it was said that the neurohermeneutic system was a structure with three parts – the antecedent attachment device (AAD), the transforming device (TD), and the subsequent attachment device (SAD) – which was why it was able to perform as a connector, creating causation and, thus, making string being in the social monism. The AAD took information about antecedent events along its afferent pathways to the TD. The SAD took transformed information from the TD along efferent pathways from the pre-motor cortex to the muscles. However, we did not know very much about the TD. Now we know a bit more. The TD is an interpretive hierarchy – operating largely, though not entirely in the case of automatic interpretations, in the PFC, association cortices, and the limbic system – that takes perceptual signs from neuronal cultural memory to construct lifeworlds and from these to calculate intentions that come with an emotional wallop. Now intention packed with an emotional wallop is a desire, and these, metaphorically speaking, might be imagined as the 'arrows' that the cultural neurohermeneutic system shoots across space to connect antecedent with subsequent E-spaces.

Consider the antecedents and subsequents that have been used to illustrate the chapter's argument. The antecedent reality in the case of Amadou Diallo was the movement of a dark man in a dark place. The subsequent reality was a dead Amadou. The arrow was the quick and dirty interpretation by the cops' neurohermeneutic systems that produced the automatic desire //shoot//. The antecedent reality in the world of Officer Turetsky, that evening in the 70th Precinct station house, was the activities of Officer Volpe. The subsequent reality was Officer Turetsky telling his questioners all he knew about Officer Volpe. The arrow was Officer Turetsky's desire to //rat// produced by his interpretive hierarchy, which was supplied by his neuronal culture with promises that he would have his 'integrity' and 'well-being' intact if he ratted. The antecedent reality in the village of Goz ed-Debib was the villagers being nice to Musa. The subsequent reality was his departure. The arrow was Musa's desire to //leave// produced by a neurohermeneutic system whose neuronal culture warned Musa of *massas* and a hideous death if he stayed. Finally, the antecedent reality in Bémbassa was Ahmet's illness. The subsequent reality was the curing ritual for him. The arrow was the villagers' desire to hold a *satega* produced by their neurohermeneutic systems, whose procedural culture told them, //Hold a *satega* for the ill//.

Perhaps a skeptic might complain that cultural neurohermeneutic systems only account for ordinary events of everyday life, not real history. With this in mind, consider Waterloo: the antecedent reality was of the Emperor Napoleon with an army. The subsequent reality was of a beaten man in desperate flight. The arrow was the operation of the interpretive hierarchy in Wellington's neurohermeneutic system that produced a desire to //first defend, next attack//. Indeed, cultural neurohermeneutics is a golden bow, lofting arrows of desire in the present, made from cultural memories of the past, into the future; and this is what makes history, be it that of an Ahmet or a Napoleon. It is time to draw this chapter to a conclusion.

CONCLUSION

> Fundamental: 1. serving as, or being an essential part of, a foundation or basis; basic underlying.
>
> (*Random House Dictionary*, 1967: 574)

Lévi-Strauss had insisted that there were 'fundamental structures of the . . . mind'. But he was more interested in what they did than in what they were. Bourdieu offered his *habitus* as a fundamental structure, but he too, like Lévi-Strauss, was preoccupied with what *habitus* did, to the detriment of what it was. This chapter has argued from the most diverse sources – Enlightenment philosophers, like Kant and Hume; neuroscientists, like Fuster and Baddeley; and cultural anthropologists, like Tylor, Tyler, and Geertz – that the material structures of the cultural neurohermeneutic system operate as an interpretive hierarchy that physically connects past with future structures.

A 'fundamental' is the 'basis' of something else. One point is utterly certain: without the different organs of the neurohermeneutic system – PFC, sensory cortex, amygdala, hippocampus, and so on – people do not represent reality. There are no automatic responses, no sensational world, no lifeworld, and no desire. People cannot act. If they cannot act, the future cannot be connected with the past. The neurohermeneutic system is the physical connector, the subway tracks of structural causality, running from the past to the present to the future of the social monism. As such, it is 'the fundamental structure of the . . . mind'. So now the 'road movie' that is the argument of this text has visited a twilight zone, fought a ghost, worked free of some cement of the universe, and, just now, fired a golden arrow. It is time to finish by cultivating a garden of Boasian social anthropology.

Part III
Coda

Chapter 6

What neurohermeneutics is not and is

Is not a biological *über*-determinism; is a knotty causation

> Pangloss sometimes said to Candide, 'All events are interconnected. . . .'
> 'Well said', replied Candide, 'But we must cultivate our garden.'
>
> (Voltaire, *Candide*)

With those words Voltaire ended *Candide*, one of the great modern 'road shows'. This chapter and the following one review some of the more general points argued along the stops of the present road show in order to contemplate what it might mean to cultivate in a neurohermeneutic garden of string being. This speculation commences by noting our road show's two most general conclusions.

The first of these is ontological. The reality in which people are involved is a social monism composed of E- and I-spaces. I-spaces make connections between E-spaces making string being. Neurohermeneutics is the investigation of what makes connections between events in E-space. The second conclusion is a contribution to neurohermeneutics, and is that a cultural neurohermeneutic system, operating through an interpretive hierarchy, is a connector linking antecedent and subsequent E-spaces. Remember that this generalization offers a causal account of making connections between earlier and later regions of time and space, and so its virtue is that it helps explain how social being is more like a movie than a fading photograph.

The following pages place neurohermeneutics within a fuller context by identifying the 'not' and the 'is' of such an approach. When addressing 'not', the discussion will be of what neurohermeneutics is not. When expounding upon 'is', the discussion will be with what the approach does concern itself and, hence, of its most sweeping characteristics.

IS NOT AN *ÜBER*-DETERMINISM

Neurohermeneutics is concerned with formulating and validating generalizations that involve neuronal culture and the neurohermeneutic system. This means that there is an interest in culture and biology, which further means that it might well be construed as some form of cultural or biological *über*-determinism. Nothing could be further from the truth. Now is the time to lay out the nots. Neurohermeneutics is not a cultural *über*-determinism. Nor is it a biological *über*-determinism in either Hobbesian, sociobiological, or reductionist forms. But the reader may be straining their memory wondering what an *über*-determinism is. In order to unravel these 'nots', let us introduce this concept.

Generally, 'Determinism is the thesis that all events and states of affairs are determined by antecedent states of affairs'. Subsequent events or states of affairs are determined by 'antecedent causes' (Mautner 1996: 137). Neurohermeneutics, as will be argued below, is a determinism. It is not an *über*-determinism. Such determinism is a rhetorical style in service of gargantuan deterministic claims. '*Über*-determinism' will be defined as insistence – in rhetorically extravagant, though often imprecise terms – that one category of causes above all other causes is somehow *the* determinant of what happens. Theology has often insisted upon *über*-determinism. In medieval Christianity, for example, you became ill, God did it. You committed a crime, God did it. You believed in God, God did it.

A danger of *über*-determinisms is that they tend to create the under-*mensch* because they discourage curiosity. Edelman, for example, back in the first chapter announced the 'beginning of the neuroscience revolution' that he claimed would be 'the largest possible scientific revolution' (1992: xiii). Hidden here was an *über*-determinism because the study of neuroscience, and neuroscience alone, was going to explain revolutionary amounts of things. Now the brain is an important structure, but it connects with other structures, about which Edelman seems incurious.

Not a cultural *über*-determinism

There is a tendency in some cultural analyses towards an *über*-determinism. In such accounts the biological and the social are either irrelevant or caused by the cultural.[1] A problem with these cultural analyses can be grasped if readers consider, for example, the assertion: Native Americans scalped their enemies because they had a procedural cultural recipe, which insisted that combat was good if it terminated with the scalping of a foe. This proposition was one I encountered a number of times growing up in New England. It was used to differentiate the Indians from us. Mrs Hosmer said one day in the fourth grade of the Louisa May Alcott School, after we had practiced 'duck and cover' preparing for the possibility of a nuclear attack, that 'They scalped, the savages. We buried, like proper Christians.'

Now it was certainly true that some Native American groups, between the seventeenth and late nineteenth century, believed it was good to scalp, and so they acted to do so. But if the analysis ends here, one does not learn that these practices appear to have begun in New England because British settlers as early as the 1600s paid bounties on the scalps of their enemies; enemies made in part because of competition over the beaver and other North Atlantic trades. The point here is that something cultural, the valuing of scalping, was part and parcel of an early modern social structure that involved Native Americans as well as the French and the English.

The social in the northeastern region of North America in early modern times included a developing capitalism based upon the fur trade. In this trade, English merchants paid their Indians (largely Iroquois) for beaver pelts which they had trapped, while French merchants did the same with their Indians (largely Hurons and Abenaki). The merchants, then, resold the pelts to hat manufacturers in Europe. Because *tout le monde* had to have their hat, demand for beaver hats was vigorous; so that, generally speaking, the more the beaver were hunted, the greater was everybody's profits. There was a problem. Beaver could not reproduce fast enough to meet the demand for the hair on their corpses. This was especially true for beaver resident among the British and their allies. This fostered an Anglo-Iroquoian policy of seeking new beaver supplies by the seizing of their competitors' beaver-hunting grounds. This led to conflict between the British and their allies versus the French and their allies (Wolf 1984). Payments for scalping were a way used by the British to reward their fighters. The cultural here, valuing of scalping, is more completely understood when it is recognized to be a component of something social, the capitalistic fur trade. The preceding illustrates that, if one studies only the cultural, one's level of understanding is less – that is, cruder – than if one seeks to understand the role of the cultural in the social of which it is an aspect. Mrs Hosmer only told us about scalping, the cultural. She never let us in on the secrets of beaver, the social. Now, there is nothing in the social monism that privileges the cultural as *the* cause of what occurs in there. In fact, because the social monism includes cultural, social, and biological realms, generalizations seek to understand all of these realms. There is nothing in the cultural neurohermeneutic system that privileges networks of neuronal cultural memory over all other networks. Rather, adequate understanding requires knowledge of how the different neuronal circuits within the brain, a system of systems, operate. However, if neurohermeneutics is not a cultural *über*-determinism, perhaps it is a biological one.

Not a biological *über*-determinism

Biological *über*-determinisms might be thought of as like prime-time television shows. Just as prime-time TV is wildly popular, so is biological determinism. This means that more is at stake in its analysis. The *cri de cœur* of biological determinism is that different aspects of individuals, societies, and cultures are governed by a chain of determinants that is biological. This is an *über*-determinism because, to appropriate a phrase from Marxism, in the last instance it is all fixed by biology. You get ill, your biology did it. You commit a crime, your biology did it. You believe in God, your biology did it. There is a considerable latitudinarianism in *über*-biological determinism. Below, three of its variants are considered, beginning with an earlier Hobbesianism.

Thomas Hobbes (1588–1679) was born in the year the Spanish Armada threatened invasion, and lived through a time of terrible strife – including the civil war between Puritans and Royalists that led to the beheading of a monarch. The times were truculent. This truculence was part and parcel of Hobbes's personality; in fact his sovereign, Charles II, called him 'the Bear' for his fractious way. Something in Hobbes's temperament disturbed his contemporary Descartes who, in a 1641 letter to a friend, resolved, 'I think the best thing would be for me to have nothing more to do with him' (in Martinich 1995: 10). The Bear may have put Descartes off, but he has had a deep influence, based upon his understanding of human nature, that continues to this day.

Hobbes concluded, in *Leviathan*, 'that in the nature of man, we find three principall causes of quarrell. First, Competition; Secondly, Diffidence; Thirdly, Glory' (1651: 185). The consequences of 'quarrell' are a *bellum omnium contra omnes*, a war of all against all, and the purpose of the social or the cultural was to regulate as best possible this reality. Thus a human nature (that is, a biology based upon 'quarrell') leads to a human condition involving 'quarrell' which leads to institutions like the Leviathan state that adjust to this quarreling. This is an *über*-determinism because everything pertaining to humanity follows from a pugnacious human nature.[2]

Neurohermeneutics is not Hobbesian. Human beings are not driven by nature driven by 'quarrell'. It is certainly true that the limbic system, especially the amygdala and the hypothalamus, make it possible for people to be angry and aggressive. However, most people most of the time are not angry and aggressive. This is true because the Hobbesian view of human nature ignores what Daniel Dennett has called the 'Great Encephalization' (1991: 190). This was an enormous growth in brain structure that occurred roughly between *Homo habilis* 2,300,000 BP and *Homo sapiens* 150,000 BP in human evolution.

The parts of the brain that were added were the association areas, especially the PFC, and their reciprocal neuronal connections with the limbic system. The point here is that, as far as neurohermeneutics is concerned, Hobbesian *über*-determinism has got its neurobiology wrong. It is ignorant of the Great Encephalization, and so does not recognize that there is a considerable neuronal circuitry in the cortex that can modulate 'quarrell'. If this is the case, then, one should be bearish on the old bear's views on the biology of human pugnaciousness. It is as much a part of human nature not to 'quarrell' as to 'quarrell'.

Perhaps, it might be imagined, that neurohermeneutics is favorable to sociobiology. Sociobiologists take over where Hobbesians left off. Hobbes asserted

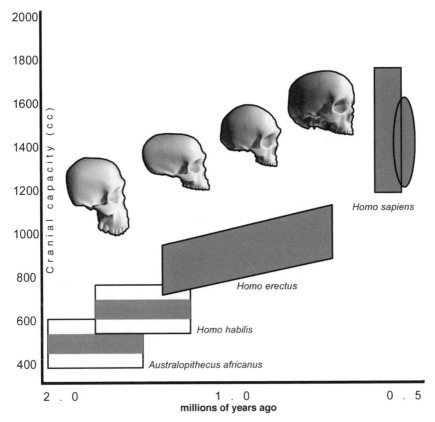

Figure 6.1 The Great Encephalization
Source: Edelman (1992: 50); *Artist:* A.N. Reyna

that human beings have a particular human nature, but gave no explanation of what caused that nature. Sociobiologists – in two central texts E.O. Wilson's *Sociobiology* (1975) and Richard Dawkins' *The Selfish Gene* (1976) – get more specific. Individuals, societies, and cultures are 'governed by a chain of determinants that runs from the gene to the individual to the sum of the behaviors of all individuals' (Lewontin et al. 1984: 6). Their position combines Darwinian with Mendelian perspectives to explain the creation of human nature. Specifically, Mendelian principles of heredity explain why genetic variability occurs in human populations. Darwinian natural selection acts upon this variability to favor the reproduction of those genes that are best adapted to the environments in which humans evolved. This pool of genes, which has survived the test of natural selection, is human nature and causes, directly or indirectly, such properties of individuals as intelligence, such social properties as crime, and such cultural properties as beliefs related to gender.[3]

There is a considerable literature expressing misgivings about sociobiology. These studies tend to fall into two categories. The first category is of investigations that demonstrate a poor validation record for sociobiological generalizations. The second category is of studies that reveal a conservative bias to sociobiological generalizations which show that the rich and powerful as well as the poor and weak are the way they are because of their biology. The politics comes in because, after all, it's in their genes and what can you do about that? So sociobiology is both unpromising and promising. On the basis of the facts, its generalizations are unpromising. On the basis of its politics, it promises to help keep the poor, and others who are disadvantaged, secure in their disadvantage.[4] But sociobiology claims to derive its positions from sound theory. After all, no generalizations would seem approximately truer than those of Darwinian evolution. However, the view that genes either directly, or somehow in some 'last instance', determine behavior seems to fly in the face of a truth of human evolutionary biology.

Certainly in lower orders of animals genes have some influence on particular behaviors. Entire species have built into them by their genes a few behavioral tricks concerning how to address reality. Sea slugs, for example, do not have many tricks; but they do have the trick of doing something when the water temperature is cold and, then again, something else when it is warmer. Birds have more tricks; most famously that of migrating when the air temperature goes down, though it is known that much of what occurs during migration is learned. However, neither birds nor sea slugs went through the Great Encephalization. This, we have just recalled, added major association areas, especially in the PFC, and the neural networks connecting these new areas to the older, previously evolved areas like the limbic system. This means that the dorsolateral, orbitofrontal, and medioventral cortices of the PFC must have greatly evolved. It means that the dense feedback networks running back and forth between the PFC, especially the orbitofrontal cortex, and amygdala were put in place. These new cortical networks are a fact of the Great Encephalization. As facts they cannot be ignored. They are terribly important because they are the material structures of a new way in which animals deal with reality.

Great Encephalization neuronal networks greatly improved human cognitive capacities. The nature and magnitude of this enhancement is a matter of speculation. Nevertheless, the following assertions seem plausible. The added association areas are places of memory storage. So hominids acquired improved memories, which meant that they could learn more about the worldly and emotional sensations in their lives. Further, the new association areas increased the ability to think categorically with symbols. This had immense implications for the acquisition of culture. Animals that cannot think categorically cannot put sensations or signs into categories, because they cannot think in categories. Animals that can think categorically can begin to associate sensations with signs, and signs with schemas; and when they do, they can begin to remember them. This meant that hominids could acquire extensive semantic – that is, cultural – memories.

Further, enlargement of the left dorsolateral cortex, as well as the associative areas in the occipital, temporal, and parietal regions allowed hominids to improve their calculations, especially probabilistically and deductively, concerning present sensations and past sensations and signs. Thus expansion of the different parts of the PFC, together with the anterior cingulate cortex allowed greater ability to have culture, to calculate, and to control calculations that use cultural memories to address present realities in the future.

These changes in brain structure had implications for the development of the interpretive hierarchy proposed in the previous chapter. They meant that a lifeworld could now be interpreted from a sensational one, and then a world of desire from the lifeworld. Dogs like Sebastian had a rich sensational world. *Homo habilis*, at the beginning of the Great Encephalization, probably equally had a rich sensational world. But neither Sebastian nor *Homo habilis* probably had much of a lifeworld. There were only rudimentary communication skills. This meant that there were no elaborate sets of schemas based upon signs associated with sensations. The improvements to executive control during the Great Encephalization made it possible for elements of past cultural memories to be retrieved into working memory and for calculations to be made on these to create intentions that people felt good about confronting present lifeworlds. In other words, the Great Encephalization made possible interpretations of desire.

Certainly, *Homo habilis* had a neurohermeneutic system that could make automatic and sensational-world interpretations. Let us call such a hermeneutic system 'acultural'. However, after the Great Encephalization, the creature, whom we earlier termed *Homo sapiens kantoboasensis*, had evolved. This animal could make interpretations of lifeworld and desire. Because it could do this, we said it had a cultural neurohermeneutic system. Certainly, no other creature on earth can make such interpretations. Possibly, if life is unique to this planet, no other structure in the universe can so address reality.

Critically, the existence of the cultural neurohermeneutic system changes human nature because it builds the signs and schemas of culture *into* their neuronal networks. Learned cultural memory is part of their biology. In sum, a key fact of human evolution was the emergence of a particular adaptation for addressing reality. This adaptation was the cultural neurohermeneutic system. Now genes have a role in making the neural networks that are the cultural neurohermeneutic system, but it is this system in humans that goes about the business of addressing reality, *not the genes that made the system*.

To illustrate the point being argued, consider that this morning I strode into a room noteworthy for the bathos of its decoration and a hulking, savage drill. The drill's operator politely, but imperatively, said, 'Open wide, this won't hurt', before applying it to shoot currents of pain throughout my body. I am terrified of pain. But while the pain raged, I docilely sat and 'took it'. Not once did I make an attempt to rip the driller's throat out. Why?

Am I some sort of obtuse sea slug who only reacts to changes in water temperature? Some might say, 'Eureka, that's it! We knew all along. Reyna *is* a sea slug!' Others, however, might observe that the interpretive hierarchy in his cultural neurohermeneutic system interpreted what was and what to do about it. His perceptual cultural memory of past such sensational worlds reassured him – that is, created a lifeworld that what was the now, the driller, was a 'dentist'. His procedural cultural memory informed his intention about what to do about what was: 'Do not butcher the gentleman because, as you may have noticed, he keeps your bloody teeth from rotting out.' So I paid the person for inflicting pain. The preceding illustrates that genes were not *über*-determinants of how I treated the dentist. In fact, they were not even determinants. So sociobiology seems an unpromising biology, one that demands that something known to be very important in human evolution – the Great Encephalization – is ignored. Neurohermeneutics is premised on understanding the implications of what sociobiology chooses to ignore.

Permit a final 'not'. Often biological determinisms are criticized for being reductionist. According to Flew reductionism: 'is any doctrine that claims to reduce the apparently more sophisticated and complex to the less' (1976: 279). Herbert Spencer (1850), followed by Alfred Kroeber (1917), in warning against reductionism when theorizing about the human condition. They found that there were inorganic, organic, and superorganic realities. Inorganic realms were those of atoms and the like, and were explained by physical laws. Organic realms were on a more complex level, being that of life forms, built up from combinations of inorganic substances. Biological explanation was appropriate at this level. Superorganic realms were at a still more complex level, being that of social and cultural forms. Sociocultural explanation was appropriate at this level.

In such a hierarchy of complexity, a reductionist position would be one that sought to explain a higher level of reality in terms of a lower one. It might, for example, seek to account for social and cultural phenomena in terms of biological ones. Biological determinisms like sociobiology are just this sort of reductionism, because what happens at the level of the social and cultural is ultimately explained at the biological level by the genes. Spencer and Kroeber both believed such reductionism to be wrong.

Neurohermeneutics is not a reductionism. It is the reverse of such a doctrine. It is an attempt to account for a social monism that includes biological phenomena like the brain in I-space that are part of individuals who are part of different practices and bundled practices in E-space. It is understood that the cultural exists both in E-space, as discursive culture, and I-space, as neuronal culture. The most complete and, hence, most satisfying theory of the social monism will involve explanation of how the different regions of structure, the spaces, all influence each other. This is an 'integrationism', not a reductionism.

IS A KNOTTY CAUSAL DETERMINISM

So, if neurohermeneutics is not a cultural determinism, not Hobbesian, not sociobiology, not a reductionism, what is it? Simply put: it is a knotty causal determinism. Such an approach is a determinism, concerned with complexity; a materialism; a structuralism; and a particular understanding of causation. These are the five 'is'es of neurohermeneutics. How it approaches these is reviewed below. Let us begin with determinism.

Determinism

The present age, at the dawn of the new millennium, is one where nothing seems to work — be it capitalism, communism, religious fundamentalism, or poverty alleviation programs — and so a hefty percentage of humanity resides within (to use Max Weber's famous image) an 'iron cage' of poverty, violence, and disease while ecosystems crumble and hopelessness mounts. Skepticism in such an age is like a powerful diet drug that people pop, pop again, and then see if they can inject, all to reduce the craving for hope. Hope for nothing, and nothing is hopeless. It is the age of the anti-Bacon, and one such anti-Baconian, Jean-François Lyotard (1979), has been good enough to inform us that skepticism extends to metanarratives and, of course, determinism is a grand metanarrative. Neurohermeneutics is a determinism, posing the question, why adopt such a theory in an age of skepticism? The short answer to this question is that the alternative is unimaginable. Let me explain why.

The argument supporting determinism is a transcendental one. Such arguments answer the question, 'What conditions must be true for a proposition that is already known to be true?' In such arguments, X is the proposition known to be true, Y is the condition or conditions that must be true for X to be true. For example, the proposition, 'under certain conditions making love makes babies', is known to be approximately true. This is the X. Now for X to be true the following condition had better be true, 'Those who make babies must have working reproductive systems.' This is the Y, and Y must be true for X to be true.

The statement 'making love makes babies' is really a causal generalization to the effect that under certain conditions 'intercourse causes offspring'. It is one of a huge variety of such propositions that are formulated because, in the world around us, antecedent events cause subsequent ones. This is another way of saying — and here even skeptics are likely to agree — that events in the world are caused because, if intercourse does not cause offspring, what is it that brings about the relationship between intercourse and offspring? People launch into mumbo-jumbo when they try to imagine alternatives to causality, because the alternatives are inconceivable. The Divine Spirit brings babies; storks bring babies; little tooth fairies – moonlighting – bring babies, all mumbo-jumbo.

So the proposition, 'under certain conditions intercourse causes babies', is an approximate truth. However, a condition that must obtain for this proposition to be true is that events and states of affairs are determined because antecedent events or states of affairs cause subsequents. The point here is that determinism makes sense because causation occurs. Without determinism it is utterly unimaginable how the world makes sense, and one is condemned to live in an iron cage of mumbo-jumbo ruled by spirits, storks, tooth fairies, and the like.

Ever-skeptical readers may wonder whether chance is the alternative to determinism they are seeking and, further, whether the acceptance of determinism means the loss of free will. Let us take up the case of chance first. One day in the 1970s I stepped out of the Printania *supermarché* in N'Djamena, Chad's capital, and who should be going by in a motorcade but President Gaddafi of Libya. I waved. No response. Nothing seemed to determine this encounter. It was a random event, pure chance. However, as was argued in the discussion of causality in Chapter 4, chance is not chance. There was a string of causes and effects that took me to Printania at that hour on that day. I needed food to return to the bush. Equally, there was a string of causes and effects that took Gaddafi to the street outside of Printania at that hour on that day. He needed to get to a meeting with the President of Chad. So there were two causal strings in operation. It was unusual that the causal strings in which Reyna and Gaddafi participate co-occurred, but once they did. Chance, then, is a particular form of determinism in which two or more causal sequences, which do not usually cohabit in space and time, do. The point being made here is that the occurrence of chance provides no grounds for skepticism vis-à-vis determinism. Let us proceed to free will.

Free will and determinism often are presented as opposed doctrines. If all human actions are determined, then, how is it possible for humans to choose and act according to the free dictates of their own wills or, in the terms of neurohermeneutics, their own desires? Some people answer this question in the negative, believing that the existence of determinism precludes that of free will. Such a position on the relationship between determinism and free will is termed 'incompatibilist'. There is a 'compatibilist' position that was famously argued by Kant.

Neurohermeneutics, while critical of skepticism towards determinism, *is* skeptical of free will. The skepticism does not concern whether there is, or is not free will, but whether the concept is useful. The concept is seen to work as a sort of narcotic of modern inequality, which like that of its premodern predecessor 'heaven', helps keep the rich and powerful rich and powerful by reducing desires to challenge them. As the Bobby McFerrin song says, 'Don't worry, be happy.' If you are poor and miserable working to make others mighty, you will get your reward in heaven. If you are poor and miserable making others mighty, you have free will and you freely willed your fate. 'Don't worry, be happy.' Who needs narcotics like free will, except those with a desire to deceive? However, if neurohermeneutics is uncomfortable with the concept of free will, it does believe that choices count in a determined universe.

This is because a 'directed determinism' operates in the social monism. Let us explain what is meant by such a view. Individuals do make choices produced by the connector. 'Choice' in this optic is the operation of the cultural neurohermeneutic system to make desires and actions; actions which are the basis of causal strings. For example, had the Greeks been beaten by the Persians at Marathon (490 BC), the causal strings of Western history might have been different, owing to a flooding of Greece with Middle Eastern institutions and culture. Conversely, had the Muslims been defeated by the Crusaders at Hattim (AD 1187), the causal strings of Middle Eastern history might have been very different, owing to a continued influx of Western institutions and culture. The choices made by the leaders of the Greeks and the Muslims that led to their victories at Marathon and Hattim had immense causal consequences. Properly speaking, these choices were both determined and determining. 'Determined', in that the choices were determined by the operation of the cultural neurohermeneutic systems of the choosers, and 'determining' of the events that followed from the choices. In a determined and determining world a notion of free will is a bit like that of God, in that it has no empirical referents. You cannot observe Him or Her. You cannot observe what it is that might exhibit free will.

However, people can sometimes know in advance what their choices will determine, though this is by no means always so. Certainly, Napoleon did not plan to have a bad winter in Russia, nor did he know he would lose at Waterloo. But one virtue of the various disciplines researching the human condition is that they do at times reveal what different choices causally entail. If you smoke cigarettes, you get sick. Perhaps more to the point, there are studies that reveal an association between poverty and illness. You are poor. You have less access to medical facilities. You get sicker. It is further known that certain policies, such as those favoring state-supported or -run health delivery systems, can alleviate this situation. In situations such as the above, a 'directed determinism' is one where the neurohermeneutic system calculates to determine desires that determine causal strings that will work towards somebody's advantage.

Directed determinisms are important in contemporary social worlds. The wealthy in the United States, for example, know at the start of the third millennium that they will get wealthier if their taxes are reduced. So their agents in places like the Congress and the Presidency calculate desires that direct action to a 'reduced taxes' determinism. Finally, it is possible to distinguish irresponsible directed determinisms. An 'irresponsible' directed determinism is one that determines choices that are determining of benefits to a very few who are advantaged and/or is one that reduces the functionality of ecosystems. It is probably of greater practical import for people to root out irresponsible directed determinisms than to spin spider webs of free will.[5]

Let us recapitulate. Neurohermeneutics is a determinism; one that views chance as an unusual concatenation of causal strings. Additionally, it is a determinism that proposes, because humans have some ability to determine how they are determined, that they should follow a procedural cultural strategy of eliminating irresponsible directed determinisms. So, if neuro-hermeneutics is a determinism, in what sort of a reality does this determinism operate?

Complexity

The answer to this question is, a complex one. Certain social, cultural, bio-logical, and physical scientists began to recognize in the late 1960s that the ways they theorized about the realities they studied simplified them too much. Different thinkers had different over-simplifications. However, there were four that everybody appreciated. The first was that reality was treated as linear, when it was anything but. The second was that reality was believed to be pre-dictable, when it often was not. The third was that reality was treated as if it were a closed system, when it was actually open to a huge number of systems. The fourth was that reality was treated as static, when it was dynamic. This book began by suggesting that I had mistaken social realities in this latter manner, seeing photographs, when what was going on around me was a movie.

So, following these realizations, a number of new theories began to develop which sought to conceptualize more complex realities. There have been three major theoretical forays into the complex. The first of these is systems theory, which was introduced into social thought by Walter Buckley in *Sociology and Modern Systems Theory* (1967). The second was structural Marxism, whose most mature expression, that of Louis Althusser in *Reading Capital* (Althusser and Balibar 1970), was an attempt to revise Marxist thought to account for a more complex social universe. Third, more recently, various forms of chaos theory try to theorize about the order in apparently chaotic complexities (Gleik 1987; Stewart 1989). Neurohermeneutics is an approach that empha-sizes the complex – posing the question, what is this complexity?

Materialism

There are a number of answers to this question. The first of these is that the complexities in which humans find themselves involve material or physical entities. This means that neurohermeneutics is explicitly a materialism.[6] Sociocultural anthropology, especially in the United States, as Mary Douglas recently made clear (1999), reiterating what Marvin Harris has said since the 1960s (1968, 1979), is dominated by idealism. This means that there is a bias against materialism in the discipline. This bias means that it is important to evaluate carefully the strength of the anti-materialist position.

There are often two sorts of arguments against materialism. The first is that social and cultural life is obviously dependent upon ideas, incorporeal abstractions. I shall not repeat all the arguments against such a view presented in the course of Chapter 3. However, the crucial point is that *ideas are material* and come in two physical forms of discursive or neuronal culture; with the former being states of sound or light waves, and the later states of neurons. As you read the words before you, and interpret the ideas they offer, material processes are occurring involving the transformation of patterns of photons in the E-space of discursive culture of the book into patterns of electrochemical signaling in the I-space of neuronal culture in your brain.

If it is insisted that ideas are not operations of photons and neurons but meanings, which have no material existence, then the immaterialist position seems saved. However, any person can conduct the following experiment in their mind. Imagine an idea, like 'dog'. Next imagine taking away the patterns of photons and neuronal firings in the dog's brain. Now what happens? You know what happens: the dog-gonest thing happens. The dog is gone. So this might be called the 'dog-gone' argument because it reveals: no patterns of photons and neuronal firings, no doggie. Otherwise put: no matter, no meaning.

A second argument against materialism is that concepts like that of the physical or material are imperfectly defined because there is no doctrine that successfully accounts for them. However, such a position seems to overlook the obvious. Humans are part of a very material reality no matter how you define matter. They are the parts of their body, material things. They are individuals, material things. They are individuals interacting with other individuals, material things. They are all the gear that humans make and use in the course of their economic, political, religious, recreational, and other lives. They are things that humans do not make but which still contact their bodies, like sunlight, rocks, elephants, what have you. All of this stuff is obviously material, whatever the material might be. Denying the materiality of the human condition because you do not know fully what the term 'material' means is a bit like denying the existence of the brain because you do not fully understand it. Neurohermeneutics, then, involves determinism concerned with a material complexity.

Structuralism

This complexity is one of structures. Structural Marxists believed, as Althusser put it, that the 'complexity' involved 'the determination of the elements of a whole by the structure of the whole' (Althusser and Balibar 1972: 187). They further believed that this recognition was an 'immense theoretical revolution' (ibid.: 182). Neurohermeneutics agrees with these two points so that, in some sense, it is a descendant of such Marxism, though there are points of disagreement. One of these concerns what is determinant 'in the last instance' in the 'structure of the whole'. Althusser and Balibar had said in *Rethinking Marxism* that the economic structure was determinant 'in the last instance' (ibid.: 99, 216–24). Actually, Althusser's views on this subject were conflicting. Earlier, in *For Marx*, he had said that the 'lonely hour of the "last instance" never comes' (1986 [1968–9]: 113). Then, towards the end of his life, he said during an interview that 'everything can be determinant "in the last instance"' (in Navarro 1988: 35). How does one deal with such inconsistencies? One way would be to insist that understanding of the structures in which humans are a part is rudimentary. Thus proclamations in this, the first instance of determination of what might in the last instance be determinate, are a form of premature (theoretical) ejaculation. Though, if anyone believes, in the halcyon days of capitalism at the beginning of the new millennium, that the economic is not hugely important, then they are living in the land of mumbo-jumbo.

Neurohermeneutics has another bone to pick with structural Marxism, though this may be more a disagreement with a Gallic approach to theory in the human sciences. Consider that the parts of individuals are structures, with one part, the brain, being the most complex structure, pound for pound, in the universe. Individuals bundled with other individuals are structures. The gear that is associated with people – their buildings, airplanes, clothing, tools, weapons – has its structures. The parts of the natural world that come into contact with humans – heat, light, sound, and so on – each have their own structures. No one, I believe, in their right mind would deny that these structures are realities.

The old British social anthropologists wanted to study the individuals bundled together with other individuals in this cosmos of structures. They called their object of study 'social structure' and what they proposed to investigate, at least according to Radcliffe-Brown, were 'the . . . actually existing relations . . . which link together human beings'. These were 'an actually existing concrete reality, to be directly observed' (1940: 190). This meant that the monographs of the social anthropologists tended to be rather descriptive. From the perspective of Lévi-Strauss, when he was explaining his notion of structure, the British were too concrete, too matter-of-fact in a way that was atheoretical. What social structure needed to be of theoretical worth was abstract 'models' (1953: 375) of the concrete. Anybody who has read the structural Marxists – with the exception, sometimes, of Godelier and C. Meillasoux – knows that they took Lévi-Strauss to heart. Reality in their work, and this is especially true of Althusser, is, to appropriate Ryle's phrase for new intellectual duty, the 'ghost in the machine'. However, I believe the old social anthropologists were absolutely correct. Any structuralism worth its salt must begin by recording what is. On the other hand, Lévi-Strauss was absolutely correct. You do not have theory unless you have abstract generalizations. The point here being that soaring Gallic theorizing grounded in Anglo-Saxon observation will be required for an agnoiologically credible theory of the role of neurohermeneutic structures in the social monism.

During the first half of the twentieth century two structuralisms comfortably dominated social science. One was British social anthropology, the other was Talcott Parsons' structural functionalism. Though there were differences between these, they tended to coexist mutually and provide a theoretical consensus – call it a problematic or a paradigm – about the nature of human social being. This consensus came apart between the 1950s and the 1980s during a new Thirty Years War, a war of the structuralisms. There were Lévi-Straussian, Lacanian, Bartheian, Althusserian, and, in his early days, Foucauldian structuralisms. Then it stopped. Post-structuralism was declared. Structuralist combatants were demobilized and sent home. But the post-structuralists should be ashamed because they are neo-Canutians. Declaring the end of structuralism in a world of structure is like joining Canute and ordering the tide not to rise. Remember, as we saw in Chapter 3, even so convinced an anti-structuralist as A.L. Kroeber admitted that 'everything' had structure. So what sort of structuralism is neurohermeneutics in a post-structuralist world?

The answer to this question is that it is a structuralism that seeks to account for the openness, non-linearity, dynamics, and unpredictability of complex realities in the social monism. Let us begin by considering openness. This discussion will lead us to causation and the way non-linearity, dynamics, and unpredictability are conceptualized. Buckley first emphasized the notion that social structures were 'open' in systems theory.

An 'open' system, or structure, for him was one where the structure not only participates 'in interchanges with the environment, but that this interchange is *an essential factor* underlying the system's viability, its reproductive ability, or continuity, and its ability to change' (Buckley 1998: 44; emphasis in the original). Structural Marxists took this assertion one inferential step further. If the 'interchange' between the structure and its environment is '*essential*', and because the environment, too, has its structure, then the structure and its environment are really linked structures; that is, structures of structures. Althusser called this 'the unity of a structural whole', and this was explicitly what he meant by 'complexity'. He further believed that the complexity had 'what can be called levels or instances which are distinct and "relatively autonomous", and co-exist within this complex structural unity, articulated with one another according to specific determinations' (Althusser and Balibar 1972: 97).

Neurohermeneutics accepts the assertions of both the systems theorists and the structural Marxists, thus maintaining that humans live in material structures of structures. However, a further conclusion to be drawn from this affirmation is that, because structures are interconnected, they are part of each other – that is, they are a monism; and, further, because there are many structures which are parts of each other, this monism is determinedly social – that is, it is a social monism.

Once it is understood that the complexity in the social monism is of a structure of structures, two sorts of investigations become vitally important. The first is how the specific structures in the structure of structures are organized and operate. Such an investigation might be said to be into the 'autonomy' of the structure. For example, specific studies of the New York legislature, and of the New York police, and of the prison system would be analyses of how each of these goes about their business autonomously.

The second sort of investigation is of how the different autonomous structures interrelate. The term 'effectivity', a structural Marxist concept, can be applied to describe this sort of investigation. Studies of the 'effectivity' of a structure are those that establish the approximate truth of how, how much, and why one structure influences another in the social monism. The New York state legislature's making of criminal laws explains, in part, how the legislature influences the police and prison systems. Specifically, it is the case that the greater the number of activities that are criminalized, the greater are the numbers of criminals to be apprehended by the police, and the greater are the numbers incarcerated by the prison system. Such studies of effectivity reveal how much the operations of one structure relate – that is are 'relative' – to another. The autonomy of a structure is increasingly 'limited' as more of its operations are dependent upon other structures. It might be said that the autonomy of the New York police and prisons is severely limited by the legislature's activities because these determine how many will be criminalized and what resources will be available to operate against the criminalized.

The result of analyses of the autonomy and effectivity of structures in the social monism is the knowledge of what, in a larger sense, they can do; with the idea here being that what gets done in a complexity like a social monism is what the component structures actually do. Theory is abstract generalizations concerning these doings. This volume has explored something of the autonomy and effectivity of various structures in I-space, hypothesizing, theoretically, that what they do is to operate a cultural neurohermeneutic system. It has said nothing of the autonomy and effectivity of structures in E-space. This is considered elsewhere (Reyna 2001). Perceptive readers will have grasped that the study of the effectivity occurring within structures of structures concerns structural causality, which brings us to the way neurohermeneutics addresses the question of causation.

Causation

Remember that a knotty approach to causation was formulated back in Chapter 4. Causation *is* connection in this approach. This means, in the con-

text of social monism, that events, which are part of the operation of a structure, are connected to other events, themselves part of the operation of
another structure, and that the events in these two structures exhibit their
connection because of causation. Hume had explained this causation as a constant conjunction that he thought of as a 'habit' of the mind. We offered a
materialist approach to constant conjunction that built upon Wesley Salmon's
and Althusser's understanding of causation. String being in this view is causal
strings. A string consists of units of antecedent causes that leads to subsequent
effects, which effects in turn become causes that lead to their own effects. The
different units of cause and effect were thought of as 'knots' that string being
together – that is, make connections.

What ties the knots? The answer to this question is that we conceived of
a unit of cause and effect as antecedent events that migrated to become
subsequent ones. This movement was made possible by the existence of a connector. The connector was some physical structure, or structures, that has the
ability to transform antecedent events migrating into it into subsequent
events migrating out of it. Connectors tie the knots. A key point to grasp here
is that effectivity concerns causation and is the study of structures knotted to
other structures in the social monism.

One of the implications of this knotty view of structural causation is that
the social monism is a dynamic structure of structures. The general meaning
of dynamic is that events are in motion. Motion means that events in an antecedent space lead to those in subsequent ones. The fact that the social
monism is *continually* in motion means that it is dynamic. Some events are
always moving to become other events because, so long as humans are alive
and awake, their connector is always turned on, and when the connector is
turned on, it is knotting antecedent events to subsequent ones. The preceding
means that the old distinction between statics and dynamics, which originally
came from the physical sciences, and which positivists like Comte said made
for fundamentally different static and dynamic theory, is not very useful.
There is only motion as connections are made, and knots are tied, and the
causal strings of the social monism grow longer and longer.

The knotty view of structural causation also has implications for linearity
and non-linearity in the social monism. The concept of linearity, like that of
dynamics, is subject to a number of definitions. Two of these will be relevant
here. A first understanding of linearity concerns the directions that causal
strings follow. This will be termed 'directed' linearity. A directed linear causal
string goes in a straight line. Of course, the notion of a 'straight line' is pretty
wobbly – that is, ambiguous. In order to reduce this ambiguity, directed
linearity will be defined in terms of intransitivity between events. This means
that if A goes to B and B goes to C, then A only gets to go to B and B only
gets to go to C. Linearity within the context of causation refers to causal
strings where something in A causes B (knot 1), something in B causes C
(knot 2), something in C causes D (knot 3); and knot 1 always precedes

knot 2 that always precedes knot 3. Non-linearity refers to causal strings where a subsequent knot has the ability to cause something in a knot that was previously an antecedent one. This, for example, is a situation where A causes B and B turns around and causes something in A. Non-linear causation will be said to be 'dialectical' when it occurs in E-space and 'feedback' when it occurs in I-space. Thus, the amygdala and the orbitofrontal cortex are causally connected in I-space by feedback causation, because what happens in the amygdala causes what happens in the orbitofrontal cortex and vice versa. Labor and capital are causally connected in E-space by dialectical causation.

It would be an over-simplification of the complexity of the social monism to say that it exhibits only non-linear causation. There is also linear causation. For example, within the I-space of the digestive system events in the mouth act as causes that migrate to the stomach, leading to digestive effects there. These digestive effects in turn become a cause that migrates from the bowel and leads to eliminative effects there. This causal string is one where eating is a cause of digestion and digestion a cause of elimination; and the events in the string never normally work the other way around. Such a causal string is intransitive. It is linear. Similarly, in E-space in the causal strings that involve what in the United States is euphemistically called the 'criminal justice system', events among the police cause certain effects in the judiciary. These effects in turn act as causes which have certain effects in the penal system; and the police have got to act before the judiciary can act and the judiciary has got to do what it does before the penal system can do what it does. This causal string is also intransitive. It is also non-linear.

There is a second meaning of 'linear' familiar to those who use linear equations that is also of interest. This usage of the term is concerned with how much causes influence effects and will be termed 'quantitative' linearity. In linear equations, 'linear' means having the same proportional effect on a sum as upon each of the summands in a series.[7] The emphasis in this view of linearity is upon having the *same* proportional effect. For those investigating effectivity within the social monism, linearity is understood to involve causal situations where the same causes have the same proportional effects. For example, in certain societies, prior to the introduction of modern health and sanitation measures, the sum of births exceeded deaths by roughly the same percentage of the total population each year. There thus might be said to have been a linear causal relationship between births and deaths and popu- lation increase. However, when radically improved health delivery and sani- tation systems were introduced, death rates fell so much that the sum of births exceeded deaths by an increasing percentage each year. Population expanded exponentially in such societies, so that there was now a non-linear causal relationship between birth and death rates and population growth. The point of the preceding is that the social monism's dynamic is especially complex because its causal strings exhibit directed and quantitative, linear and non- linear connections.

Causation can be highly predictable in physical reality: same cause, same effects; split an atom, get energy release. Always. Causation tends to be less predictable in the social monism. Often it seems there is a common cause, and who knows what effect. Put Napoleon at the head of an army, get an attack; put Wellington at the head of an army, get a defense. Here there is the same cause (a general at the head of an army) and different effects: attack, in one case; defense in the other. This raises the question, what explains the social monism's unpredictability? One answer to this question concerns the nature of the connector in the social monism. All causal knots in string being consist of antecedent events in E-space, the causes, which because of the connector, the cultural neurohermeneutic system, are knotted to subsequent events, the effects. It was theorized that there were different sorts of basic, locational, and individual cultural memories in the cultural neurohermeneutic system. These individual cultural memories are likely to be just that, individual, and the singular is difficult to predict. Every person in E-space will have a singular cultural neurohermeneutic system. Thus same causes do not predictably have same effects because the connectors that knot cause to effect are different due to the unique concatenation of neuronal memories in the cultural neurohermeneutic system of each person.

So what is neurohermeneutics? Most emphatically, it is not a biological determinism. In fact it offers an alternative to such determinisms. Rather, it is a part of string-being theory that offers generalizations made by using a knotty structural causal determinism to explain how connections are made in an open and complex social monism. It is time now to consider the sort of discipline anthropology might be, if it studied neurohermeneutics and the social monism.

Chapter 7

A Boasian social anthropology

[B]iological and cultural life is a whole.

(Boas, *General Anthropology*, 1938)

The beginnings of revolutions and ends of books tend to raise the question, what is to be done? Voltaire, at the end of his inquiry into the human condition in *Candide*, suggested to his readers that they should go to cultivate their gardens. Here at the end of *Connections*, I have a similar suggestion. What is to be done is to cultivate a Boasian social anthropology. As was noted in the introduction, this might strike some readers as oxymoronic. After all, practitioners of the two traditions regarded each other with some disdain, each believing they were practicing a different, and far better, anthropology. But readers may recall how, back in the second chapter, the philosopher Mario Bunge asserted that anthropology, because it was the 'broadest', should be the 'central' social science. Of course, it turned out that this was not the case because anthropologists, like youthful lovers, bungled making connections. So readers, the aspiration of this chapter is to persuade you that a Boasian social anthropology is desirable in order to give the discipline its proper, central place.

First, however, we must address a minor stumbling block to this aspiration. Boasian anthropology is in decline, even where it began. US anthropologists were strongly committed to a four-field approach in their discipline by the middle of the twentieth century. This meant that the discipline would involve a unified study of four fields: cultural anthropology, archeology, biological anthropology, and linguistics. It was this four-field approach that defined Boasian anthropology. However, commitment to it has waned in the United States because fewer undergraduate and graduate programs systematically staff with people in all four fields, or require that their students acquire rigorous knowledge of them. The reasons for declining commitment to the four fields are complex, but reflect a rejection of the (subdisciplinary) Other. Rejection occurs because practitioners in the different subfields perceive that the canons of other subfields reduce their own to irrelevance. Rejection is fiercest between biological and cultural anthropology; especially, it seems, in certain Californian universities where bitter intradepartmental wars have split programs into warring factions.[1]

Firing up these factions are the rise of *über*-biological and -cultural stances. The biological anthropologist who is a sociobiologist sees little need to consider culture except as a consequence of the expression of genes. Conversely, *über*-cultural analysts tend to deny any relevance of biology because all things human, even biological processes, are cultural constructs. This means that *über*-biological anthropologists view cultural anthropology as irrelevant to the study of culture; and their *über*-cultural counterparts view biology as irrelevant to the study of biological processes. Such views are hardly likely to make for congenial department meetings. So the old Boasian anthropology is disintegrating, in a world of dueling irrelevancies. What good can come from not letting this disintegration run its course?

The response to this question will have its irony. Boasian anthropology should continue for precisely the opposite reason for which Boas created it in the first place. Boas's original justifications for creating a four-field approach were evident throughout his work but were, perhaps, presented most compellingly in *The Mind of Primitive Man* (1911). Here he made it clear that he was first and foremost interested in opposing the racism prevalent at the end of the nineteenth century. Explicitly, anthropology was to invalidate the racist generalization that 'race causes culture'. This was to be accomplished in two ways. First, evidence was to be adduced which would reveal that there was no relationship between race and culture.[2] Because the concept of 'race' was a biological one, a biological anthropology was desirable in order to have scientists who were competent to make the observations that made the invalidation.

The second way this invalidation was to proceed was to validate alternative, non-racist generalizations that provided accounts of what caused events in the cultural domain. These generalizations were twofold: 'culture is acquired by learning', and 'culture causes culture'. This latter generalization was not as glaringly tautological as it appears; because what was meant by it was that 'certain aspects of culture (understood in the broad Tylorian sense) were the cause of other aspects of culture'. Cultural anthropology, archeology, and linguistics were desirable in order to have scientists who could make the observations that validated these generalizations. So the four-field approach was created to provide credible evidence that there is *not* a relationship between something biological, race, and culture.

I believe that the human sciences require a Boasian anthropology precisely because there *is* a relationship between the biological and cultural, so that if one ignores this relationship one imperfectly explains the human condition. The Boasians ignored questions of causation even though their project was based upon causal generalizations. Social anthropologists, for that matter, also eschewed explicit discussions of causation. This meant that the anthropology that had developed by the mid-twentieth century lacked understanding of how humans go about making connections. Certainly, this tradition of disciplinary ignorance contributed to the incompetence of more recent anthropological theory in explaining the making of connections that was documented in Chapter 2. But making connections is what people do in all places and all times, so the chapters after the second one have sought to help account for how this might be possible.

These chapters argued that people live in a social monism. In this monism, reality consists of things that get connected and things that are the connectors, knotting together strands of string being. So in the end, even though the social monism is complex, its analysis is simple. It is interested in explaining the connected and the connectors. What gets connected are the structures that exist in E-space. What do the connecting are the connectors in I-space. E-space is being where there are structures based on individual actions bundled to practices which are themselves bundled with other practices, and one of the actions which occurs in this reality is that of producing discursive cultural texts. Social and cultural anthropologists, together with archeologists and linguists, are needed to provide knowledge of how these E-space structures work.

I-space is being where there are structures that do the connecting. But I-space involves biological structures, especially those of the CNS. This means that biological anthropologists are required to study the connector. Further, however, what is requisite is a new type of biological anthropologist; one interested in the biology of cognition. This is because the connector has been theorized to be a cultural neurohermeneutic system. This is a structure of structures which has built into it neuronal culture. If this view of what does the connecting is to be further explored, biological anthropologists will need to be trained both in neuroscience and culture. Such thinkers might be called 'neuroanthropologists'.

Additionally, what will be desirable in this Boasian anthropology is extensive collaboration between neuroanthropologists and cognitive anthropology. Explanation of the analytic procedures used in Chapters 4 and 5 to formulate the view that a cultural neurohermeneutic system accounted for the connections made in I-space will help readers to understand why such collaboration can be fruitful. These procedures may be said to have followed a 'mind–brain' approach.

Some cognitive anthropologists, such as Maurice Bloch, appreciate that their object of study is the 'mind–brain' (1998: 12). 'Mind', it will be recalled from the third chapter, was the functions performed by the brain; and 'brain' was the neuronal structures that performed these functions. In such an approach mind and brain are the *same thing* differently conceived from functional and structural perspectives. The foundation of such an approach is to reveal how mind and brain are different parts of a common reality, and the key to this is to demonstrate their unification. This involves the formulation of generalizations concerning different functions of the brain, especially of its cognitive functions, and, then, the discovery of whether there are different brain structures that actually perform these functions, and how they do what they do. Thus, when both these research practices are coordinated it is possible to know better how the activities of the mind are unified with those of the brain.

The domain-specific modularity theorists discussed in the introduction – Sperber, Boyer, Atran, Hirschfeld – implicitly take such a mind–brain approach. Mind for them is their generalizations concerning the domain-specific cognition; brain is the different modules that perform such cognitive functions. Perhaps there is difficulty with such understandings of both brain and mind. Sperber's modules are autonomous. Each module appears to do its own thing with a liberal individualism, marching to the beat of its domain-specific function; fully as 'insensitive to central cognitive goals' as a US Republican president is to central planning. This is because, as Fodor explained it, 'I don't see how there could be a module for doing that' (1998: 12), with 'that' being organizing central cognitive goals. Now domain-specific modularists do not really include brain neurobiology in their analyses and, as a result, their understanding of the brain is perhaps a bit behind the times.

The notion that there might be a modular brain was popular in the neuroscience of the 1960s and 1970s, prior to the increased understanding that came about after the introduction of the new brain imaging technologies in the 1980s. These revealed, among other things, the importance of the PFC in planning action. Further, the domain-specific modularists' view that mind is insensitive to central cognitive goals seems remarkably insensitive to evidence that people actually do make plans, calculate strategies, plot intentions, hatch schemes, or what have you.

So the mind–brain approach proposed in this text offers an alternative to domain-specific modularity. Mind in this alternative is an interpretive hierarchy going about its increasingly complex interpretations to arrive at conscious desires – emotionally charged intentions that function to guide action. Brain in this optic is the operation of the different structures – modules, circuits, pathways, and so on – throughout the CNS that operate the interpretive hierarchy, with the PFC being especially important, operating as a central executive to coordinate desire formation. Such an approach to might be called an 'interpretive hierarchy/PFC' theory. In this approach the PFC is a whole gaggle of modules arranged in circuits, which Fodor just could not 'see', that *is* sensitive to central cognitive goals.

The two imperatives, then, of a mind–brain approach are, first, formulate and test generalizations concerning mind, a job for cognitive anthropologists; and, second, do the same for generalizations concerning how the brain minds the store of cognition, a job for neuroanthropologists. However, all observers agree that 'knowledge of the different parts of the brain is still very primitive' (Crick 1994: 89). Some sense of just how much is unknown is important.

Consider, for example, that the amygdala is in some way central to both emotion and reinforcement. However, a recent article asks, 'What is the amygdala?' It answers this question by suggesting that it may be an 'arbitrary name describing a series of structures that are heterogeneous' (Lanuza and Martinez-Marcos 1999: 207). Thus, even though the region where there is supposed to be an amygdala is involved in emotion and reinforcement, maybe there is no amygdala.

Consider, further, the retrosplenial cortex, that is supposed to operate when there are symbols with emotional values. This conclusion was that of Maddock following the review of a number of studies, which led him to conclude that it was 'activated by emotionally salient words' (1999: 310). However, B.A. Vogt, who has researched this area of the brain extensively, has answered Maddock's claim with his own, that Maddock does not know where the retrosplenial cortex is located and, additionally, that, regardless of its whereabouts, 'nothing is known about its function' (Vogt 2000: 196). Maddock has responded (2000: 196) to Vogt's critique by asserting that Vogt does not understand 'the functional imaging literature and the method of meta-analysis' used by Maddock and his colleagues. These debates indicate that neuroscientists squabble over everything in the brain from where the parts are located to what they actually do.

Further, consider five matters that are known. It is known that memory is stored and retrieved in the brain. It is known that memory includes sensations of the world as well as those of symbols. It is known that the symbols are the signs and schemas of neuronal culture. It is known that these signs and symbols become associated with worldly sensations that tell people what is and what to do about it. Finally, it is known that there is no systematic investigation of the role of culture in the brain. So, given such knowledge, it is clear that the type of neuroanthropologists who will be needed are cultural neuroanthropologists.

The problem that the previous three paragraphs expose is that there is an agnoiological hole in the understanding of cognition and culture in the brain. The questions about the location, structure, and function of the amygdala and retrosplenial cortex indicate voids. There probably are amygdala and retrosplenial cortices, but exactly what they do and how they function has not been fully observed, which means that they are voids. Similarly, there are certainly parts of the brain where there is neuronal culture, but just what goes on there is not known. This is especially true, as indicated earlier in Chapter 3, for the PFC. In short, there is another void. A gaggle of voids such as these suggests a hole. Holes, readers will recall from the discussion in Chapter 2, because they were deep spaces of known ignorance, were said to be great places for scientific Vulcans to set up shop.

One type of research project, for example, that could be envisioned would involve collaboration between primatologists, cognitive anthropologists, and cultural neuroscientists. The former would arrive at knowledge concerning primate cognition and culture, especially in primate species like chimpanzees. Cognitive anthropologists would analyze the role of culture and cognition in humans. The goal of these researches would be to discover what is distinctive about human culture and cognition. Then the cultural neuroscientists would explain the brain biology that produced this particularity. Otherwise put, the collaboration of these different subfields of anthropology may fill a hole by completing an understanding of how our connector connects us with the world. Perhaps they would confirm that this connector is a cultural neuro-hermeneutic system operating an interpretive hierarchy.

The preceding suggests that one needs all four fields of anthropology – with cultural and social anthropologists, linguists, and archeologists to account for what gets connected in E-space, and cultural neuroscientists to account for what does the connecting in I-space. This means one needs a *Boasian* anthropology – Boasian in the spirit of the quotation from the *Docturaluk* that began this chapter that, somehow, the biological and cultural are 'a whole'. However, it should never be forgotten that this Boasian anthropology has as its object of study the explanation of how structures of structures go about making connections; which means that this Boasian anthropology is a *social* anthropology. Such an intellectual discipline, its generalizations tempered to truthful edges by the application of agnoiological methods, would be central to understanding the human condition in all places and all times.

Finally, and this gets us into the garden, Edelman believed that the 'neuro-scientific revolution' might be a 'prelude to the largest possible scientific revolution, one with inevitable and important social consequences' (1992: xiii). Edelman's focus solely upon the brain was argued to be the evidence of an *über*-deterministic personality. However, integrative investigations by new social anthropologists making connections between biological, social, and cultural realms in the social monism might just have the desired revolutionary effects. Thus, if you want to cultivate your garden and maybe make a little revolution, get yourself to a honeysuckle or a tamarind. Sit under it, and make Boasian social anthropology.

Notes

1 Introduction

1 Stocking (1965) first described the importance of Boas's Arctic period for the development of anthropology. Cole (1999) has written about Boas's formative years. Müller-Wille (1998) has edited Boas's journals and letters from Baffin Island.
2 One view of social anthropology can be found in Reyna (2001).
3 The approach to abstraction in the text is indebted to Kaplan (1964).

2 Conjectural hermeneutics and 'insurmountable dualism'

1 Some might wonder why Giddens and Habermas are not discussed. This is because, even though their work is of great theoretical import, it has less occupied anthropology than that of those considered.
2 Though I believe science to be an art based upon imagination, this does not mean, as the text makes clear, that all arts are identical. I share with Levine the view that 'Science Isn't Literature' (1994: 65). It is by discovering the differences between different artistic practices that one sharpens the work of particular imaginations. This approach is different from Geertz with his interest in 'blurred genres'. After all, a blur is a blur – something vaguely apprehended.
3 Practicing scientists have not been especially concerned with Truth even though they are keenly interested in truth. Truth, with a capital T, concerns explanations of truth. However, it is fairly straightforward that some statements are truer than others: 'Water freezes at 35 degrees Fahrenheit' is less true than 'Water freezes at 32 degrees Fahrenheit'. Scientific practice is concerned to discover such truths. It leaves to philosophers explanation of why they are True. Philosophers have been in lively debate over the nature of Truth. Recently, correspondence theories of Truth have begun to make a comeback (see Alston 1996).
4 Kant in *Critique of Pure Reason* (1781) was important in establishing the term 'objectivity'. Megill (1994) provides a point of entry into current discussions of it. These tend to be heated. One reason for this is that the term is so polysemic that people employing it are often oblivious to what others mean by it. Cunningham (1973) remains useful for unraveling the term's meanings. Fabian has considered (1971) and re-considered (1994) the analysis of objectivity in anthropology. He believed 'discussions' of the term were absent in 1971, and that twenty years later they were still 'disappointing' (ibid.: 81, 85). O'Meara (2001) discusses the prospects for objectivity in anthropology.

5 This section is based on a literature that is skeptical of Geertz's hermeneutics (see Bazin 1998; Descombes 1998; Reyna 1994, 1997, 1998).

6 Important conjecturalist texts have been those of Boon (1982), Clifford and Marcus (1986), Clifford (1988), Marcus and Fischer (1986), Rabinow (1977), Rosaldo (1989) and Tyler (1987).

7 Pérez-Ramos (1988) is useful for grasping Bacon's science; Faulkner (1993) his project of progress; and Whitney (1986), his modernity.

8 Clarke (1982) discusses Descartes's science, Ariew (1999) his connections with the later scholastics.

9 Practice theory as an explicit theory began in post-World War II France as a structural Marxist project with Althusser's rethinking of the concept of social formation. Classical Marxism understood a social formation to include a base of the mode of production upon which was erected the superstructure. Social formations in Althusser were 'articulations' of different practices (1986).

10 Hénaff (1998: 94–119) has argued that Lévi-Strauss's mind is less vague than Descombes believes. I am not convinced.

11 To be fair to Sahlins, even dictionaries tend to be vague about the actualities of schema. For example, one technical dictionary of cultural studies defines a schema 'as a *model* . . . by which we internalize structure and make sense of an event' (O'Sullivan et al. 1994: 276). An exasperated reader of this definition might ask, a model of what? The dictionary does not answer this question.

3 Confronting the 'insurmountable'

1 The history of neuroscience, especially cognitive neuroscience, can be found in Jeannerod (1985) and Gross (1998). Discussion of EEG is the subject of Kutas and Dale (1997). Neuroimaging techniques are presented in Kandel et al. (1991), and Frith and Friston (1997).

2 A current strand in anthropology urges analysis of 'embodiment' (Csordas 1990, 1994). Embodiment theory is phenomenological and tends to ignore neuroscience. For example, Andrew Strathern's work on the topic mentions the brain on only one page in the index (1996). Merleau-Ponty, a phenomenologist to whom the embodiment theorists frequently refer, wrote that 'It would conform better to the facts . . . to consider the central nervous system as a place where an overall "image" of the organism is developed' (1942: 22). Here Merleau-Ponty indicates that those interested in embodiment should 'consider' the CNS.

3 The PFC is 29 percent of the total cortex in humans, 11.5 percent in chimpanzees, and 7 percent in dogs (Fuster 1989: 5).

4 There is debate on this issue. Recently, Duncan et al. (2000) claim that a region in the PFC is responsible for general intelligence. This finding is disputed by Sternberg (2000) in the same journal in which it is announced.

5 Readers interested in the prefrontal cortex might wish to consult Nauta (1971), Stuss and Benson (1986), Perecman (1987), Fuster (1989), Passingham (1993), Krasnegor et al. (1997), and Roberts et al. (1998).

6 More complete accounts of the CNS can be found in Brodal (1998) and of the cerebral cortex in the fourteen volumes of Jones and Peters (1984–99).

7 A staple of neuroscience has been that, 'At birth, the primate nervous system has virtually all the neurons it will ever have' (Patricia Churchland 1986: 38). Recent research indicates this may be untrue (Gould et al. 1999).

8 The African involved in this incident was Amadou Diallo. His death is described in the *New York Times* (February 9, 1999: A 31).

9 Neuroscientific treatments of memory can be found in Martinez and Kesner (1998), Fuster (1995), Metcalfe (1993), Schacter (1996), Squire (1987), Schacter and Tulving (1994), and Tulving (1983)

10 Deacon (1997) and Pinker (1994) have published useful introductions to the nature and evolution of language.

11 Associationist approaches to memory can be found in Hinton and Anderson (1981); Kohonen (1977, 1984); Palm (1982).

12 Important contributors to a cognitive neuroscientific approach to emotion include A. Damasio (1999), Rolls (1999), Ekman (1992), Frijda (1993), Gaffan et al. (1993).

13 Not all consciousness research is sweet smelling. Purves, for example, remarks that there are a lot of recent 'flatulent books . . . on consciousness' (1999: 370). Influential discussions of consciousness since 1980 include Dennett (1991), Johnson-Laird (1988), Minsky (1985), Penrose (1989), Humphrey (1992), Gazzaniga (1992), Shallice (1988), Kinsbourne (1988), Churchland (1988), Baars (1988), Kosslyn and Koenig (1992), Mandler (1988), Edelman (1992), Searle (1992), Eccles (1989), Chalmers (1996), Crick (1994), Crick and Koch (1992), Weiskrantz (1997), Metzinger (2000).

4 Neurohermeneutics

1 Introduction to work explicating different causal positions roughly from 1950 through the 1980s can be found in Beauchamp (1974), Harré and Madden (1975), Kitcher (1989), Mackie (1974), Suppes (1970), and Wallace (1972). Texts in the social sciences that responded to eliminationist critiques with pro-causal arguments were MacIver (1943) and Sorokin (1943) followed by Blalock (1964) and Simon (1957).

2 Althusser was a Marxist and a long-time member of the French Communist Party. He believed in revolution. This, in conjunction with the fact that he became paranoid and murdered his wife, made him unthinkable to many. There might even be an inclination to classify Althusser with Martin Heidegger and to pair them on a television program entitled 'Good Philosophers Gone Bad'. However, there was a difference between the two. Althusser's problem was that he went insane. This was a tragedy. However, Althusser was never crazy enough to volunteer for duty in a Nazi regime as Heidegger did. There has been some attempt to revitalize the Althusserian tradition (Callari and Ruccio 1996). Balibar (1996) in particular has sought to explicate the notion of structural causality.

3 Spinoza presents his notion of God as the immanent cause of reality in Book I, Proposition XVIII of his *Ethics* (1951). A useful discussion of Althusser's utilization of Spinoza's thought can be found in Smith (1984: 187–92).

4 Dilthey, as far back as 1860, wrote an essay indicating his awareness of Schleiermacher's ties to German Reformation religious hermeneutics, and of this latter's rise owing to the exigencies of challenging the legitimacy of Catholic biblical exegesis (see Makkreel 1975: 259).

5 For general discussions of hermeneutics, consult Bauman (1978), Hoy (1982), Shapiro and Sica (1984), and Wachterhauser (1986), for presentations of Heidegger within the context of other hermeneutics, see Bleicher (1980, 1982). Steiner (1978) offers a fine account of Heidegger's writings. For analyses of the relationship between Heidegger's Nazism and his hermeneutics, see Farias (1987), Wolin (1991), and Rockmore and Margolis (1992). There is an explosive issue here. Is a Heideggerian hermeneutic conducive to Nazi-like ideologies? Löwith, a student of Heidegger's, during a 1936 meeting with him, asked the Hermes of Being about this

matter. Löwith reports that Heidegger agreed 'without reservation' with the suggestion that 'his partisanship for national socialism lay in the essence of his philosphy' (1991: 142).

5 A neurohermeneutic theory of culture

1 Research concerning the cognitive neuroscience of categorization normally involves the study of language. Reviews of these studies can be found in Deacon (1997), Brown and Hagoort (1999), Smith and Jonides (2000), Martin et al. (2000), and Caramazza (2000).

2 There is a critique of the domain-specific modularity theory that questions the innateness of modules (Karmiloff-Smith, 1992; Quartz and Sejnowsky 1997; Rose 1997). So, if Kant's a priori categories resemble domain-specific cognition, then this critique applies to the Kantian a priori.

3 The argument just advanced in the text does not assert that Boas consciously sought to improve anthropological theory by fixing a problem in Kantian thought. Boas was not a close scholar of Kant. He makes no mention of him in *The Mind of Primitive Man* (1938), *Anthropology and Modern Life* (1932), or in the articles collected in *Race, Language and Culture* (1940). Indeed, one wonder's just how much of the *Critique of Pure Reason* Boas actually studied while on Baffin Island. However, when Boas moved away from his original intellectual base in physics, he moved into one that was deeply influenced by Kant (see Cole 1999: 125). My hunch is that Boas acquired in this milieu the idea that minds work categorically. However, once he began to recognize the different ways that Eskimo, Kwakiutl, and Euro-Americans categorized, it became clear that different cultures had different specific categories for classifying experience.

4 Recent significant discussions of the nature of culture begin with Kroeber and Kluckhohn (1952). Since then the following have contributed to continuing debates: Harris (1964), Goodenough (1964), Geertz (1973), Keesing (1974), D'Andrade (1984), and more recently, Gupta and Ferguson (1997), Nuckolls (1998), Bloch (1998), Kuper (1999).

5 Constructivism is currently hotly contested. A good way to build understanding of it is to read some of its classics (especially Schutz 1970; Berger and Luckman 1967), then some overviews (Sarbin and Kitsuse 1994; Watzlawick 1984), followed by works of the antagonists in the contests. Glasersfeld (1995) offers a radical constructivism. Herrnstein-Smith (1997) begs to differ.

6 There is considerable support for the associative nature of memory and Hebb's explanation of it reviewed in Fuster (1995: 22–44).

7 Excellent discussion of the concept of 'schema' can be found in D'Andrade (1995: 122–50). There is deliberation concerning the proper spelling of the plural for 'schema'. Some fancy schemata. I shall follow D'Andrade (ibid.: 124) and simply add the 's' to schema.

8 Permit an aside that shows the relevance of perceptual and procedural cultural signs for discussions of hypocrisy. There is no guarantee that any cultural sign accurately represents and rehearses being. In fact, they often do not. There does appear to be a reality that is pretty well represented by 'dog'. 'Consciousness' is more problematic, and there does not appear to be any reality represented by 'ghost'. The concept of 'hypocrisy' may be proposed as a measure of the degree to which cultural information does not accurately represent realities that benefit certain persons. The more cultural signs misrepresent being in the favor of somebody, the greater the hypocrisy of that information. Racial cultural information which favors certain racial groups over others – privileging for which there is no basis in reality – is

hypocritical. There is ample evidence that information asserting that blacks or hispanics are 'inferior', a sign of perceptual culture, and should be denied good jobs, an intention of procedural culture, has benefitted powerful folk in different ways and at different times. Seen in this light, a racist cultural schema is part of the hypocrisy of the powerful.

9 Throughout much of contemporary anthropology a person judged to be essentialist is considered to have committed a horrible crime. However, there are a variety of essentialist positions, and they cannot all be dismissed out of hand. For example, Saul Kripke (1982) has applied essentialist considerations to issues in the philosophy of logic, science, and language. This work is important. So critics of essentialism need to specify whose essentialism they are against. In the above text my concern is with an Aristotelian essentialism of certain social and cultural thinkers.

10 Has US anthropology encouraged essentialist notions of culture? This is a question whose response requires further research. However, my sense is that the Boasians can be read two ways. When Boas emphasized the historical nature of culture he was taking a fairly anti-essentialist line. Cultural items existed in a population due to their histories. Change the history and they were gone. However, when Kroeber and Benedict began insisting that there were enduring 'configurations' or 'patterns' of culture, they took a more essentialist position. Benedict, for example, in *Patterns of Culture* (1934) seemed to be saying that there was a megalomaniacal pattern to Kwakiutl culture that survived the vicissitudes of history, and was at the essence of the Kwakiutl. So, on one reading, the Boasians were pretty essentialist, on another they were not. This provides grounds for subsequent scholars to take more or less essentialist notions of culture. Current US cultural anthropology is steadfastly anti-essentialist; see, for example, Knauft, who sees culture as 'shifting and contested' (1996: 44). However, there seems to be a vigorous essentialism, especially in conservative scholars outside of anthropology. For example, Huntington (1996), a political scientist, warns of global wars arising from the 'clash' of essentially different cultures.

11 The term 'intracultural variation' appears on one page for a few lines in Tyler's introduction to *Cognitive Anthropolgy* (1969). Intracultural variation plays no part in the substantive analyses of those articles. David Schneider, in a retrospective discussion of his *American Kinship*, is candid about its failings with regard to locational contingents, announcing, 'my claim that there is only one American kinship system tripped over the fact that the "family" means something different to the lower class from what it does to the middle class' (1980: 122).

12 What are the implications of the recognition that neuronal culture is a thing of shreds and patches for the construction of formal cultural models based upon discursive culture? There is nothing in the recognition of individual cultural mobility and particularity that condemns such modeling. However, such models would more accurately account for neuronal culture, and be better able to predict individual action, if they included the patches as well as the shreds. This means that locational and individual contingents need to be built into them.

13 The following works are important in confrontational critiques of Freudian theory: Cioffi (1970), Edelson (1984), Fisher and Greenberg (1977), Grünbaum (1984), Lieberson (1985), Masson (1984), Nagel (1959), Prioleau et al. (1983).

14 Readers may wonder why the criticism of the psychoanalytic view of desire in the text is so severe. A case can be made that psychoanalysts are crooks. Remember that psychoanalysis is a business. It sells a service, therapy, on the basis of its knowledge of the therapeutic benefits of its concepts. It has been known for a considerable period that this knowledge is not validated. Hence, theirs is a therapy based on no particular knowledge of how to cure. So, when they charge for it, they are

paid for a service they do not provide. This is fraud. Fraud is a crime, theft by deception.

15 Nietzsche's concept of will in *Beyond Good and Evil* closely resembles the concept of desire employed in the text. Nietzsche's will involves both 'a commanding thought' and 'the emotion of command' (1973: 300). However, when the person in the street thinks of 'will', it is rarely in the exact, Nietzschean sense. So, because I emphasize the generalization 'no intention without its emotion', I prefer the term 'desire'.

6 What neurohermeneutics is not and is

1 Sahlins verges towards an *über*-cultural determinism in *Culture and Practical Reason* when he insists that culture is autonomous and that it 'constitutes utility' (1976a: viii).

2 Hobbes's opinion of human nature and its impact upon subsequent thinkers is discussed in Green (1993). Johnson (1993) shows similarities – that Hobbes acknowledged in his lifetime – between Hobbes's and Thucydides' views of human nature. Thus, more accurately, Hobbes's biological determinism is Thucydidean. The facts of Hobbes's life would seem to provide evidence against his position. The Bear lived in truculent times, so his bearishness would seem explained by these times and not by his biology.

3 The question might be posed, are Sperber's neo-Darwinists propagators of a socio-biological *über*-determinism? Guille-Escuret (2000) thinks this is so, especially of Hirschfeld. Hirschfeld protests this designation (2000). Further, a statement like Boyer's, that 'evolution is relevant to all domains of culture' (1999: 877), certainly has an *über*-determinist ring to it because it claims that evolution, and evolution alone, is 'relevant' to explaining 'all domains of culture'. Fodor notes that the 'direct evidence' for their views is 'very slim' (1998: 13).

4 Useful introductions to the critical literature on sociobiology can be found in Sahlins (1976b), Montagu (1980), Leeds and Dusek (1981–82), and Kitcher (1985). Lewontin et al. (1984) show how sociobiological notions support conservative agendas. Ferguson (2001) reveals the empirical incredibility of sociobiological claims concerning warfare and crime. Sociobiological claims concerning intelligence have been made frequently. Generally, these argue that intelligence is overwhelmingly acquired through genes and that poor 'races', usually those of people of color, do not make the genetic grade for higher intelligence. Lewontin et al. (1984: 83–139) is useful for countering Jensen's (1969) iteration of this view. Frazer (1995), Gould (1996), and Jacoby and Glauberman (1995) demolish the Herrnstein and Murray (1994) reiteration of it. Graves (2001) does the same on the latest Rushton (1995) re-reiteration.

5 Hook is a useful introduction to debates concerning free will and determinism (1961). Double (1991) takes pro-free-will views, and claims to refute them and then does the same for free will. Wright (1974), Dennett (1984), Honderich (1993), and O'Connor (2000) have made contributions of note. 'Contemporary philosophers appear to be divided into roughly equal camps' in the compatibalist versus incompatibilist controversy (O'Connor 1995: 4). Carnois (1987) offers an excellent assessment of what has arguably been the most influential compatibilist position, that of Kant.

Crick (1994) and Eccles (1982, 1989) offer neuroscientific accounts of free will. Both suggest that the 'seat' of free will may be the anterior cingulate cortex. However, regardless of what its exact functions may turn out to be, my judgment is that it is part of the machinery of the neurohermeneutic system which is part of the structures that determine human action. The *eccles*-iastical position is compatibilist. He states:

> To claim freedom of will does not mean that actions are uncaused. It means that some are not caused or controlled solely by purely physical events in the neuronal machinery of the brain, but that the events in this neuronal machinery are to some extent modulated by the ego or self in the mental act of willing.
>
> (1972: 153)

The problem here is twofold. As I read Eccles, it seems that concepts of 'ego' and 'self' have no reality. They are something that is nothing. Further, the term, 'modulation' usually implies causation. Thus actions are caused by 'ego', whatever it might be, and neuronal machinery. Where is the freedom here?

6 Materialist positions were common in the ancient world. Some Pre-Socratics, like Empedocles, discussed in Chapter 3, were materialists. Aristotle was a materialist. The Epicureans held an especially modern materialism, with Lucretius (*c*.99–*c*.54) insisting that nature was composed of objects, which have their 'basic atoms' (1966: 26). Materialism was well represented in early modern thought. Hobbes was a materialist. Descartes insisted that humans could not be thought of as like material machines, which may explain his distaste for Hobbes. La Mettrie, who did not like Descartes, wrote a famous materialist manifesto, *Man a Machine* (1748). Nineteenth- and twentieth-century materialism have been associated with Marxism. This has been a problem because for many it means that if you are a materialist, then you are a Marxist; a connection which Harris (1968) – a materialist but an anti-Marxist – has been at pains to dispute. Moser and Trout (1995) present an overview of contemporary materialism. Robinson (1982, 1993) presents the case against; Poland (1994) the case for it. Callari and Ruccio (1996) present articles arguing for a postmodern, Marxist materialism.

7 Y is related to X in a linear fashion if $Y = AX + B$, where A and B are constants.

7 A Boasian social anthropology

1 Rabinow (1996: 163–7) reveals the intensity of these debates at the University of California at Berkeley.

2 A reading of Boas reveals that he believed that races exist as biological entities (1940). However, contemporary Boasian biological anthropology challenges the notion of race as a useful biological concept (Livingstone 1962; Reynolds and Lieberman 1996).

References

Aldington, Richard (1943) *The Duke: Being an Account of the Life and Achievements of Arthur Wellesley, 1st Duke of Wellington*, New York: Viking Press.

Allman, J.M. (1998) *Evolving Brains*, New York: W.H. Freeman.

Alston, W.P. (1996) *A Realist Conception of Truth*, Ithaca, NY: Cornell University Press.

Althusser, Louis (1986; 1968–69) *For Marx*, trans. Ben Brewster, London: New Left Books.

Althusser, Louis and Balibar, Etienne (1972; 1970) *Reading Capital*, trans. Ben Brewster, London: New Left Books.

Appadurai, Arjun (1996) *Modernity at Large, Cultural Dimensions of Globalization*, Minneapolis: University of Minnesota Press.

Ariew, Roger (1999) *Descartes and the Last Scholastics*, Ithaca, NY: Cornell University Press.

Atran, Scott (1990) *Cognitive Foundations of Natural History: Towards an Anthropology of Science*, New York: Cambridge University Press.

—— (1998) 'Folk Biology and the Anthropology of Science: Cognitive Universals and Cultural Particulars', *Brain and Behavioral Sciences*, 21: 547–609.

Baars, Bernard J. (1988) *A Cognitive Theory of Consciousness*, New York: Cambridge University Press.

Bacon, Francis (1980; 1620) *The Great Instauration*, in J. Weinberger (ed.) *The Great Instauration; and New Atlantis/Francis Bacon*, Arlington Heights, IL: AHM Publishing Co.

Baddeley, Alan (1988) 'Cognitive Psychology and Human Memory', *Trends in Neurosciences*, 11(4[118]): 176–81.

Balibar, Etienne (1996) 'Structural Causality, Overdetermination, and Antagonism', in Antonio Callari and David F. Ruccio (eds) *Postmodern Materialism and the Future of Marxist Theory: Essays in the Althusserian Tradition*, Hanover, NH: University Press of New England.

Baron, Robert (1987) *The Cerebral Computer: An Introduction to the Computational Structure of the Human Brain*, Hillsdale, NJ: Erlbaum.

Barthes, Roland (1975) *The Pleasure of the Text*, trans. Richard Miller, New York: Hill & Wang.

Bauman, Zygmunt (1978) *Hermeneutics and Social Science: Approaches to Understanding*, London: Hutchinson.

Bazin, Jean (1998) 'Questions de Sens', *Enquête*, 6: 13–34.

Beauchamp, Tom L. (ed.) (1974) *Philosophical Problems of Causation*, Encio, CA: Dickenson Publishing Company, Inc.

Benedict, Ruth (1959; 1934) *Patterns of Culture*, New York: Mentor Books.

Berger, P.L. and Luckmann, Thomas (1967) 'Sociological Aspects of Pluralism', *Archives de Sociologie des Religions*, 12(23): 117–27.

Blake, William (1950) *Jerusalem*, London: Published by the Trianon Press for the William Blake Trust.

Blalock, Hubert M., Jr (1964; 1961) *Causal Inferences in Nonexperimental Research*, New York: W.W. Norton & Company, Inc.

Bleicher, Josef (1982) *The Hermeneutic Imagination: Outline of a Positive Critique of Scientism and Sociology*, London and Boston: Routledge & Kegan Paul.

—— (1993; 1980) *Contemporary Hermeneutics: Hermeneutics as Method, Philosophy and Critique*, London and New York: Routledge.

Bliss, T.V.P. and Lømo, T. (1973) 'Long-lasting Potentiation of Synaptic Transmission in the Dentate Area of the Anaesthetized Rabbit Following Stimulation of the Perforant Path', *Journal of Physiology*, 232: 331–56.

Bloch, Maurice (1998) *How We Think They Think: Anthropological Approaches to Cognition, Memory, and Literacy*, Boulder, CO: Westview.

Boas, Franz (1932) *Anthropology and Modern Life*, New York: W.W. Norton & Co.

—— (1938) *General Anthropology*, Boston: Heath.

—— (1938; 1911) *The Mind of Primitive Man*, New York: Macmillan.

—— (1940) *Race, Language and Culture*, New York: Macmillan.

Boon, James A. (1982) *Other Tribes, Other Scribes: Symbolic Anthropology in the Comparative Study of Cultures, Histories, Religions and Texts*, New York: Cambridge University Press.

Botvinick, Matthew, Nystrom, Leigh E., Fissell, Kate, Carter, Cameron S., and Cohen, Jonathan D. (1999) 'Conflicting Monitoring versus Selection-for-action in Anterior Cingulate Cortex', *Nature*, 402(6758): 179–181.

Bouissac, Paul (ed.) (1998) *Encyclopedia of Semiotics*, New York: Oxford University Press.

Bourdieu, P. (1977) *Outline of a Theory of Practice*, New York: Cambridge University Press.

—— (1984) *Distinction, A Social Critique of the Judgment of Taste*, Cambridge, MA: Harvard University Press.

—— (1986) 'The Forms of Capital', in John G. Richardson (ed.) *Handbook of Theory and Research for the Sociology of Education*, pp. 241–58. New York: Greenwood Press.

—— (1987) 'The Force of Law: Toward a Sociology of the Juridical Field', *Hastings Journal of Law*, 38: 209–48.

—— (1988) 'Vive la Crise! For Heterodoxy in Social Science', *Theory and Society*, 17: 773–87.

—— (1989a) 'Social Space and Symbolic Power', *Sociological Theory*, 7(1): 14–25.

—— (1989b) 'Réproduction interdite. La dimension symbolique de la domination économique', *Etudes Rurales*, 113–14: 15–36.

—— (1990) *The Logic of Social Practice*, Stanford, CA: Stanford University Press.

—— (1993) *La Misère du monde*, Paris: Seuil.

Boutonier, J.F. (1951) 'A propos du "problème" de la psychogenèse des nèvroses et des psychoses', *L'Evolution Psychiatrique*, pp. 335–63.

Boyer, Pascal (1994) *The Naturalness of Religious Ideas: A Cognitive Theory of Religion*, Berkeley: University of California Press.

—— (1999) 'Cognitive Tracks of Cultural Inheritance: How Evolved Intuitive Ontology Governs Cultural Transmission', *American Anthropologist*, 1000: 876–89.

Brodal, Per (1998) *The Central Nervous System: Structure and Function*, New York: Oxford University Press.

Brown, Colin M. and Hagoort, Peter (eds) (1999) *The Neurocognition of Language*, New York: Oxford University Press.

Buckley, Walter F. (1967) *Sociology and Modern Systems Theory*, Englewood Cliffs, NJ: Prentice-Hall.

—— (1998) *Society – A Complex Adaptive System: Essays in Social Theory*, Australia: Gordon & Breach.

Bunge, Mario (1963; 1959) *Causality*, Cleveland, OH: World Publishing Co.

—— (1996) *Finding Philosophy in Social Science*, New Haven, CT: Yale University Press.

—— (1998) *Social Science under Debate: A Philosophical Perspective*, Toronto: University of Toronto Press.

Bush, G., Luu, P., and Posner, M.I. (2000) 'Cognitive and Emotional Influences in the Anterior Cingulate Cortex', *Trends in Cognitive Neuroscience*, 4: 215–22.

Butterworth, Brian (1999) *What Counts: How Every Brain is Hardwired for Math*, New York: Free Press.

Bynum, W.F., Browne, E.J., and Porter, R. (1981) *The Dictionary of the History of Science*, Princeton, NJ: Princeton University Press.

Callari, Antonio and Ruccio, David F. (eds) (1996) *Postmodern Materialism and the Future of Marxist Theory: Essays in the Althusserian Tradition*, Hanover, NH: University Press of New England

Caputo, John (1978) *The Mystical Element in Heidegger's Thought*, Athens: Ohio University Press.

—— (1992) 'Heidegger's Scandal: Thinking and the Essence of the Victim', in Tom Rockmore and Joseph Margolis (eds) *The Heidegger Case: On Philosophy and Politics*, pp. 265–81. Philadelphia, PA: Temple University Press.

Caramazza, Alfonso (2000) 'The Organization of Conceptual Knowledge in the Brain', in Michael S. Gazzaniga *et al.* (eds) *The New Cognitive Neurosciences*, 2nd edn, Cambridge, MA: MIT Press.

Carnois, Bernard (1987) *The Coherence of Kant's Doctrine of Freedom*, trans. David Booth, Chicago: University of Chicago Press.

Carter, Cameron S., Braver, T.S., Barch, D.M., Botvinick, M.M., Noll, D., and Cohen, J.D. (1998) 'Anterior Cingulate Cortex, Error Detection, and the On-line Monitoring of Performance', *Science*, 280: 747–9.

Carter, Rita (1998) *Mapping the Mind*, Berkeley and Los Angeles: University of California Press.

Chalmers, David J. (1996) *The Conscious Mind: In Search of a Fundamental Theory*, New York: Oxford University Press.

Child, William (1994) *Causality, Interpretation and the Mind*, New York: Oxford University Press.

Chomsky, Noam (1980) *Rules and Representations*, New York: Columbia University Press.

Churchland, Patricia S. (1986) *Neurophilosophy: Toward a Unified Philosophy of the Mind–Brain*, Cambridge, MA: MIT Press.

Churchland, Paul M. (1988; 1984) *Matter and Consciousness*, Cambridge, MA: MIT Press.

—— (1995) *The Engine of Reason, the Seat of the Soul: A Philosophical Journey into the Brain*, Cambridge, MA: MIT Press.

Cioffi, F. (1970) 'Freud and the Idea of a Pseudo-Science', in R. Borger and F. Cioffi (eds) *Explanation in the Behavioral Sciences*, New York: Cambridge University Press.

Clarke, Desmond (1982) *Descartes' Philosophy of Science*, University Park, PA: Penn State University Press.

Clifford, J. (1988) *The Predicament of Culture: Twentieth-century Ethnography, Literature and Art*, Cambridge, MA: Harvard University Press.

Clifford, J. and Marcus, G. (eds) (1986) *Writing Culture: The Poetics and Politics of Ethnography*, Los Angeles: University of California Press.

Cohen, A. (1974) *Two-dimensional Man: An Essay on the Anthropology of Power and Symbolism in Complex Society*, Los Angeles: University of California Press.

Colapietro, Vincent M. (1993) *Glossary of Semiotics*, New York: Paragon House.

Cole, Douglas (1999) *Franz Boas: The Early Years, 1858–1906*, Seattle: University of Washington Press.

Collins, Henry B. (1964) 'Introduction', in Franz Boas, *The Central Eskimo*, Lincoln: University of Nebraska Press.

The Columbia Dictionary of Modern Literary and Cultural Criticism Joseph Childers and Gary Hentzi (general editors) (1995), New York: Columbia University Press.

Comaroff, Jean (1985) *Body of Power, Spirit of Resistance: The Culture and History of a South African People*, Chicago: University of Chicago Press.

Comaroff, Jean and Comaroff, John (1991) *Of Revelation and Revolution: Christianity, Colonialism and Consciousness in South Africa*, vol. 1, Chicago: University of Chicago Press.

Comte, Auguste (1896; 1853) *The Positive Philosophy of Auguste Comte*, London: G. Bell & Sons.

Cottingham, John (1986) *Descartes*, Oxford: Blackwell.

Crapanzano, V. (1992) *Hermes' Dilemma and Hamlet's Desire: On the Epistemology of Interpretation*, Cambridge, MA: Harvard University Press.

Crews, Frederick (1986) *Skeptical Engagements*, New York: Oxford University Press.

Crick, Francis (1994) *The Astonishing Hypothesis: The Scientific Search for the Soul*, New York: Maxwell Macmillan International.

Crick, Francis and Koch, Cristof (1992) 'The Problem of Consciousness', *Scientific American*, 267(3): 152–9.

—— (1995) 'Why Neuroscience May be Able to Explain Consciousness', *Scientific American*, 273(6): 84–6.

Csordas, Thomas J. (1990) 'The 1988 Stirling Award Essay: Embodiment as a Paradigm for Anthropology', *Ethos*, 18(1): 5–47.

—— (ed.) (1994) *Embodiment and Experience: The Existential Ground of Culture and Self*, Cambridge and New York: Cambridge University Press.

Cunningham, F. (1973) *Objectivity in Social Science*, Toronto: Toronto University Press.

Damasio, Antonio R. (1994) *Descartes' Error: Emotion, Reason, and the Human Brain*, New York: Avon Books, Inc.

—— (1999) *The Feeling of What Happens: Body and Emotion in the Making of Consciousness*, New York: Harcourt Brace.

Damasio, Antonio R. and Damasio, Hanna (1992) 'Brain and Language', *Scientific American*, 267(3): 89–95.

D'Andrade, Roy (1984) 'Cultural Meaning Systems', in Richard Shweder and Robert A. Le Vine (eds) *Culture Theory*, Cambridge: Cambridge University Press.

—— (1995) *The Development of Cognitive Anthropology*, Cambridge: Cambridge University Press.

Dannhauer, Johann (1630) *Idea boni interpretis et malitici caluminiatoris*, Strasbourg: Glaser.

Darwin, Charles (1872) *The Expression of the Emotions in Man and Animals*, London: Murray.

Davidson, Donald (1963) 'Actions, Reactions, Causes', *Journal of Philosophy*, 60: 685–700.

Dawkins, Richard (1976) *The Selfish Gene*, New York: Oxford University Press.

Deacon, Terrence W. (1997) *The Symbolic Species: The Co-evolution of Language and the Brain*, New York: W.W. Norton & Co.

Dehaene, Stanislas, Dehaene-Lambertz, Ghislaine, and Cohen, Laurent (1998) 'Abstract Representation of Numbers in the Animal and Human Brain', *Trends in Neuroscience*, 21(8): 355–61.

Deleuze, G. and Guattari, F. (1977) *Anti-Oedipus: Capitalism and Schizophrenia*, New York: Viking.

Dennett, Daniel C. (1984) *Elbow Room: The Varieties of Free Will Worth Wanting*, Cambridge, MA: MIT Press.

—— (1991) *Consciousness Explained*, Boston: Little Brown.

Derrida, J. (1981) *Positions*, Chicago: University of Chicago Press.

Descartes, René (1985; 1649) *A Discourse on Method*, in John Cottingham, Robert Stoothoff, and Dugald Murdoch, *The Philosophical Writings of Descartes*, vol. 1, pp. 109–152, New York: Cambridge University Press.

—— (1988; 1637) 'Discours de la méthode pour bien conduire sa raison, et Recherches de la vérité dans les sciences', in *Selected Philosophical Writings*, Cambridge: Cambridge University Press.

Descombes, Vincent (1980) *Modern French Philosophy*, trans. L. Scott-Fox and J.M. Harding, Cambridge: Cambridge University Press.

—— (1998) 'The Confusion of Tongues', *Enquête*, 6: 35–56.

Dilthey, Wilhelm (1883) *Introduction to the Human Sciences: An Attempt to Lay a Foundation for the Study of Society and History*, Leipzig: Duncker & Humblot.

—— (1894) 'Ideen über eine beschreibende und zergliedernde Psychologie', *Gesammelte Schriften*, vol. V, 139–237, Göttingen: Vandenhoeck & Ruprecht.

—— (1900) 'Die Entstehung der Hermeneutik', *Gesammelte Schriften*, vol. V, 317–31, Göttingen: Vandenhoeck & Ruprecht.

—— (1962) *Pattern and Meaning in History: Thoughts on History and Society*, H.P. Rickman (ed. and intro.), New York: Harper & Row.

Double, Richard (1991) *The Non-reality of Free Will*, New York: Oxford University Press.

Douglas, Mary (1999) 'Culture Clash in American Anthropology', *Nature*, 400(6745): 631–3.

Dowe, Phil (1992) 'An Empiricist Defence of the Causal Account of Explanation', *International Studies in the Philosophy of Science*, 6: 123–8.

—— (1995) 'Causality and Conserved Quantities: A Reply to Salmon', *Philosophy of Science*, 62: 321–33.

Dowling, John E. (1998) *Creating Mind: How the Brain Works*, New York: W.W. Norton.

Droysen, Johan Gustav (1977; 1858) *Historik*, Darmstadt: Wissenschaftliche Buchgesellschaft.

Duncan, J. and Owen, A.M. (2000) 'Common Regions of the Human Frontal Lobe Recruited by Diverse Cognitive Demands', *Trends in Neuroscience*, 23: 475–83.

Duncan, J., Seitz, J.R., Kolodny, J., Bor, D., Herzog, H., Ahmed, A., Newell, F.N., and Emslie, H. (2000) 'A Neural Basis for General Intelligence', *Science*, 289: 457–60.

Durkheim, Émile and Mauss, Marcel (1963; 1903) *Primitive Classification*, Chicago: University of Chicago Press.

Eccles, John C. (ed.) (1982) *Mind and Brain: The Many-faceted Problems: Selected Readings from the Proceedings of the International Conferences on the Unity of the Sciences*, Washington, DC: Paragon House.

Eccles, John C. (1989) *Evolution of the Brain: Creation of the Self*, New York: Routledge.

Eccles, John C. and Karczmar, A.G. (eds) (1972) *Brain and Human Behavior*, New York: Springer-Verlag.

Eccles, J.C. and Popper, K.R. (1977) *The Self and its Brain: An Argument for Interactionism*, New York: Springer International.

Eccles, J.C., Deeke, L., and Mountcastle, V.B. (eds) (1990) *From Neuron to Action: An Appraisal of Fundamental and Clinical Research*, New York: Springer-Verlag.

Edelman, Gerald M. (1992) *Bright Air, Brilliant Fire: On the Matter of the Mind*, New York: Basic Books.

Edelson, Marshall (1984) *Hypothesis and Evidence in Psychoanalysis*, Chicago: University of Chicago Press.

Eiser, J. Richard (1994) *Attitudes, Chaos, and the Connectionist Mind*, Cambridge, MA: Blackwell.

Ekman, Paul (1992) 'Are there Basic Emotions?' *Psychological Review*, 99(3): 550–4.

Elman, J.L., Bates, E.A., Johnson, M.H., Karmiloff-Smith, A., Parisi, D. and Plinkett, K. (1996) *Rethinking Innateness: A Connectionist Perspective on Development*, Cambridge, MA: MIT Press.

Erikson, Erik H. (1962) *Young Man Luther: A Study in Psychoanalysis and History*, New York: Norton.

Fabian, Johannes (1971) 'Language, History and Anthropology', *Philosophy of the Social Sciences*, 1(1): 19–47.

—— (1994) 'Ethnographic Objectivity Revisited: From Rigor to Vigor', in Allan Megill (ed.) *Rethinking Objectivity*, pp. 81–108, Durham, NC: Duke University Press.

Farias, Victor (1987) *Heidegger and Nazism*, Philadelphia, PA: Temple University Press.

Faulkner, Robert (1993) *Francis Bacon and the Project of Progress*, London: Brown & Littlefield

Ferguson, Brian (2001) 'Anthropological Theory on War: Yanomami Reflections', *Anthropological Theory*, 1: 99–116.

Ferrier, J.F. (1854) *Institutes of Metaphysic: The Theory of Knowing and Being*, London: Blackwood

Fetzer, James H. and Almeder, Robert F. (1993) *Glossary of Epistemology/Philosophy of Science*, New York: Paragon House.

Firth, Raymond (1963; 1951) *Elements of Social Organization*, Boston, MA: Beacon.

Fisher, Seymour and Greenberg, Roger P. (1977) *The Scientific Credibility of Freud's Theories and Therapy*, New York: Basic Books.

Flew, Antony (1976) *Sociology, Equality and Education: Philosophical Essays in Defense of a Variety of Differences*, New York: Barnes & Noble Books.

—— (1979) *A Dictionary of Philosophy*, New York: St Martin's Press.

Fodor, J.A. (1983) *The Modularity of Mind*, Cambridge, MA: MIT Press.

—— (1998) 'The Trouble with Psychological Darwinism', *London Review of Books*, 20: 11–13.

Fodor, J.A. and Pylyshyn, Z.W. (1988) 'Connections and Cognitive Architecture: A Critical Analysis', in Steven Pinker and J. Mehler (eds) *Connections and Symbols*, Cambridge, MA: MIT Press.

Frazer, Steven (ed.) (1995) *The Bell Curve Wars: Race, Intelligence, and the Future of America*, New York: Basic Books.

Friedman, Jonathan (1987) 'Beyond Otherness: The Spectacularization of Anthropology', *Telos*, 71: 161–70.

Frijda, Nico H. (1993) 'The Place of Appraisal in Emotion', *Cognition and Emotion*, 7(3–4): 357–87.

Frith, Christopher D. and Friston, Karl J. (1997) 'Studying Brain Function with Neuroimaging', in Michael D. Rugg et al. (eds) *Cognitive Neurosciences: Studies in Cognition*, pp. 169–95, Cambridge, MA: MIT Press.

Fuster, Joaquín M. (1989) *The Prefrontal Cortex: Anatomy, Physiology, and Neuropsychology of the Frontal Lobe*, New York: Raven Press.

—— (1995) *Memory in the Cerebral Cortex*, Cambridge, MA: MIT Press.

—— (1997) 'Network Memory', *Trends in Neuroscience*, 20(10): 451–9.

—— (1998) 'Linkage at the Top', *Neuron*, 21(6): 1223–4.

Gadamer, H.G. (1987) 'The Problem of Historical Consciousness', in P. Rabinow and W. Sullivan (eds) *Interpretive Social Science: A Second Look*, pp. 82–140, Los Angeles: University of California Press.

Gaffan, David (1992) 'Amygdala and the Memory of Reward', in John P. Aggleton et al. (eds) *The Amygdala: Neurobiological Aspects of Emotion, Memory, and Mental Dysfunction*, pp. 471–83, New York: Wiley-Liss.

Gaffan, David, Murray, E.A., and Fabre-Thorpe, M. (1993) 'Interaction of the Amygdala with the Frontal Lobe in Reward Memory', *European Journal of Neuroscience*, 5: 968–75.

Gazzaniga, Michael S. (1985) *The Social Brain: Discovering the Networks of the Mind*, New York: Basic Books, Inc.

—— (1992) *Nature's Mind: The Biological Roots of Thinking, Emotions, Sexuality, Language and Intelligence*, Harmondsworth: Penguin Books.

—— (ed.) (1997) *Conversations in the Cognitive Neurosciences*, Cambridge, MA: MIT Press.

—— (1999) *Cognitive Neuroscience: A Reader*, Malden, MA: Blackwell.

Gazzaniga, Michael S. *et al.* (1995) *The Cognitive Neurosciences*, Cambridge, MA: MIT Press.

Geertz, C. (1973) *The Interpretation of Cultures*, New York: Basic Books.

—— (1983) *Local Knowledge: Further Essays in Interpretive Anthropology*, New York: Basic Books.

—— (1988) *Works and Lives*, Stanford, CA: Stanford University Press.

—— (1995) *After the Fact: Two Countries, Four Decades, One Anthropologist*, Cambridge, MA: Harvard University Press.

Gelman, Susan (1999) 'Domain Specificity', in R.A. Wilson and F.C. Keil (eds) *The MIT Encyclopedia of the Cognitive Sciences*, pp. 238–9, Cambridge, MA: MIT Press.

Giddens, Anthony (1984) *The Constitution of Society: Introduction to the Theory of Structuration*, Los Angeles: University of California Press.

Gilson, Etienne, Langan, Thomas, and Maurer, Armand (1966) *Recent Philosophy: Hegel to the Present*, New York: Random House.

Glasersfeld, Ernst von (1995) *Radical Constructivism: A Way of Knowing and Learning*, Washington, DC: Falmer Press.

Gleik, James (1987) *Chaos: Making a New Science*, New York: Viking.

Glucksmann, André (1967) *Le Discours de la guerre*, Paris: l'Herne.

Glymour, Clark (1997) 'A Review of Recent Work on the Foundations of Causal Interference', in Vaughn R. McKim and Stephen P. Turner (eds) *Causality in Crisis? Statistical Methods and the Search for Causal Knowledge in the Social Sciences*, pp. 201–48, Notre Dame, IN: University of Notre Dame Press.

(Comte de) Gobineau (1856) *The Moral and Intellectual Diversity of Races*, Philadelphia, PA: Lippincott.

Goel, V., Gold, B., Kapur, S., and Houle, S. (1997) 'The Seats of Reason: A Localization Study of Deductive and Inductive Reasoning Using PET (015) Blood Flow Technique', *Neuroreport*, 8: 1305–10.

Goldman-Rakic, P.S. (1987) 'Circuitry of Primate Prefrontal Cortex and Regulation of Behavior by Representational Knowledge', in F. Plum (vol. ed) and V.B. Mountcastle (sec. ed) *Handbook of Physiology, Section 1: The Nervous System*, vol. 5: *Higher Functions of the Brain*, Bethesda, MD: American Physiological Society.

—— (1992) 'Working Memory and the Mind', *Scientific American*, 267(3): 110–17.

Goodenough, Ward (ed.) (1964) *Explorations in Cultural Anthropology*, New York: McGraw-Hill Book Co.

Gould, E., Gross, C.G., Reeves, A.J., and Graziano, M.S. (1999) 'Neurogenesis in the Neocortex of Adult Primates', *Science*, 286(5439): 548–52.

Gould, Stephen J. (1996; 1981) *The Mismeasure of Man: The Definitive Refutation of the Argument of the Bell Curve*, New York: Norton.

Gramsci, A. (1971) *Selections from the Prison Notebooks*, New York: International Publishing.

—— (1988) *An Antonio Gramsci Reader: Selected Writings 1916–1935* (D. Forgacs, ed.), New York: Schocken.

Grant, Robert (1997) 'No Conjuring Tricks', *Times Literary Supplement*, 4937: 3–4.

Graves, Joseph L. (2002) 'What a Tangled Web He Weaves: Race, Reproductive Strategies and Rushton's Life History Theory', *Anthropological Theory*, 2(4).

Green, Arnold W. (1993) *Hobbes and Human Nature*, New Brunswick, NJ: Transaction Publishers.

Gregory, Richard L. (ed.) (1987) *The Oxford Companion to the Mind*, New York: Oxford University Press.

Greimas, Algirdas J. (1990) *The Social Sciences, A Semiotic View*, trans. Paul Perron and Frank H. Collins, Minneapolis: University of Minnesota Press.

Griffen, Donald R. (1987) 'Mind, Animal', in George Adelman (ed.) *Encyclopedia of Neuroscience*, pp. 669–72, Boston, MA: Birkhäuser.

Gross, Charles G. (1998) *Brain, Vision, Memory: Tales in the History of Neuroscience*, Cambridge, MA: MIT Press.

Grünbaum, Adolf (1984) *The Foundations of Psychoanalysis: A Philosophical Critique*, Berkeley: University of California Press.

Guille-Escuret, Georges (2000) 'L'Enfant, la race et la hiérarchie', *L'Homme*, 153: 291–9.

Gupta, Akhil and Ferguson, James (eds) (1997) *Culture, Power, Place: Explorations in Critical Anthropology*, Durham, NC: Duke University Press.

Hall, S. (1986) 'Gramsci's Relevance for the Study of Race and Ethnicity', *Journal of Communication Inquiry*, 10: 5–27.

Handler, R. (1991) 'An Interview with Clifford Geertz', *Current Anthropology*, 32(5): 603–13.

Harré, Rom and Madden, Edward (1975) *Causal Powers*, Oxford: Basil Blackwell.

Harris, Marvin (1964) *The Nature of Cultural Things*, New York: Random House.

—— (1968) *The Rise of Anthropological Theory*, New York: Crowell.

—— (1979) *Cultural Materialism*, New York: Viking.

Hebb, Donald O. (1949) *The Organization of Behavior: A Neuropsychological Theory*, New York: Wiley.

Hegel, G. (1967; 1807) *The Phenomenology of Mind*, New York: Harper.

Heidegger, M. (1996; 1972/27) *Being and Time*, New York: Harper & Row.

—— (1953; 1929) *Einführung in die Metaphysik*, Tübingen: Niemeyer.

Heisenberg, Werner (1930) *The Physical Principles of the Quantum Theory*, trans. Carl Eckhart and Frank C. Hoyt, Chicago, IL: University of Chicago Press.

Hempel, Carl and Oppenheim, Paul (1965; 1948) 'Studies in the Logic of Explanation', in Carl Hempel, *Aspects of Scientific Explanation and other Essays in the Philosophy of Science*, pp. 245–96, New York: Free Press.

Hénaff, Michael (1998) *Claude Lévi-Strauss and the Making of Structural Anthropology*, Minneapolis: University of Minnesota Press.

Herold, J. Christopher (ed.) (1955) *The Mind of Napoleon: A Selection from his Written and Spoken Words*, New York: Columbia University Press.

Herrnstein, Richard J. and Murray, Charles (1994) *The Bell Curve: Intelligence and Class Structure in American Life*, New York: Free Press.

Herrnstein-Smith, Barbara (1997) *Belief and Resistance: Dynamics of Contemporary Intellectual Controversy*, Cambridge, MA: Harvard University Press.

Hinton, Geoffrey E. and Anderson, James A. (eds) (1981) *Parallel Models of Associative Memory*, Hillsdale, NJ: Lawrence Erlbaum Associates.

Hirschfeld, Lawrence (1996) *Race in the Making: Cognition, Culture and the Child's Construction of Human Kinds*, Cambridge, MA: MIT Press.

—— (1999) 'La Règle de la goutte de sang ou comment l'idée de race vient aux enfants', *L'Homme*, 150: 14–40.

—— (2000) 'Race et reductionism: réponse à Georges Guille-Escuret', *L'Homme*, 153: 299–303.

Hirschfeld, Lawrence and Gelman, Susan (1994) *Mapping the Mind*, New York: Cambridge University Press.

Hobbes, Thomas (1651) *Leviathan: The Matter, Form and Power of a Common Wealth, Ecclesiastical and Civil*, London, printed for A. Crooke.

Holland, Dorothy and Skinner, Debra (1987) 'Prestige and Intimacy: The Cultural Models Behind America's Talk about Gender Types', in Dorothy Holland, Naomi Quinn *et al.* (eds) *Cultural Models in Language and Thought*, pp. 78–111, New York: Cambridge University Press.

Holloway, R.L. (1966) 'Dendritic Branching: Some Preliminary Results of Training and Complexity in the Visual Cortex', *Brain Research*, 2: 393–6.

Honderich, Ted (1993) *How Free Are You? The Determinism Problem*, New York: Oxford University Press.

Hook, Sidney (ed.) (1979; 1961) *Determinism and Freedom in the Age of Modern Science*, New York: Collier Books.

Hoy, David C. (1982) *The Critical Circle: Literature, History, and Philosophical Hermeneutics*, Berkeley: University of California Press.

Hume, David (1739) *A Treatise of Human Nature*, London: John Noon.

—— (1958; 1748) *An Enquiry Concerning Human Understanding*, LaSalle, IL: Open Court Press.

Humphrey, N. (1992) *A History of the Mind*, London: Chatto & Windus.

Hundert, Edward M. (1989) *Philosophy, Psychiatry and Neuroscience: Three Approaches to the Mind*, Oxford: Clarendon Press.

Huntington, Samuel P. (1996) *The Clash of Civilizations and the Remaking of World Order*, New York: Simon & Schuster.

Husserl, Edmund (1962; 1931) *Ideas*, New York: Collier.

—— (1970) *Logical Investigations*, New York: Humanities Press.

Hutchins, Edwin (1980) *Culture and Influence: A Trobriand Case Study*, Cambridge, MA: Harvard University Press.

Jacoby, Russell and Glauberman, Naomi (eds) (1995) *The Bell Curve Debate: History, Documents, Opinions*, New York: Times Books.

James, William (1890) *The Principles of Psychology*, New York: H. Holt & Co.

Jeannerod, Marc (1985) *The Brain Machine: The Development of Neurophysiological Thought*, Cambridge, MA: Harvard University Press.

Jensen, A.R. (1969) 'How Much can we Boost IQ and Scholastic Achievement?', *Harvard Educational Review*, 39: 1–123.

Johnson, Laurie M. (1993) *Thucydides, Hobbes and the Interpretation of Realism*, DeKalb, IL: Northern Illinois University Press.

Johnson-Laird, Philip Nicholas (1988) *The Computer and the Mind: An Introduction to Cognitive Science*, Cambridge, MA: Harvard University Press.

Jones, Edward G. and Peters, Alan (1984–99) *Cerebral Cortex*, vols 1–14, New York: Plenum Press.

Judovitz, Dalia (1988) *Subjectivity and Representation in Descartes: The Origins of Modernity*, Cambridge and New York: Cambridge University Press.

Juraska, Janice M. (1984) 'Sex Differences in Dendritic Response to Differential Experience in the Rat Visual Cortex', *Brain Research*, 295(1): 27–34.

Kandel, Eric R., Schwartz, James H., and Jessell, Thomas M. (eds) (1991) *Principles of Neural Science*, 3rd edn, New York: Elsevier Science Publishing Co., Inc.

—— (1995) *Essentials of Neural Science and Behavior*, Norwalk, CT: Appleton & Lange.

Kant, I. (1991; 1781) *Critique of Pure Reason*, trans. J.M.D. Meiklejohn, London: J.M. Dent & Sons, Ltd

—— (1956; 1788) *Critique of Practical Reason*, New York: Bobbs-Merrill.

Kaplan, A. (1964) *The Conduct of Inquiry: Methodology for Behavioral Science*, San Francisco: Chandler.

Karmiloff-Smith, Annette (1999) 'Modularity of Mind', in R.A. Wilson and F.C Keil (eds) *The MIT Encyclopedia of the Cognitive Sciences*, pp. 558–60, Cambridge, MA: MIT Press.

—— (1992) *Beyond Modularity*. Cambridge, MA: MIT Press.

Keesing, Roger (1974) 'Theories of Culture', *Annual Review of Anthropology*, 3: 73–97.

Kinsbourne, Marcel (1988) 'Integrated Field Theory of Consciousness', in Anthony J. Marcel and Edoardo Bisiach (eds) *Consciousness in Contemporary Science*, pp. 239–56, Oxford: Oxford University Press.

Kitcher, Philip (1985) *Vaulting Ambition: Sociobiology and the Quest for Human Nature*, Cambridge, MA: MIT Press.

—— (1989) 'Explanatory Unification and the Causal Structure of the World', in P. Kitcher (ed.) *Scientific Explanation*, Minnesota Studies in the Philosophy of Science, vol. 13, pp. 410–505, Minneapolis: University of Minnesota Press.

Knauft, B.M. (1996) *Genealogies for the Present in Cultural Anthropology*, New York: Routledge.

Kohonen, Teuvo (1977) *Associative Memory: A System-Theoretical Approach*, Berlin, New York: Springer-Verlag.

—— (1984) *Self-organization and Associative Memory*, Berlin, New York: Springer-Verlag.

Kolb, Bryan and Whishaw, Ian Q. (1990) *Fundamentals of Human Neuropsychology*, 3rd edn, New York: W.H. Freeman & Co.

Kosslyn, Stephen M. and Andersen, Richard A. (eds) (1995) *Frontiers in Cognitive Neuroscience*, Cambridge, MA: MIT Press.

Kosslyn, Stephen M. and Koenig, Olivier (1992) *Wet Mind: The New Cognitive Neuroscience*, New York: The Free Press.

Krasnegor, Norman A., Lyon, G. Reid, and Goldman-Rakic, Patricia S. (eds) (1997) *Development of the Prefrontal Cortex: Evolution, Neurobiology, and Behavior*, Baltimore, MD: Paul H. Brookes Publishing Co.

Kripke, Saul A. (1982) *Wittgenstein on Rules and Private Language: An Elementary Exposition*, Cambridge, MA: Harvard University Press.

Kroeber, Alfred (1917) 'The Superorganic', *American Anthropologist*, 19: 163–213.

—— (1948) *Anthropology*, New York: Harcourt Brace.

Kroeber, Alfred and Kluckhohn, Clyde (1952) *Culture: A Critical Review of Concepts and Definitions*, Cambridge, MA: The Museum.

Kuper, Adam (1999) *Culture: The Anthropologists' Account*, Cambridge, MA: Harvard University Press.

Kutas, Marta and Dale, Anders (1997) 'Electrical and Magnetic Readings of Mental Functions', in Michael D. Rugg *et al.* (eds) *Cognitive Neurosciences: Studies in Cognition*, pp. 169–95, Cambridge, MA: MIT Press.

Kuznar, L.A. (1997) *Reclaiming a Scientific Anthropology*, Walnut Creek, CA: Altamira.

Lacan, Jaques (1977) *Ecrits*, New York: Norton.

La Mettrie, Julien Offray de (1912; 1748) *Man a Machine*, LaSalle, IL: Open Court.

Lanuza, Enrique and Martinez-Marcos, Alino (1999) 'What is the Amyglada? A Comparative Approach', *Trends in Neurosciences*, 22(5): 207–9.

Lave, Jean (1988) *Cognition in Practice: Mind, Mathematics and Culture in Everyday Life*, New York: Cambridge University Press.

Leach, Edmund R. (1966; 1961) *Rethinking Anthropology*, New York: Humanities Press, Inc.

Lears, T.J.H. (1985) 'The Concept of Cultural Hegemony: Problems and Possibilities', in *American Historical Review*, 9: 567–93.

LeDoux, Joseph (1996) *The Emotional Brain*, New York: Simon & Schuster.

Leeds, Anthony and Dusek, Val (eds) (1981–2) 'Sociobiology: A Paradigm's Unnatural Selection through Science, Philosophy and Ideology', in 'Sociobiology: The Debate Evolves', double issue, *The Philosophical Forum*, vol. XIII, nos. 2–3, pp. i–xxv.

Lefebvre, Henri (1991; 1974) *The Production of Space*, Oxford: Blackwell.

LeMay, Eric and Pitts, Jennifer A. (1994) *Heidegger for Beginners*, New York: Writers & Readers Publishers.

Levine, George (1994) 'Why Science Isn't Literature: The Importance of Differences', in Allan Megill, *Rethinking Objectivity*, pp. 65–80, Durham, NC: Duke University Press.

Lévi-Strauss, Claude (1948) *La Vie familiale et sociale des indiens Nambiikwara*, Paris.

—— (1953) 'Social Structure', in A.L. Kroeber (ed.), *Anthropology Today*, Chicago: University of Chicago Press.

—— (1966; 1962) *The Savage Mind*. [*La Pensée Sauvage*], Chicago: University of Chicago Press.

—— (1967) *Totemism*, Boston, MA: Beacon Press.

—— (1969; 1949) *The Elementary Structures of Kinship*. [*Les Structures élémentaires de la parenté*], Boston, MA: Beacon.

Levitan, Irwin B. and Kaczmarek, L.B. (1997) *The Neuron, Cell and Molecular Biology*, New York: Oxford University Press.

Lewontin, R.C., Rose, Steven, and Kamin, Leon J. (1984) *Not in our Genes: Biology, Ideology and Human Nature*, New York: Pantheon Books.

Lieberson, J. (1985) 'Putting Freud to the Test', *New York Review of Books*, pp. 24–8.

Lister, Richard G. and Weingartner, Herbert J. (eds) (1991) *Perspectives on Cognitive Neuroscience*, New York: Oxford University Press.

Livingstone, Frank (1962) 'On the Non-existence of Human Races', *Current Anthropology*, 3: 279–81.

Llewellyn, K.N. and Hoebel, E. Adamson (1967; 1941) *The Cheyenne Way: Conflict and Case Law in Primitive Jurisprudence*, Norman: University of Oklahoma Press.

Locke, John (1975; 1690) *An Essay Concerning Human Understanding*, with intro. and glossary by P.H. Nidditch, Oxford: Clarendon Press.

Lowie, Robert H. (1920) *Primitive Society*, New York: Liveright.

Löwith, Karl (1991) 'My Last Meeting with Heidegger in Rome, 1936', in Richard Wolin (ed.) *The Heidegger Controversy: A Critical Reader*, pp. 140–4, New York: Columbia University Press.

Lucretius Caras, Titus (1966; 1964) *On the Nature of Things*, Oxford: Clarendon Press.

Luria, A.R. (1966) *Higher Cortical Functions in Man*, trans. B. Haigh, New York: Basic Books.

Luther, Martin (1970) *Three Treatises*, trans. Charles M. Jacobs, A.T.W. Steinhäuser, and W.A. Lambert, Philadelphia, PA: Fortress Press.

Lyotard, J.-F. (1984; 1979) *The Postmodern Condition: A Report on Knowledge*, Minneapolis: University of Minnesota Press.

MacDonald, A.W., Cohen, J.D., Stenger, V.A., and Carter, C.S. (2000) 'Dissociating the Role of the Dorsolateral Prefrontal and Anterior Cingulate Cortex in Cognitive Control', *Science*, 288: 1835–8.

MacDonald, Cynthia and MacDonald, Graham (eds) (1995) *Connectionism: Debates on Psychological Explanation*, vol. 2, Cambridge, MA: Blackwell Publishers.

MacIver, R.M. (1943) *Social Causation*, New York: Harper & Row.

Mackie, J.L. (1974) 'Counterfactuals and Causal Laws', in Tom L. Beauchamp (ed.) *Philosophical Problems of Causation*, Encio, CA: Dickenson Publishing Co., Inc.

MacLean, P.D. (1952) 'Some Psychiatric Implications of Physiological Studies on Frontotemporal Portion of Limbic System (Visceral Brain)', *Electroencephalography and Clinical Neurophysiology*, 4: 407–18.

Maddock, Richard J. (1999) 'The Retrosplenial Cortex and Emotion: New Insights from Functional Neuroimaging of the Human Brain', *Trends in Neuroscience*, 22(7): 310–16.

—— (2000) 'The Retrosplenial Cortex and Emotion: New Insights from Functional Neuroimaging of the Human Brain. Commentary Reply', *Trends in Neurosciences*, 23(5): 196–7.

Makkreel, Rudolf A. (1975) *Dilthey: Philosopher of the Human Studies*, Princeton, NJ: Princeton University Press.

Malinowski, B. (1962; 1922) *Argonauts of the Western Pacific*, New York: Dutton.

Mandler, George (1988) 'Problems and Directions in the Study of Consciousness', in Mardi J. Horowitz *et al.* (eds) *Psychodynamics and Cognition*, pp. 21–45, Chicago: University of Chicago Press.

Marcus, G. (1994) 'After the Critique of Ethnography: Faith, Hope and Charity, but the Greatest of these is Charity', in R. Borofsky (ed.) *Assessing Cultural Anthropology*, New York: McGraw Hill.

Marcus, G. and Fischer, M. (1986) *Anthropology as Cultural Critique: An Experimental Moment in the Human Sciences*, Chicago: University of Chicago Press.

Martin, Alex, Ungerleider, Leslie, and Haxby, James (2000) 'Category Specificity and the Brain: The Sensory/Motor Model of Semantic Representations of Objects', in Michael S. Gazzaniga *et al.* (eds) *The New Cognitive Neurosciences*, 2nd edn, Cambridge, MA: MIT Press.

Martin, Alex, Wiggs, Cheri, Ungerleider, Leslie, and Haxby, James (1996) 'Neural Correlates of Category Specific Knowledge', *Nature* 379(6566): 649–52.

Martindale, Don (1960) *The Nature and Types of Sociological Theory*, Boston: Houghton Mifflin.

Martinez, Joe L., Jr and Kesner, Raymond P. (eds) (1998) *Neurobiology of Learning and Memory*, San Diego: Academic Press.

Martinich, Aloysius P. (1995) *A Hobbes Dictionary*, Cambridge, MA: Blackwell Publishers.

Masson, Jefferey M. (1984) *The Assault on Truth: Freud's Suppression of the Seduction Theory*, New York: Farrar, Straus & Giroux.

Mautner, T. (1996) *A Dictionary of Philosophy*, Oxford: Blackwell.

Mayer, Richard (1983) *Thinking, Problem Solving, Cognition* New York: W.H. Freeman.

McKim, Vaughn R. (1997) 'Causality in Crisis? Introduction', in Vaughn R. McKim and Stephen P. Turner (eds) *Causality in Crisis?: Statistical Methods and the Search for Causal Knowledge in the Social Sciences*, Notre Dame, IN: University of Notre Dame Press.

Mead, George H. (1977) *On Social Psychology*, Chicago: University of Chicago Press.

Megill, A. (1994) *Rethinking Objectivity*, Durham, NC: Duke University Press.

Merleau-Ponty, M. (1942) *La Structure du comportement*, Paris: NF.

Metcalfe, Janet (1993) 'Monitoring and Gain Control in an Episodic Memory Model: Relation to the P300 Event-related Potential', in A.F. Collins, S.E. Gathercole, M.A. Conway, and P.E. Morris (eds) *Theories of Memory*, Hove, UK: Lawrence Erlbaum.

Metzinger, Thomas (ed.) (2000) *Neural Correlates of Consciousness: Empirical and Conceptual Questions*, Cambridge, MA: MIT Press.

Mill, J.S. (1843) *System of Logic*, vol. 1, London: John Parker.

Miller, G.A., Galanter, E.H. and Pribram, K.H. (1960) *Plans and the Structure of Behavior*, New York: Holt, Rinehart & Winston.

Miller, R.W. (1987) *Fact and Method, Confirmation and Reality in the Natural and Social Sciences*, Princeton, NJ: Princeton University Press.

Minsky, Marvin (1985) *The Society of Mind*, New York: Simon & Schuster.

Montagu, Ashley (ed.) (1980) *Sociobiology Examined*, New York: Oxford University Press.

Moser, Paul K. and Trout, J.D. (eds) (1995) *Contemporary Materialism: A Reader*, New York: Routledge.

Mountcastle, V.B. (1979) 'An Organizing Principle for Cerebral Function: The Unit Module and the Distributed System', in F.O. Schmitt and F.G. Worden (eds) *The Neurosciences Fourth Study Program*, pp. 21–42, Cambridge, MA: MIT Press.

Mozzuri, G. and Magoun, H. W. (1949) 'Brain Stem Reticular Formation and Activation of the EEG', *Electroencephalogy and Clinical Neurophysiology*, 1: 455–73.

Müller-Wille, Ludger (ed.) (1998) *Franz Boas among the Inuit of Baffin Island, 1883–1884: Journals and Letters*, Toronto: University of Toronto Press.

Myrdal, G. (1969) *Objectivity in Social Research*, Middletown, CT: Wesleyan University Press.

Nagel, Ernest, Baron, Salo W., and Pinson, Koppel S. (eds) (1951) *Freedom and Reason: Studies in Philosophy and Jewish Culture* (in memory of Morris Raphael Cohen), Glencoe, IL: Free Press.

—— (1959) 'Methodological Issues in Psychoanalytic Theory', in S. Hook (ed.) *Psychoanalysis, Scientific Method and Philosophy*, New York: New York University Press.

Nauta, W.J.H. (1971) 'The Problem of the Frontal Lobe: A Reinterpretation', *Journal of Psychiatric Research*, 8: 167–87.

Navarro, Fernanda (1988) *Filosofia y Marxismo: Entrevista a Louis Althusser*, Mexico, DF: Siglo Veintiuno Editores.

New York Times (February 9, 1999) Berger, Joel, 'The Police Misconduct We Never See', p. A31.

—— (May 12, 1999) 'Louima Trial Postponed by Juror's Illness', p. A22.

—— (May 13, 1999) Fried, Joseph P. 'Officer Testifies in Torture Case: Tells of a Defendant Escorting Accuser and Carrying Stick', p. A1 and A 29.

—— (May 15, 1999) Barstow, David and Flynn, Kevin 'Officer who Broke Code of Silence Defies Labels: In Torture Case, a Witness under Scrutiny', p. A13.

Nichols, M.J. and Newsome, W.T. (1999) 'The Neurobiology of Cognition', *Nature* Supplement to vol. 402(6761): c35–c41.

Nietzsche, Friedrich W. (1973) *Beyond Good and Evil: Prelude to a Philosophy of the Future*, trans. R.J. Hollingdale, Harmondsworth: Penguin Books.

Norman, D. A. and Shallice, T. (1986) 'Attention to Action: Willed and Automatic Control of Behaviour', in R.J. Davidson, G.E. Schwartz, and D.E. Shapiro (eds) *Consciousness and Self-regulation*, vol. 4, New York: Plenum Press.

Nuckolls, Charles W. (1998) *Culture: A Problem that Cannot be Solved*, Madison: University of Wisconsin Press, c1998.

Obeyesekere, Gananath (1992) *The Apotheosis of Captain Cook*, Princeton, NJ: Princeton University Press.

O'Connor, Timothy (ed.) (1995) *Agents, Causes and Events: Essays on Indeterminism and Free Will*, New York: Oxford University Press.

—— (2000) *Persons and Causes: The Metaphysics of Free Will*, New York: Oxford University Press.

O'Keefe, J. (1985) 'Is Consciousness the Gateway to the Hippocampal Cognitive Map? A Speculative Essay on the Neural Basis of Mind', in D.A. Oakley (ed.) *Brain and Mind*, London and New York: Methuen.

O'Meara, J. Tim (2001) 'Causation and the Postmodern Critique of Objectivity', *Anthropological Theory*, 1(1).

Ortner, S. (1984) 'Theory in Anthropology since the Sixties', *Comparative Studies in Society and History*, 26: 126–66.

Osherson, Daniel, Perani, Daniela, Cappa, Stefano, Schnur, Tatiana, Grassi, Franco, and Fazio, Ferruccio (1998) 'Distinct Brain Loci in Deductive versus Probabilistic Reasoning', *Neuropsychologia* 36(4): 369–76, Great Britain: Elsevier Science, Ltd.

O'Sullivan, Tim, Hartley, John, Sanders, Danny, Montgomery, Martin, and Fiske, John (1994) *Key Concepts in Communication and Cultural Studies*, London: Routledge.

Palm, G. (1982) *Neural Assemblies*, Berlin: Springer-Verlag.

Parkin, Alan J. (1996) *Explorations in Cognitive Neuropsychology*, Cambridge: Blackwell Publishers.

Passingham, R.E. (1993) *The Frontal Lobes and Voluntary Action*, Oxford: Oxford University Press.

Pearl, Judea (2000) *Causality: Models, Reasoning and Inference*, New York: Cambridge University Press.

Pearson, Karl (1957; 1911) *The Grammar of Science*, 3rd edn, New York: Meridian Books.

Peirce, Charles S. (1958) *Values in a Universe of Chance: Selected Writings of Charles S. Peirce*, Garden City, NY: Doubleday.

Penfield, W. (1947) 'Some Observations on the Cerebral Cortex of Man', *Proceedings, Royal Society, Series B*, 134: 329–47.

Penfield, W. and Roberts, L. (1959) *Speech and Brain Mechanisms*, Princeton, NJ: Princeton University Press.

Penrose, Roger (1989) *The Emperor's New Mind: Concerning Computers, Minds, and the Laws of Physics*, New York: Oxford University Press.

Perecman, Ellen (ed.) (1987) *The Frontal Lobes Revisited*, New York: IRBN Press.

Pérez-Ramos, Antonio (1988) *Francis Bacon's Idea of Science and the Maker's Knowledge Tradition*, New York: Oxford University Press.

Persinger, Michael A. (1987) *Neuropsychological Bases of God Beliefs*, New York: Praeger.

Piaget, Jean (1983) 'Piaget's Theory', in W. Kessen (ed.) *Handbook of Child Psychology*, vol. 1, New York: Wiley.

Pinker, Steven (1994) *The Language Instinct*, New York: W. Morrow & Co.

—— (1997) *How the Mind Works*, New York: W.W. Norton.

Pinker, S. and Prince, A. (1988) 'On Language and Connectionism: Analysis of a Parallel Distributed Processing Model of Language Acquisition', *Cognition*, 28: 73–113.

Plato (1949) *Meno*, trans. Benjamin Jaratt. Indianapolis: Bobbs-Merrill.

Poland, Jeff (1994) *Physicalism: The Philosophical Foundations*, New York: Oxford University Press.

Posner, Michael and Raichle, Marcus E. (eds) (1994) *Images of Mind*, New York: W.H. Freeman.

Pribram, Karl H. (1997) 'The Work in Working Memory: Implications for Development', in Norman A. Krasnegor, G. Reid Lyon, and Goldman-Rakic, Patricia S. (eds) *Development of the Prefrontal Cortex: Evolution, Neurobiology, and Behavior*, pp. 359–77, Baltimore, MD: Paul H. Brookes Publishing Co.

Prioleau, Leslie, Murdock, Martha, and Brody, Nathan (1983) 'An Analysis of Psychotherapy versus Placebo Studies', *The Behavioral and Brain Sciences*, 6(2): 275–85.

Purves, Dale (1999) 'Brain and Mind: Evolutionary Perspectives (Human Frontier Workshop V)', *Trends in Neurosciences*, 22(8): 370.

Quartz, S.R. and Sejnowsky, T.J. (1997) 'A Neural Basis of Cognitive Development: A Constructivist Manifesto', *Behavioral and Brain Sciences*, 20: 537–56.

Rabinow, Paul (1977) *Reflections on Fieldwork in Morocco*, Los Angeles: University California Press.

—— (1996) *Essays on the Anthropology of Reason*, Princeton, NJ: Princeton University Press.

Rabinow, Paul and Sullivan, William (1987) 'The Interpretive Turn', in P. Rabinow and W. Sullivan (eds) *Interpretive Social Science, a Second Look*, Berkeley: University of California Press.

Radcliffe-Brown, A.R. (1940) 'On Social Structure', *Journal of the Royal Anthropological Institute*, 70: 1–12.

—— (1948; 1922) *The Andaman Islanders*, Glencoe, IL: Free Press.

Ramon y Cajal, Santiago (1988) *Cajal on the Cerebral Cortex: An Annotated Translation of the Complete Writings*, ed. by Javier DeFelipe and Edward G. Jones, New York: Oxford University Press.

The Random House Dictionary of the English Language (1967) Jess Stein (editor in chief), Lawrence Urdang (managing editor), New York: Random House.

Restak, Richard (1979) *The Brain*, New York: Warner Books.

—— (1994) *The Modular Brain: How New Discoveries in Neuroscience are Answering Age-old Questions about Memory, Free Will, Consciousness, and Personal Identity*, New York: Simon & Schuster, Inc.

Reyna, S.P. (1994) 'Literary Anthropology and the Case against Science', *Man*, 29(3): 555–81.

—— (1997) 'Theory in Anthropology in the Nineties', *Cultural Dynamics*, 9(3): 325–51.

—— (1998) 'Right and Might: Of Approximate Truths and Moral Judgments', *Identities*, 4(3–4): 431–65.

—— (2001) 'Theory Counts: (Discounting) Discourse to the Contrary by Adopting a Confrontational Stance', *Anthropological Theory*, 1: 9–29.

Reynolds, L.J. and Lieberman, L. (1996) *Race and Other Misadventures*, Dix Hills, NY: General Hall.

Rickman, H.P. (ed.) (1962) *Pattern and Meaning in History: Thoughts on History and Society*, New York: Harper & Row.

Roberts, A.C., Robbins, T.W. and Weiskrantz, L. (eds) (1998) *The Prefrontal Cortex: Executive and Cognitive Functions*, New York: Oxford University Press.

Robinson, Howard (1982) *Matter and Sense: A Critique of Contemporary Materialism*, New York: Cambridge University Press.

—— (ed.) (1993) *Objections to Physicalism*, New York: Oxford University Press.

Rockmore, Tom and Margolis, Joseph (eds) (1992) *The Heidegger Case: On Philosophy and Politics*, Philadelphia, PA: Temple University Press.

Roland, P.E. (1993) *Brain Activation*, New York: Wiley-Liss.

Roland, P.E. and Friberg, L. (1995) 'Localization of Cortical Areas Activated by Thinking', *Journal of Neuropsychology*, 53(5): 1219–43.

Rolls, Edmund T. (1998) 'The Orbitofrontal Cortex', in Angela C. Roberts, Trevor W. Robbins *et al.* (eds) *The Prefrontal Cortex: Executive and Cognitive Functions*, pp. 67–86, New York: Oxford University Press.

—— (1999) *The Brain and Emotion*, Oxford and New York: Oxford University Press.

Rorty, Richard (1979) *Philosophy and the Mirror of Nature*, Princeton, NJ: Princeton University Press.

Rosaldo, R. (1989) *Culture and Truth: The Remaking of Social Analysis*, Boston, MA: Beacon Press.

Rose, S. (1997) *Lifelines: Biology, Freedom, Determinism*, London: Lane.

Rosenau, Pauline Marie (1992) *Post-modernism and the Social Sciences: Insights, Inroads and Intrusions*, Princeton, NJ: Princeton University Press.

Rousseau, Jean Jacques (1984; 1754) *A Discourse on the Origins of Inequality*, Harmondsworth: Penguin.

Rowe, J.B., Toni, I., Josephs, O., Frackowick, R., and Passing, R. (2000) 'The Prefrontal Center: Response Selection or Maintenance within Working Memory?' *Science*, 288: 1656–60.

Rozemond, Marleen (1998) *Descartes' Dualism*, Cambridge, MA: Harvard University Press.

Rummelhart, David E. and McClelland, James L. and the PDP Research Group (1986) *Parallel Distributed Processing: Explorations in the Microstructure of Cognition*, Cambridge, MA: MIT Press.

Runes, Dagobert (1970; 1960) *Dictionary of Philosophy*, New York: Philosophical Library.

Rushton, J. Phillippe (1995) *Race, Evolution, and Behavior: A Life History Perspective*, New Brunswick, NJ: Transaction Publishers.

Russell, Bertrand (1981; 1953/1929) 'On the Notion of Cause', in Bertrand Russell, *Mysticism and Logic, and other Essays*, pp. 180–208, New York: W.W. Norton.

Ryle, Gilbert (1949) *The Concept of Mind*, London and New York: Hutchinson's University Library.

Sahlins, M. (1976a) *Culture and Practical Reason*, Chicago: University of Chicago Press.

—— (1976b) *The Use and Abuse of Biology: An Anthropological Critique of Sociobiology*, Ann Arbor: University of Michigan Press.

—— (1981) *Historical Metaphors and Mythical Realities*, Ann Arbor: University of Michigan Press.

—— (1985) *Islands of History*, Chicago: University of Chicago Press.

—— (1995) *How 'Natives' Think – About Captain Cook, for Example*, Chicago: University of Chicago Press.

Salmon, Wesley C. (1984) *Scientific Explanation and the Causal Structure of the World*, Princeton, NJ: Princeton University Press.

—— (1998) *Causality and Explanation*, New York: Oxford University Press.

Sarbin, Theodore R. and Kitsuse, John I. (eds) (1994) *Constructing the Social*, London: Sage.

Sartre, J.-P. (1966; 1943) *Being and Nothingness*, New York: Washington Square Press.

Saussure, Ferdinand de (1959; 1916) *Course in General Linguistics*, ed. by Charles Bally and Albert Sechehaye in collaboration with Albert Reidlinger, trans. Wade Baskin, New York: Philosophical Library.

Schacter, D.L. (1996) *Searching for Memory: The Brain, the Mind, and the Past*, New York: Basic Books.

Schacter, D.L. and Tulving, E. (1994) 'What are the Memory Systems of 1994?' in D.L. Schacter and E. Tulving (eds) *Memory Systems 1994*, Cambridge, MA: MIT Press.

Scheines, Richard (1997) 'An Introduction to Causal Interference', in Vaughn R. McKim and Stephen P. Turner (eds) *Causality in Crisis? Statistical Methods and the Search for Causal Knowledge in the Social Sciences*, pp. 185–99, Notre Dame, IN: University of Notre Dame Press.

Schleiermacher, Friedrich (1998; 1811) 'General Hermeneutics', in Friedrich Schleiermacher, trans. and ed. by Andrew Bowie, *Hermeneutics and Criticism and Other Writings*, pp. 225–68, New York: Cambridge University Press.

—— (1836) *Schleiermacher's Introductions to the Dialogues of Plato*, trans. William Dobson, Cambridge: J. & J.J. Deighton.

—— (1998; 1838) 'Hermeneutics and Criticism', in Friedrich Schleiermacher, trans. and ed. by Andrew Bowie, *Hermeneutics and Criticism and Other Writings*, pp. 1–224, New York: Cambridge University Press,

Schneider, David M. (1980) *American Kinship: A Cultural Account*, Chicago: University of Chicago Press.

Schutz, Alfred (1970) *On Phenomenology and Social Relations: Selected Writings*, Chicago: University of Chicago Press.

Searle, John R. (1983) *Intentionality, An Essay in the Philosophy of Mind*, New York: Cambridge University Press.

—— (1992) *The Rediscovery of the Mind*, Cambridge, MA: MIT Press.

—— (1995) *The Construction of Social Reality*, New York: Free Press.

Shallice, Tim (1988) *From Neuropsychology to Mental Structure*, Cambridge and New York: Cambridge University Press.

Shapiro, Gary and Sica, Alan (eds) (1984) *Hermeneutics: Questions and Prospects*, Amherst: University of Massachusetts Press.

Simon, Herbert A. (1957) *Models of Man*, New York: John Wiley & Sons.

Singer, W. (1993) 'Synchronization of Cortical Activity and its Putative Role in Information Processing and Learning', *Annual Review of Physiology*, 55: 349–74.

Skinner, B.F. (1961) *Cumulative Record*, New York: Appleton-Century-Crofts.

Smith, Edward E. and Jonides, J. (1999) 'Storage and Executive Processes in the Frontal Lobe', *Science*, 283: 1657–61.

—— (2000) 'The Cognitive Neuroscience of Categorization', in Michael S. Gazzaniga *et al.* (eds) *The New Cognitive Neurosciences*, 2nd edn, Cambridge, MA: MIT Press.

Smith, S.B. (1984) *Reading Althusser*, Ithaca, NY: Cornell University Press.

Sorokin, Pitirim A. (1964; 1943) *Sociocultural Causality, Space, Time: A Study of Referential Principles of Sociology and Social Science*, New York: Russell & Russell.

Spencer, Herbert (1883; 1850) *Social Statics*, New York: D. Appleton.

Spencer, J. (1989) 'Anthropology as a Kind of Warning', *Man*, 24(4): 145–64.

Sperber, Dan (1996) *Explaining Culture: A Naturalistic Approach*, Oxford: Blackwell.

Spinoza, Benedictus de (1951) *Ethics*, Mineola, NY: Dover Publications, Inc.

Squire, Larry R. (1987) *Memory and Brain*, New York: Oxford University Press.

Steiner, George (1978) *Heidegger*, Hassocks, UK: Harvester Press.

Stent, G.S. (1973) 'A Physiological Mechanism for Hebb's Postulate of Learning', *Proceedings of the National Academy of Science, USA*, 70: 997–1001.

Sternberg, Robert J. (2000) 'Cognition: The Holy Grail of General Intelligence', *Science*, 289: 399–401.

Stewart, Ian (1989) *Does God Play Dice? The Mathematics of Chaos*, New York: B. Blackwell.

Stocking, George W., Jr (1965) 'From Physics to Ethnology: Franz Boas' Arctic Expedition as a Problem in the Historiography of the Behavioral Sciences', *Journal of the History of the Behavioral Sciences*, 1(3): 53–66.

—— (1968) *Race, Culture and Evolution: Essays in the History of Anthropology*, New York: Free Press.

Strathern, Andrew (1996) *Body Thoughts*, Ann Arbor: University of Michigan Press.

Strauss, Claudia and Quinn, Naomi (1997) *A Cognitive Theory of Cultural Meaning*, Cambridge: Cambridge University Press.

Stuss, D. and Benson, D. (1986) *The Frontal Lobes*, New York: Raven Press.

—— (1987) 'The Frontal Lobes and Control of Cognition and Memory', in Ellen Perecman (ed.), *The Frontal Lobes Revisited*, pp. 141–58, New York: Erlbaum.

Suppes, Patrick (1970) *A Probabilistic Theory of Causality*, Amsterdam: North-Holland.

Surber, Jere Paul (1998) *Culture and Critique: An Introduction to the Critical Discourses of Cultural Studies*, Boulder, CO: Westview Press.

Sutton, S., Braren, M., Zubin, J., and John, E.R. (1965) 'Evoked Potential Correlate of Stimulus Uncertainty', *Science*, 150: 1187–8.

Tallis, Raymond (1988) *Not Saussure*, London: Macmillan.

Thompson, E.P. (1979) *The Poverty of Theory and other Essays*, New York: Monthly Review Press.

Toni, Nicolas and Buchs, P.A. (1999) 'LTP Promotes Formation of Multiple Spine Synapses Between a Single Axon Terminal and a Dendrite', *Nature*, 402(6760): 421–6.

Toren, Christina (1990) *Making Sense of Hierarchy: Cognition as Social Process in Fiji*, London: Athlone Press.

—— (1999) *Mind, Materiality and History: Explorations in Fijian Ethnography*, London: Routledge.

Trimmer, John D. (1950) *Response of Physical Systems*, New York: John Wiley & Sons.

Tulving, Endel (1983) *Elements of Episodic Memory*, New York: Oxford University Press.

—— (1972) 'Episodic and Semantic Memory', in Endel Tulving and Wayne Donaldson (eds) *Organization of Memory*, pp. 381–403, New York: Academic Press.

Tulving, Endel and Lepage, Martin (2000) 'Where in the Brain is the Awareness of One's Past', in D.L. Schacter and Elaine Scarry (eds) *Memory, Brain and Belief*, pp. 208–30, Cambridge, MA: Harvard University Press.

Turner, Victor (1985) *On the Edge of the Bush: Anthropology as Experience*, Tucson, AZ: University of Arizona Press.

Tyler, S. (1969) *Cognitive Anthropology*, New York: Holt, Rinehart & Winston.

—— (1986) 'Post-modern Ethnography: From Document of the Occult to Occult Document', in J. Clifford and G. Marcus (eds) *Writing Culture, the Poetics and Politics of Ethnography*, Los Angeles: University of California Press.

—— (1987) *The Unspeakable: Discourse, Dialogue, and Rhetoric in the Postmodern World*, Madison, WI: University of Wisconsin Press.

Tylor, Edward B. (1958; 1871) *The Origins of Culture*, vols I and II, New York: Harper Torch Books.

Vogt, Brent A. (2000) 'Human Retrosplenial Cortex: Where Is It and Is It Involved in Emotion?' *Trends in Neurosciences*, 23(5): 195–8.

Volkmar, Fred R. and Greenough, William T. (1972) 'Rearing Complexity Affects Branching of Dendrites in the Visual Cortex of the Rat', *Science* 176(4042): 1445–6.

Voltaire (1959) *Candide*, trans. Lowell Bair, New York: Bantam Books.

Wachterhauser, Brice R. (ed.) (1986) *Hermeneutics and Modern Philosophy*, Albany, NY: State University of New York Press.

Wacquant, L.J.D. (1989) 'Toward a Reflexive Sociology: A Workshop with Pierre Bourdieu', *Sociological Theory* 7(1): 26–63.

Wallace, William A. (1972) *Causality and Scientific Explanation*, Ann Arbor: University of Michigan Press.

Wallenstein, Gene V., Eichenbaum, Howard and Hasselmo, Michael E. (1998) 'The Hippocampus of an Associator of Discontiguous Events', *Trends in Neurosciences*, 21(8): 317–23.

Washington Post (Friday, May 28, 1999), Raspberry, William 'The Mystery of Officer Justin Volpe', p. A35.

Watzlawick, Paul (ed.) (1984) *The Invented Reality: How Do We Know What We Believe We Know? Contributions to Constructivism*, New York: Norton.

Weber, Max (1968a; 1913) *Economy and Society: An Outline of Interpretive Sociology*, edited by Guenther Roth and Claus Wittich, New York: Bedminster Press.

—— (1968b) '"Objectivity" in Social Science', in May Brodbeck (ed.) *Readings in the Philosophy of the Social Sciences*, New York: Macmillan.

Weinberger, J. (ed.) (1980) *The Great Instauration; and, New Atlantis/Francis Bacon*, Arlington Heights, IL: AHM Publishing Co.

Weiskrantz, L. (1956) 'Behavioral Changes Associated with Ablation of the Amygdaloid Complex in Monkeys', *Journal of Comparative Physiology and Psychology*, 49: 381–91.

—— (1997) *Consciousness Lost and Found: A Neuropsychological Exploration*, Oxford: Oxford University Press.

Westphal, K.R. (1984) 'Was Nietzsche a Cognitivist?' *Journal of the History of Philosophy* 26(3): 343–63.

Whitehead, Harriet (2000) *Food Rules: Hunting, Sharing, and Tabooing Game in Papua New Guinea*, Ann Arbor, MI: University of Michigan Press.

Whitney, Charles (1986) *Francis Bacon and Modernity*, New Haven, CT: Yale University Press.

Wilden, A. (1981) 'Translator's Introduction', in J. Lacan, *Speech and Language in Psychoanalysis*, Baltimore, MD: Johns Hopkins University Press.

Williams, R. (1977) *Marxism and Literature*, New York: Oxford University Press.

Wilson, Edward O. (1975) *Sociobiology: The New Synthesis*, Cambridge, MA: Belknap Press of Harvard University.

Wolf, Eric R. (1984; 1982) *Europe and the People without History*, Berkeley: University of California Press.

Wolin, Richard (ed.) (1991) *The Heidegger Controversy: A Critical Reader*, New York: Columbia University Press.

Wright, Georg H. von (1971) *Explanation and Understanding*, Ithaca, NY: Cornell University Press.

—— (1974) *Causality and Determinism*, New York: Columbia University Press.

Index